WATER RESOURCES OF CANADA

RESSOURCES HYDRAULIQUES DU CANADA

Thoughtful people everywhere, but particularly in North America, are disturbed by the increasing number and seriousness of the problems associated with water resources. The Royal Society of Canada, impressed by the gravity of this situation, and by the multi-disciplinary nature of the specialized knowledge needed to cope with it, chose Water Resources as the main theme for its 1966 annual meeting.

The topic has been broadly interpreted here: most of the papers were presented by the Science Section of the Society but contributions from all its Sections are included, covering political, historical and sociological aspects of the problem in addition to the physical, biological and even mathematical aspects. The contents comprise twenty-three essays, grouped into six parts under self-explanatory headings. The contributors to this volume include Senator Frank E. Moss, the late General A.G.L. McNaughton, Pierre Camu, Hilda Neatby, Benoit Brouillette, A.D. Misener, and F.R. Hayes.

This work is authoritative without being highly technical. It can be read profitably by all scientists and health workers professionally involved in the conservation of water resources everywhere. In addition, the non-scientific citizen can find much in this book that is enlightening and impressive about this inescapable and vital problem.

(Royal Society of Canada Studia Varia Series No. 11)

CLAUDE E. DOLMAN was Research Scholar at St. Mary's Hospital Institute of Pathology and Research. He came to Canada in 1931 to work at the Connaught Medical Research Laboratories, University of Toronto, and still retains a Research Membership in that institution. In 1935 Dr. Dolman became Director, Division of Laboratories, Department of Health and Welfare of British Columbia and head of the Department of Bacteriology and Preventative Medicine at the University of British Columbia. In 1965 he resigned and became Research Professor of Microbiology in order to devote full time to scholarly essays in the history of microbiology.

ROYAL SOCIETY OF CANADA
"STUDIA VARIA"

SOCIÉTÉ ROYALE DU CANADA
"STUDIA VARIA"

1. *Studia Varia: Literary and Scientific Papers—Etudes littéraires et scientifiques* (1956). Edited by E. G. D. MURRAY
2. *Our Debt to the Future: Symposium presented on the Seventy-Fifth Anniversary, 1957—Présence de Demain : Colloque présenté au Soixante-quinzième Anniversaire, 1957.* Edited by E. G. D. MURRAY
3. *The Canadian Northwest: Its Potentialities; Symposium presented to the Royal Society of Canada in 1958—L'Avenir du Nord-Ouest Canadien; Colloque présenté à la Société royale du Canada en 1958.* Edited by FRANK H. UNDERHILL
4. *Evolution: Its Science and Doctrine; Symposium presented to the Royal Society of Canada in 1959—L'Evolution : La Science et la Doctrine; Colloque presénté à la Société royale du Canada en 1959.* Edited by THOMAS W. M. CAMERON
5. *Aux sources du présent : Etudes présentées à la Section I de la Société royale du Canada—The Roots of the Present: Studies presented to Section I of the Royal Society of Canada* (1960). Sous la direction de LÉON LORTIE et ADRIEN PLOUFFE
6. *Canadian Universities Today: Symposium presented to the Royal Society of Canada in 1960—Les Universités canadiennes aujourd'hui; Colloque présenté à la Société royale du Canada en 1960.* Edited by GEORGE STANLEY and GUY SYLVESTRE
7. *Canadian Population and Northern Colonization: Symposium presented to the Royal Society of Canada in 1961—La Population canadienne et la colonization du Grand Nord : Colloque présenté à la Société royale du Canada en 1961.* Edited by V. W. BLADEN
8. *Higher Education in a Changing Canada: Symposium presented to the Royal Society of Canada in 1965—L'Enseignement supérieur dans un Canada en évolution : Colloque présenté à la Société royale du Canada en 1965.* Edited by J. E. HODGETTS
9. *Pioneers of Canadian Science: Symposium presented to the Royal Society of Canada in 1964—Les Pionniers de la science canadienne : Colloque présenté à la Société royale du Canada en 1964.* Edited by G. F. G. STANLEY
10. *Structures sociales du Canada français : Etudes de membres de la Section I de la Société royale du Canada.* Edité par GUY SYLVESTRE
11. *Water Resources of Canada: Symposia presented to the Royal Society of Canada in 1966—Ressources hydrauliques du Canada : Colloques présentés à la Société royale du Canada en 1966.* Edited by CLAUDE E. DOLMAN

Water Resources of Canada

Symposia presented to the
ROYAL SOCIETY OF CANADA
in 1966

Ressources Hydrauliques du Canada

Colloques présentés à la
SOCIÉTÉ ROYALE DU CANADA
en 1966

EDITED BY
CLAUDE E. DOLMAN, F.R.S.C.

PUBLISHED FOR THE SOCIETY
BY UNIVERSITY OF TORONTO PRESS
1967

University of Toronto Press
Reprinted in paperback 2015
ISBN 978-1-4426-3121-2 (paper)

FINANCIAL ASSISTANCE FROM THE CANADA COUNCIL TOWARDS THE PUBLICATION OF THE STUDIA VARIA SERIES IS GRATEFULLY ACKNOWLEDGED BY THE ROYAL SOCIETY OF CANADA. THE FACT THAT A GRANT HAS BEEN MADE DOES NOT IMPLY, HOWEVER, THAT THE CANADA COUNCIL ENDORSES OR IS RESPONSIBLE FOR THE STATEMENTS OR VIEWS EXPRESSED IN THE PARTICULAR VOLUMES

CONTENTS

Introduction
CLAUDE E. DOLMAN, F.R.S.C., *Research Professor, Department of Microbiology, University of British Columbia, and Research Member, Connaught Medical Research Laboratories, University of Toronto* ix

PART I. PROS AND CONS OF CANADIAN WATER EXPORT

Toward a North American Water Policy
SENATOR FRANK E. MOSS, *United States Senate* 3

A Monstrous Concept, a Diabolic Thesis
GENERAL A. G. L. MCNAUGHTON, F.R.S.C. 16

The McNaughton–Moss Confrontation
C. E. DOLMAN, F.R.S.C. 25

NAWAPA and Muskeg
NORMAN W. RADFORTH, F.R.S.C., *Chairman of Department of Biology and of Organic and Associated Terrain Research Unit, McMaster University* 27

PART II. WATER, AN INDISPENSABLE RESOURCE

L'eau, ressource indispensable
PIERRE CAMU, M.S.R.C., *Président, Administration de la Voie maritime du Saint-Laurent, Ottawa* 31

Water, a Physical Resource
W. M. CAMERON, *Director, Marine Sciences Branch, Canada Department of Transport, Ottawa* 37

Water Resources
J. M. HARRISON, F.R.S.C., *Assistant Deputy Minister (Research), Department of Energy, Mines and Resources, Ottawa* 44

PART III. THE ST. LAWRENCE, THEN AND NOW

That Great Street: The St. Lawrence
HILDA NEATBY, F.R.S.C., *Professor of History, University of Saskatchewan* 49

Le rôle du Québec dans le trafic maritime au Canada
BENOÎT BROUILLETTE, M.S.R.C., *Ecole des Hautes Etudes Commerciales, Montréal* 63

PART IV. THE GREAT LAKES: UNIQUE FEATURES AND PECULIAR PROBLEMS

The Uniqueness of the Great Lakes
A. D. MISENER, F.R.S.C., *Director, Great Lakes Institute, University of Toronto* 73

Unique Research Opportunities Afforded by the Great Lakes
DAVID C. CHANDLER, *Director, Great Lakes Research Division, University of Michigan* 76

Environmental Control in the Great Lakes–St. Lawrence Region of North America
E. G. PLEVA, *Professor and Head, Department of Geography, University of Western Ontario* 83

Thermal Régime and Circulation in the Great Lakes
G. K. RODGERS, *Hydrophysicist, Great Lakes Institute, University of Toronto* 87

Meteorological Problems on the Great Lakes
T. L. RICHARDS, *Lakes Investigation Unit, Meteorological Branch, Canada Department of Transport, Toronto* 96

PART V. PHYSICO-MATHEMATICAL STUDIES OF WATER

Meteorology and Water Resources
J. P. BRUCE, *Superintendent of Hydrometeorology, Meteorological Branch, Canada Department of Transport, Toronto* 111

L'aspect mathématique de l'océanographie
PAUL H. LEBLOND, *Institute of Oceanography, University of British Columbia, Vancouver* 116

Estimates of Groundwater Recharge on the Prairies
P. MEYBOOM, *Water Research Branch, Department of Energy, Mines and Resources, Calgary* 128

The Reverse Osmosis Membrane Separation Process and Its Application for Water Purification
S. SOURIRAJAN, *Division of Applied Chemistry, National Research Council of Canada, Ottawa* 154

PART VI. THE BIOLOGICAL NECESSITIES AND HAZARDS OF WATER

Biological Aspects of the Water Problem
F. R. HAYES, F.R.S.C., *Chairman, Fisheries Research Board of Canada, Ottawa* 185

Aquatic Communities and Their Adaptations to Their Environment
GORDON A. RILEY, *Institute of Oceanography, Dalhousie University, Halifax* 191

Présence de bactéries réductrices du soufre dans les rivières polluées par les eaux résiduaires des usines de préparation des pâtes à papier
RAYMOND DESROCHERS, *Professeur de microbiologie, Université de Sherbrooke* 203

Water-Borne Viral Infections
DONALD M. MCLEAN, *Professor of Medical Microbiology in the Department of Microbiology, University of British Columbia* (formerly *Virologist, Hospital for Sick Children, Toronto)* 212

The Waters of Wide Agony
C. E. DOLMAN, F.R.S.C., *Research Professor, Department of Microbiology, University of British Columbia, and Research Member, Connaught Medical Research Laboratories, University of Toronto* 228

Die Masse könnt ihr nur durch Masse zwingen,
Ein jeder sucht sich endlich selbst was aus.
Wer vieles bringt, wird manchem etwas bringen;
Und jeder geht zufrieden aus dem Haus.

GOETHE, *Faust: Vorspiel auf dem Theater*

INTRODUCTION

Claude E. Dolman, F.R.S.C.

I

SHORTLY BEFORE the First World War began, the annual meeting of the Royal Society of Canada was addressed by its President, Dr. Frank D. Adams,[1] on the topic "The National Domain in Canada and Its Proper Conservation." Perusal of the text of this address[2] has prompted some reflections.

First—a trivial point—the limits of endurance of Fellows two generations ago were set apparently higher than they are today, for Dean Adams' discourse, punctuated by lantern slides, graphs, and maps, must have taken at least two hours to deliver. A more significant reflection is that this Society has never been preoccupied exclusively with matters of scholarly, esoteric, or only theoretical interest. There is instead a long history of indirect involvement, through the expert knowledge and dedication of individual Fellows, in many issues of the utmost practical import to the nation's welfare and integrity. In the past, the Society's direct concern with such issues may have been rather haphazardly displayed and sporadically expressed; but in recent years, the Council and the various committees responsible for programme planning have selected for attention at each annual meeting some problem of deep significance to all Canadians that lends itself to interdisciplinary analysis and elucidation.

In those days, it was possible for one man to speak and write authoritatively on the necessity to conserve the country's resources—ranging from oysters and whales to migratory birds and the musk-ox, from soil and forest cover to natural gas—and yet to say nothing about water. This omission must have been drawn to Dean Adams' attention, for a later, revised version of his address (recently found by chance in a

[1]Dr. Adams, a distinguished geologist, was Dean of Applied Science at McGill University from 1908 to 1923.

[2]F. D. Adams, "The National Domain in Canada and Its Proper Conservation," *Proc. & Trans. Roy. Soc. Canada, 3rd Ser.* VIII (1914): xli–lxxii.

second-hand bookshop) contained a short section on "water-powers."[3] But an insertion of almost equal length was devoted to describing the importation of Lapland reindeer into Labrador, initiated by Dr. Wilfred Grenfell in 1907–8, and to urging that this reindeer experiment be extended to the barrens of far northern Canada. The ebullient enthusiasms which must underlie such versatility as his perhaps account largely for the fact that half a century ago the Society's President could give such scant attention to the nation's water resources. Another factor contributing to this imbalance no doubt was complacency, the prevalence of which is suggested by the following truisms quoted from the revised address: "It is doubtful if there is any country in the world which is so abundantly supplied with water-power as the Dominion of Canada. . . . Water-power is perhaps unique among the resources of a country in that it is not diminished by use nor conserved by non-use."

Complacent attitudes about water resources cannot be justified anywhere today, for most parts of the world are either threatened by or already suffering from inadequate reserves of clean fresh water for the essential purposes of civilized life. No lake, from Abitibi to Zürich, and no river, from the Ab-i-Diz to the Zuni, appears immune to man-made pollution. North America in particular is creating, to use Julian Huxley's phrase, an "effluent society"; and there is more sad prophecy than bad scansion in Tom Lehrer's raucous ditty on Pollution:

> If you visit American City
> You will find it very pretty,
> Just two things of which you must beware,
> Don't drink the water and don't breathe the air. . . .

If current population trends persist, while commercial and recreational demands for water continue insatiable, every continent (except Antarctica) will face acute shortages well before another half century has passed. Such crises can only be averted by the imposition of enlightened but rigorous controls, backed by sound, stern legislation.

The Royal Society of Canada, impressed by the gravity of this situation, and by the multidisciplinary nature of the specialized knowledge and viewpoints needed to comprehend and cope with it, designated Water Resources as the main theme for the 1966 annual meeting held in Sherbrooke, Quebec. An editor was appointed at the same time for the monograph in the *Studia Varia* series which it was hoped might be compiled from the various contributions by Fellows and invited guests. This volume is an outcome of those decisions.

[3]F. D. Adams, *The National Domain in Canada and Its Proper Conservation* (Ottawa: Lowe-Martin Co. Ltd., 1915).

II

From the outset it was intended that Water Resources should be broadly interpreted, in order to preclude the development of several symposia devoted mainly to various aspects of the pollution problem, and to encourage the many-sided approach for which the Royal Society of Canada is constitutionally well fitted. To have limited the scope of the programme to what are basically public health aspects of water resources, thus focusing upon control campaigns that were already receiving much attention, would have done the Society less than justice.

Pollution control in certain areas of North America has become indeed so inescapable a necessity that it may be engaging the concern of too many agencies to secure prompt, clear-cut, and effective decisions. This situation probably helped to ensure passage of the United States Water Quality Act in 1965, under which a Federal Water Pollution Control Administration was established. Many years are likely to elapse before a comparable centralized authority can be set up in Canada. Meanwhile, the Canadian Council of Resource Ministers, comprising representatives of the federal and all the provincial governments, does its best to serve as clearing-house, sounding-board, and instigator of research on resource problems.

This Council sponsored a conference on "Pollution and Our Environment," held at Montreal early in November 1966, some five months after the Society's annual meeting, and about one year after President Johnson signed the U.S. Water Quality Act. Over 500 appointed and invited delegates registered for the five-day conference. The writer was privileged to attend as the Royal Society of Canada's representative, and is thus able to aver that although some contributions in the present volume inevitably deal with water pollution, there will be no duplication and very little overlapping in content between this book and any proceedings of the Montreal conference that might be published eventually.

In their overall reserves of clean, safe water, Canadians still enjoy the enviable abundance referred to by Adams. But of course the fact that enormous quantities of water are flowing wastefully into the Beaufort Sea and Hudson Bay does nothing to irrigate the sage-brush desert of parts of southeastern British Columbia, or to alleviate the intermittent droughts of southern Saskatchewan. Large-scale diversion or redistribution is the only possible solution to this sort of difficulty. The tremendous costs of redistributing the country's water resources provide no excuse for tardiness in appraising them or in laying long-term plans. Ironically, it is the covetous avidity for water of our great southern neighbour that may force us without delay to take stock of these resources in terms of the estimated needs of many generations of Canadians. Should the most thorough and cautious surveys reveal a superabundance of total available water—not just for tomorrow but for the foreseeable future—it seems reasonable to anticipate that many of our countrymen would be sympathetic to a plan of redistribution, provided that all beneficiaries within the borders of Canada paid their fair share of the costs, and that the government treasuries concerned were adequately recompensed for all exported surplus. Granted these provisos, it is difficult to imagine politicians finding it still expedient to cry: "Not a drop of our water for sale to anyone!," especially if (as happened for example at Chanute, Kansas during the 1956–57 drought) many cities are by then reduced to subsisting for water supplies upon their own recycled sewage.[4]

Such conjectures are as yet academic, but it would be foolish to underestimate or ignore the portent of recent polemic skirmishes, so far confined to vanguards, that might expand eventually into well-nigh irresistible demands upon Canada for water export. Perhaps those responsible for initiating the Water Resources theme had this in mind when it was decided to have the issue laid bare before a plenary session of the Society. Initially, one or two additional representatives of government were to have been invited; but force of circumstances narrowed the field to Senator Moss and General McNaughton, who proved thoroughly worthy and well-chosen protagonists.

III

The detailed organization of additional thematic contributions was mainly delegated to Section III's Programme Committee, under the chairmanship of Dr. J. S. Marshall, Vice-President of that Section. This Committee, comprising the conveners of all eight Subject-Divisions, endorsed another general symposium, planned and chaired by Dr. J. M. Harrison, in which various scientific problems connected with Canadian water resources were to be introduced in non-technical terms. Other papers on specialized biological aspects of this question were sponsored jointly by the Plant Pathology, Animal Pathology, and Microbiology and Biochemistry Divisions, under the guidance of Dr. B. A. Eagles, convener of the last-named Division. The Mathematics Division, with

[4]D. F. Metzler, *et al.*, "Emergency Use of Reclaimed Water for Potable Supply at Chanute, Kansas," *J. Am. Water Works Assoc. 50* (1958): 1021–60.

Dr. G. F. D. Duff as convener, arranged a symposium entitled "Waves, Tides, and Currents." Again, Section III as a whole combined forces with the Royal Mathematical Society and the Canadian Association of Physicists to present a series of reports under the heading "Problems of the Great Lakes." This symposium was organized and chaired by Dr. A. D. Misener.

The Geology Division, though preoccupied with a different symposial topic, had one study on its programme that was sufficiently related to water resources to be incorporated in this volume. The Presidential Address to Section III was also dedicated to a watery theme. Ultimately, every Subject Division of the Section either participated in one or other of these symposia, or at least made helpful suggestions about suitable guest speakers. Nor was the unusual extent of this cooperative involvement limited to Section III. We are delighted to be able to include three papers from Sections I and II, two of which were presented at a joint session on "The St. Lawrence River."

Thus it came about that in due course a heterogeneous collection of over twenty papers on water resources reached the editor's desk. The fact that the majority of them were distinctively Canadian in viewpoint, if not in subject matter, settled the final choice of title for this volume of essays. Fortunately, the miscellany lent itself to subdivision into six parts of uneven lengths under a series of self-explanatory headings, and within each part the topics could be arranged in fairly logical sequence. Any further discussion of the genesis of the book would seem superfluous, but a few comments on its scope and purport may be warranted.

IV

The volume begins with the addresses of Senator Moss and General McNaughton. Thus we pay our respects to a distinguished visitor and make a gesture of homage to a great Canadian, and also acknowledge the outstanding magnitude of the political and technical issues raised during their confrontation. As that debate has been accorded a separate editorial comment, no more need be said about it here, except to note that the denunciatory title of General McNaughton's address should not be laid at his door, for his typescript was untitled. However, the epithets supplied (which it is safe to assume he would not have disavowed) were culled from his own text.

Part II includes eloquent addresses by Dr. Pierre Camu and Dr. W. M. Cameron, which in quite different styles define the uses and abuses of water and remind us of its absolute indispensability to life on earth.

Dr. J. M. Harrison's succinct statement finds its place here because it so clearly underlines the main problematic issues.

Part III comprises two essays illustrating the undiminished importance of the St. Lawrence as a highway of provincial and international commerce over a span of 200 years. Professor Hilda Neatby has provided a painstakingly detailed, evocative portrayal of that great river in the 1760–90 era, based on her scrutiny of many collections of official documents, as well as of business and personal correspondence, in the Public Archives of Canada. Dr. Benôit Brouillette reveals some surprising facts about the tonnage and value of commercial goods shipped through present-day ports of the province of Quebec, derived from a careful analysis of the relevant statistics for 1963 and 1964.

Five topics relating specifically to the Great Lakes were assigned to Part IV. The mounting pollution and falling water-levels in this vast area of expanding industrialization, and the relatively substantial support now available from the governments of Canada and the United States for Great Lakes surveys and research projects, are providing incentives for wide-ranging efforts. Fittingly, Dr. A. D. Misener, representing the University of Toronto's Great Lakes Institute, had invited Dr. D. C. Chandler of the University of Michigan's Great Lakes Research Division to participate in this almost exclusively Canadian programme, which could only be truly meaningful if international cooperation were assured. Both of these contributors emphasize the many unique physical features of the Great Lakes and the remarkable research opportunities they present. Professor Pleva amplifies Dr. Misener's warning that no satisfactory solution to the complex problems of the Great Lakes can be reached by any group acting in isolation and partial ignorance. He stresses the socio-economic factors to be reckoned with before the quality of the regional environment can be improved, and laments the fragmented political jurisdictions which interfere with unitary control programmes. Dr. G. K. Rodger's paper on the temperature structure and circulation patterns of the Great Lakes impressively illustrates their uniqueness for highly specialized physical studies. He describes how intensive observations, carried out on Lake Ontario over the past few years, led to recognition of a sharp horizontal temperature gradient at the lake surface, known as the "thermal bar." Finally, in an illuminating review, Mr. T. L. Richards describes the influences exerted by the Great Lakes upon the regional weather patterns and, conversely, the effects of meteorological factors on the lakes themselves. He advocates an expanded research programme in hydrology, physical limnology, and meteorology, in order to improve our understanding of the critical problem of water-level variations.

Part V contains a mixed group of studies to which the adjective "physico-mathematical" seems applicable. Mr. J. P. Bruce argues persuasively that more meteorological knowledge and research is essential for a realistic assessment of Canadian water resources, as well as for predicting floods and droughts. He outlines some of the hydrological projects now under way across the country, or about to be started, in connection with Canada's programme for the International Hydrologic Decade, launched in 1965 under United Nations auspices. The other three contributions in this group will doubtless strike the general reader as highly specialized and even abstruse. However, their authoritative approach to unusual aspects of water behaviour adds a dash of reconditeness to the volume, which can harm nobody and should please the initiated. Dr. Paul H. LeBlond expounds some mathematical difficulties arising from the turbulent nature of oceanic flows. Because of these mathematical obstacles and the paucity of data, accurate predictions of oceanic behaviour are still impossible, even on an empirical basis. Successful oceanic engineering projects will be possible only when a clearer understanding of large-scale turbulent interactions is gained. Dr. P. Meyboom presents multiple evidence that groundwater on the Prairies is a renewable resource. His report describes how groundwater flow systems are now being delineated, and how measurements at the boundaries of the flow system are used to solve the hydrologic equation with respect to groundwater replenishment on the Prairies. Dr. S. Sourirajan's paper examines the fundamental mathematical considerations bearing on the mechanisms of the reverse osmosis process. This is a technique, whose development he has vigorously furthered, whereby a mixture of substances in fluid solution can be separated by passing the fluid under pressure through an appropriate porous membrane. The process has important potentialities in water purification and pollution control.

Finally, the papers assembled in Part VI discuss and illustrate from various biological standpoints the proposition implicit and occasionally enunciated in many of the foregoing submissions, that water is the essence of life, but may be a medium of death. Dr. F. R. Hayes reviews in general terms the biological effects, particularly upon fish, of waters containing soluble substances carelessly introduced by man. Bodies of water made excessively fertile through addition of large quantities of phosphate and nitrate, originating in human sewage and animal manure and in industrial waters, develop obnoxious algal scums, undergo increased silting, and lose their better-quality fish. Dr. Gordon A. Riley analyses some of the complex mechanisms of adaptation which the aquatic environment imposes on its animal, plant, and bacterial inhabitants. Drastic alterations in this environment, induced by severe pollution, may encourage disruptive proliferation of species that hitherto were harmless. Dr. Raymond Desrochers reports careful observations on changes in the bacterial flora of the Ottawa River resulting from pollution by pulp mill effluents, with specific reference to the malodorous activities of sulphate-reducing bacteria. Dr. D. M. McLean describes ingenious experimental investigations of the mechanisms, extent, and rate of dispersal of an innocuous virus introduced into swimming-pools, lakes, and creeks. Viruses deliberately added to sewage survived passage through a laboratory model of an aeration tank and treatment columns. Chlorination of effluents from sewage plants, and continuous maintenance of adequate halogen residuals in swimming-pools, are advisable precautions against water-borne virus hazards.

The last item in the book recounts some highlights in the triumphant yet often tragic story of man's control of epidemic water-borne disease, as epitomized especially by cholera. Were it not for the curiosity, courage, self-sacrifice, and unadvertised achievements of successive pioneers, the process of human enlightenment about the causation of such disasters would have been far more halting and painful than it was. When so elemental an agent as water stands accused of being the vehicle, some inadequately informed and emotionally unstable people apparently sense a challenge to certain primordial affinities. They then become easily provoked, by those having special interests or claims to defend, into resentful opposition to measures that most of their fellow-citizens recognize as in the public interest. The hysterical campaign against chlorination of Vancouver's water supply is recent enough to remind us that expert knowledge, adequate funds, and valid legislation will not alone suffice to ensure rapid progress in purifying, conserving, or redistributing our water resources. In democratic communities, apart from the average voter, a minority of noisy protestors may also need to be convinced that those who advocate these measures are on the side of the angels.

V

The foregoing synopsis, it is hoped, indicates the unusually broad coverage of this collection of essays. Despite the high degree of specialization displayed in some of the contributions, the book as a whole is animated by an interdisciplinary spirit, operating both within and beyond the bounds of science. This is fully in keeping with the Society's purposes in establishing the *Studia Varia* series. Admittedly there are many gaps in this volume, which it would be futile to bewail and uncalled for to specify. The Society's constitution and its organizational system, as well as the traditional programme structure and the prevailing attitudes of its membership, are not conducive to the production of sufficient material at a single annual meeting for a definitive monograph on such a complex theme. To assign supplemental topics *post hoc* to well-known authorities would delay publication and dilute the Society's sponsorship. An editor of such a work as this should therefore subject himself, as cheerfully as possible, to Francis Bacon's definition of a scientist, as one who "works according to his stuff and is limited thereby."

There are in fact grounds for hope that this volume will prove worthy of the *Studia Varia* series, in literacy, authority, and timeliness. More important, the purport of the assembled contents is ultimately optimistic. The historical essays and allusions remind us how far we have come since, for instance, Edwin Chadwick published his 1842 report—a model of zealous acerbity—on the Sanitary Conditions of the Labouring Population of Great Britain, in which a description of the revolting nuisances, indignities, and health hazards then so prevalent ends with the words: "The Civic Officers sat still amidst the pollution with the resignation of Turkish fatalists."

Again, the many references to current and projected research in diverse fields of science, and to the need for much more of it, are in themselves a contingent testimony of confidence from scientists that a way can be found out of the maze of problems bearing on water resources. Already there is evidence that the second half of the twentieth century may see consigned to final oblivion a 700-year-old assertion of Roger Bacon: "The greatest obstacle to the progress of science and to the undertaking of new tasks and provinces therein, is found in this—that men despair and think things impossible." That dictum, though always challenged by a scattering of alchemists and natural philosophers, has held true of the generality of mankind until recently. Now suddenly mountains are moved, rivers diverted, huge dams erected, and artificial lakes impounded, tunnels built under the sea, atomic energy harnessed, and astronauts prepared to land on the moon. Faced with such staggering present realities, there is plenty of excuse if the layman begins to imagine that all physical problems are resolvable by applied science.

Terminal comments seem called for on two fundamental fallacies or lacunae in this assumption. Life in our times offers not only exhilarating opportunities for mind-stretching but also seductive temptations to head-swelling and conscience-blunting. There are grave dangers in fostering the unqualified conceit that no physical problem is too enormous, too refractory, or too costly for mankind to tackle. In the very year of the Royal Society of Canada's programme on water resources, there were many humbling reminders of man's impotency when that element is unleashed—devastating floods and deadly avalanches, villages swept away through broken dams and tidal waves, and inestimable havoc wrought in Florence by the rampaging Arno. These tragic events do not negate the power of science, for scientific thought, like Greek drama, as Whitehead has pointed out, is pervaded by "remorseless inevitableness." Such disasters serve rather as frightful reinforcements of the warnings now multiplying from various sources that in the long run mankind does not "win" any "battle" with Nature.

To ensure the maximum share of security, comfort, and loveliness that most of us yearn to harvest from the world's resources, it is now becoming self-evident to scientists and engineers, as it has long been to many poets and philosophers, that men must learn to cooperate with Nature and live in harmony with it. As George Sarton has put it: "The man of science who has the real *feu sacré* in him feels that though he is but an infinitestimal part of the whole, yet his own endeavour may contribute, however little, to the fulfilment of man's purpose: a deeper understanding of nature, a closer adaptation to it, a better guidance, a more intelligent devotion."

But to live at peace with Nature is not enough. A paramount lesson of our time is that man must ardently believe in and practise international cooperation in all fields of human endeavour. Over 300 years ago, Fulke Greville, the first Baron Brooke, described in moving verse the proper applications of human knowledge:

> The chief Use then in man of that he Knowes,
> Is his paines taking for the good of all,
> Not fleshly weeping for our owne made woes,
> Not laughing from a Melancholy gall,
> Not hating from a soule that overflowes
> With bitternesse, breath'd out from inward thrall;
> But sweetly rather to ease, loose, or binde,
> *As need requires*, this fraile fall'n humane kinde.[5]

Of course there is nothing new in the doctrine of the brotherhood of man: it is at least as old as Christianity. But throughout history it has needed constantly to be restated. The percipient reader will be glad and perhaps surprised to find some unobtrusive reminders of its essential truth within the pages of this volume.

[5]From *Certain Learned and Elegant Workes of Lord Brooke* (1633), p. 50. Quoted by Henry W. Acland, Regius Professor of Medicine at Oxford, opposite the title page of his *Memoir on the Cholera at Oxford in the year 1854* (London: John Churchill, 1856).

PART I

PROS AND CONS OF CANADIAN WATER EXPORT

TOWARD A NORTH AMERICAN WATER POLICY

Frank E. Moss

IT IS A SINGULAR HONOUR to be invited to address the Royal Society of Canada, the senior learned society of your country and one of the world's leading associations of scientists and men of letters. I do not know whether some of my colleagues in the United States Senate have preceded me on this platform, or whether my appearance here today sets some sort of precedent. But I am sure that such an appearance is rare, and I shall treat it with respect.

I am by custom and courtesy in a position to bring you greetings from the American people. I do so with warmth. We Canadians and Americans have inherited jointly the loveliest and most richly endowed of all continents. We share the job of preserving its beauty and the responsibility of developing its natural resources for the greatest benefit, not only of this generation, but of unborn millions who will follow us.

At the beginning, let me make my position clear. I do not speak as the representative of the Executive Branch of the United States government. I speak as a member of the United States Senate—as the Senator from the water-conscious state of Utah. I will try to set forth what I believe *should be* the policies of my government. Many in my country share these views.

I alway feel very much at home in your country. A recent U.S. Department of the Interior publication describes Utah as a panorama of peaked mountains, lush valleys, and wind-swept plains, where the taming of the wilderness made "the history of Utah an epic of hardship, determination, and triumph." I am sure those same words could have been written about many parts of Canada. Timber, trapping, minerals, farming, and incredible beauty have been as much a part of our Utah lives as of yours. One of the first white men to see the Great Salt Lake, nature's identifying monument in my state, was a Canadian trapper named Etienne Provost. The first white settler in Utah came from St. Louis, whence he had come from Quebec. His name was Antoine

Robidou—I am told there are still Robidous in Quebec. Again, just as the railroads helped knit Canada, Utah is proud to be the place where the last spike was driven in the bands of steel which first linked our western and eastern coasts of America.

What is more to the point in today's discussion, however, is the nature and intensity of our common interest in the preservation of our natural resources. Our lives and our future depend upon the care we take of them, particularly the care we take of our water. In Utah we have an almost sacred respect for water, which shares the indispensability of its life-giving role only with the air we breathe. Its value is determined everywhere by nature's pattern of distribution. In my state there is no more precious thing.

I am sure that Canada, which has a very large portion of the earth's freshwater supplies, does not value water less. The problem of assuring an adequate supply of water for Canada's future differs from the problem in the United States more in degree than in substance. The pollution and levels of the Great Lakes, for example, are bringing as many grey hairs to you as to us, and the flow in the St. Lawrence is as vital to the Port of Montreal as the flow of the Hudson is to New York. Time may be crowding you less, but the challenge of preserving your water resource is clear and near. The challenge looms larger and closer for us. We are already feeling the sharp pinch of necessity. Our demands are quantitatively greater than yours, and the pattern of population growth and industrial development in the United States is putting tremendous pressure on us.

Two factors must be weighed in considering the speed and manner of growth of economic development in the United States and Canada, and the intensity of the exploitation of natural resources in the two countries. First, there is considerable disparity between our two countries in total population and in gross national product. This is unavoidably a source of strain between Canadians and Americans. Such disparity tests the skills of professional diplomats as much as it calls for good manners and broad understanding on the part of all of us. We beg your understanding of our problems and expect you to ask the same of us. Secondly, there is a melancholy lesson for Canada in the economic and natural resource history of the United States. This is a lesson in the importance of taking care of water resources. We in the United States are learning it late and under stress. You have the opportunity to learn it in time to apply it purposefully and according to plan.

The thrust of my message today is a plea to you as members of the influential Royal Society of Canada to support the long-range studies, the surveys, the appraisals, and the planning, which will provide without unnecessary delay a sound basis for effective management of your vast water resources. In order that there be no misunderstanding in this area, let me state my position clearly. After you in Canada have measured your water and projected your own ultimate requirements, it is my hope that you will find that you have water for export, over and above your own foreseeable needs. I assure you that you will find a profitable market for it south of the border in both the United States and in Mexico.

Preliminary studies indicate that it is technically feasible and economically sound to collect, store, and redistribute *unused* runoff water from the northern reaches of the continent. Unlike oil and uranium, water can be marketed on a sustained yield basis. If the producing areas are properly managed, they will continue without depletion to produce a profitable "crop" for export. But first you must answer the basic question as to whether it is clearly to your advantage to export water. This question cannot be answered definitively until Canada's water-harvesting capabilities are fully and accurately measured.

Let me clarify a few points of possible misunderstanding. Borrowing from the techniques of the practice of law in both our countries, I want to remove from argument, by stipulation, two very important assumptions which underlie my discussion today. These assumptions should constitute the permanent foundation for continuing relations between our two countries.

The first stipulated assumption is that we Americans and Canadians are mutually desirous of living together in peace on this continent for a very long time to come, preserving the sovereign values of *both* our nations and our societies, and developing our respective talents constructively for the greatest good of the greatest number. The second stipulation is that we two peoples, in addition to all of our intangible blessings, have been endowed and entrusted with a very valuable piece of real estate, a section of the earth which is conducive to life and worthy of our care and affection, and that we are equally interested in preserving it and enhancing it as a region for human habitation.

Now, these are not assumptions to be stipulated in isolation. They are not points to be agreed upon in passing, and separated from the real world of politics, economics, and diplomacy. If you agree to such a dual stipulation, then the course ahead should be carefully plotted in both countries and clearly coordinated for the mutual benefit of both. In other words, if we want to continue to live in constructive peace on this richly endowed continent of North America, and to grow "in wisdom and stature," then we must cooperate in taking care of it.

I would not dare to come here and utter such seeming platitudes were it not for my confidence in the traditional good manners of Canadians. If this audience were to indulge in the habits of old-fashioned American politics, you might drown my voice in loud guffaws and say "Look who's talking! Why don't you clean your own house first?" Indeed, I must plead guilty to this basic charge made against the United States: that we have not taken proper care of our own waters. How then can we qualify to address our neighbours on the subject? I answer on two grounds. First, we have tardily learned our lesson and are doing something about our wasted waters. Secondly, we can help Canada to avoid the onerous costs of trying to recover lost ground after too many years of neglect. Our experience should be valuable to you.

A Canadian businessman recently observed to an American associate, in a friendly but meaningful sally: "You Americans have muddied your own water, now you want to muddy ours." He added (I hope more in jest than justice) that to part of the U.S. press, Idaho water was "American" but British Columbia water was "continental." My response is that really we are not the reprobates we are sometimes made to appear. In my own discussions I have been careful to talk about continental *planning* and not continental *water*. I trust most of my countrymen intended to do the same.

A certain amount of Canadian scepticism is a normal reaction to the widespread discussion in the United States on continental water planning, and particularly to the great attention that has been given to the North American Water and Power Alliance—the NAWAPA concept. Let me point out first of all that the concept relates to a continent-wide water *system*, and not to continental *water*. Then allow me to put into proper perspective the actual status of NAWAPA in the United States.

The concept was developed by the Ralph M. Parsons Company of Los Angeles. Its central idea came from one of the outstanding water-planning engineers of the West. Over the years it has been broadened to include parts of many regional plans which have been discussed on both sides of the border, and expanded into an integrated system. The resulting proposal or concept is based entirely on maps and analysis of published topographical, climatographical, and hydrological data. In many areas there have been no on-site investigations.

The Parsons Company has put the concept or plan in the public domain. While no funds other than his own have been invested in it, Ralph M. Parsons, the head of the company, makes no proprietary claims. The project has been entirely an in-house research and development effort in a field of special competence of the firm. The concept is, I understand, still being revised and refined. When it was brought to my attention, it seemed to me to warrant the attention of the Senate Committees on water resources. At my request, a Special Subcommittee on Western Water Development was appointed and directed to look into the matter. I was named Chairman. The Subcommittee made a rough comparison of this NAWAPA plan with an inventory of all the water projects anticipated by our U.S. federal agencies over the next twenty years.[1] The Committee's general conclusion was that for about 25 per cent greater total cost, the NAWAPA concept could deliver nearly twice as much water as could be provided by the large number of American projects envisioned by the four U.S. federal agencies having water resource development responsibilities.

Our review admittedly was hasty. The degree of refinement of the NAWAPA concept at that time did not warrant more detailed study. I believe that now it does. The United States still has a lot of homework to do. I hope Canada will feel that she does too. Before discussing this homework, let me review for you the essentials of the NAWAPA concept.

In one sentence, it is a continent-wide plan for collection, redistribution, and efficient utilization of waters now running off to the seas totally unused or only partially used. It would collect about 15 to 18 per cent of the excess runoff from the high-precipitation, medium-elevation areas of Alaska and of western and northern Canada. It is important to keep in mind that the concept deals with *surplus* water. By proper diversion and storage, optimal flows can be maintained downstream and flood peaks levelled. This collected, surplus water would be diverted southward and eastward through a continent-serving system of tunnels, canals, and improved natural channels, linking chains of reservoirs. Such controlled distribution of the waters from the North, pooled with waters from the interconnected producing areas of both countries, would benefit one territory and seven provinces of Canada, thirty-five states of the United States, and three states of Mexico.

NAWAPA would create a vast power generation system across Canada, pivoted in the West on your great Peace River Project. It would supply new industrial and agricultural water and would provide low-cost water transportation to the Prairie Provinces. It would stabilize flows in both the Columbia and the St. Lawrence rivers—with protection for the port

[1] *Western Water Development*, Compiled by the Special Subcommittee on Western Water Development of the Committee on Public Works, United States Senate (Washington: U.S. Government Printing Office, 1964).

of Montreal—and permit stabilization of the levels of the Great Lakes with living new water from both the Northwest and from the James Bay watershed.

In the United States, NAWAPA would permit increased flow in the upper Missouri and upper Mississippi rivers during low-flow periods. It would provide ample supplies of clean water for all the arid states of the West, including supplies for restoration of groundwater where it has been depleted. NAWAPA would also provide new high-quality water for Mexico in amounts many times greater than those the Egyptians will garner from the Aswan high dam.

Although Canada and the United States share the benefits of all the water in the Great Lakes, in case additional Canadian water were to become available from the North, the question of actual water export via the Lakes is worthy of investigation. Undoubtedly, the system of stabilized optimal levels in the Lakes would aid gradual restoration of their biological health.

The proposal to transfer James Bay water to the Great Lakes is not exclusive to NAWAPA. The idea has been proposed in only slightly different form by Thomas W. Kierans of Sudbury, Ontario, whose GRAND canal scheme embodies the possibility of converting most of James Bay into a great freshwater reservoir. Mr. Kierans' expanded plan now covers almost as much territory as does NAWAPA; but NAWAPA would add water from the Northwest as well as from the James Bay watershed. There is no point at this time in attempting to make a choice between the Kierans and NAWAPA proposals for diversion of water into the Great Lakes. There is certainly sufficient promise in both proposals, however, to warrant the detailed survey and appraisal work which is necessary. Once these studies are completed, Canada may then want either to develop one of these plans or a combination of the two, to design a third plan, or to reject the whole idea.

One undeniable value of the NAWAPA idea is that it stimulates resource study. The least that should be said for continental water planning is that it justifies investigation of all the water resources which might be incorporated in the system. Rational discussion of the specifics of any and all of the plans must await more precise technical data. Assuming that Canada actually produces the surplus water which today's sketchy climatological and hydrological data indicate she does—and I believe detailed engineering studies will confirm and expand the amount—NAWAPA would substantially benefit *both* countries, and bring direct profitable return to Canada.

Thus the bulk of that homework mentioned earlier involves the actual

NORTH AMERICAN WATER AND POWER ALLIANCE
CONCEPTUAL PLAN

field engineering determination of whether the initial assumptions are true. A determination of real precision—one in which the public can have confidence—must be made and it must demonstrate clearly that Canada does, in fact, have sufficient water-harvesting capability to consider export to her neighbours to the south. It would make little sense for us to debate further at this time any of the details of the continental planning concept, or even the question of whether it is a good idea for either country. But it makes a lot of sense to go after the facts on which to base definitive judgments. It also makes sense to examine the condition of the continent we share, to survey and appraise its total life-support capability in terms of water supply. Then we should plan the best way to preserve and, if possible, expand this resource. Finally, we must plan its most advantageous use for both our countries and for Mexico.

Let me now stipulate a third point: the people of the United States cannot expect the people of Canada to consider entering any arrangement such as this unless it is demonstrably and unquestionably in Canada's long-term best interest—and is so found by Canadians. We Americans have no right to suggest or to expect any water transfer scheme which might provide water in the United States for the next thirty or forty years, but which would leave Canada too little to meet her own future requirements.

I want to emphasize this point because the engineers, administrators, and parliamentarians who are scrutinizing the NAWAPA concept as a conceivable long-range answer to water supply problems in the United States are *not* conspiring to steal Canada's water. We are not devising a scheme to trick Canada. We are not even trying to arrive at a minimum price at which we might cajole and persuade you into selling us some of your water. As a matter of fact, we are working with dedication to *avoid* the prospect of dependence on imported water. The United States is now embarking on every possible venture to stretch our own water, creatively and ingeniously, and to find out whether we might have enough to see us through. We realize that only through an intensive effort can we find out just how much we can do on our own. After that we will know whether we must seek to import water and if so, how, where, and at what cost?

Our labours have a strange duality. The things we must do to get ready to import water, in case it *is* offered, are, to a very large extent, the things we must do if the water is *not* offered. In my opinion, however, transportation of unused water from an area where usability is meagre or impossible is all but inevitable. Population, economics, and common sense demand it.

Historically, there have been three great surges of federal interest and activity in water resource protection and development in the United States. One was under Theodore Roosevelt, when Gifford Pinchot led the movement for protection of forests. The second was under Franklin Roosevelt, when conservation received a mighty boost from depression-stimulated economic recovery programmes. Neither of these efforts, however, compares in scope or pace with the third surge now taking place under President Johnson. I think it is safe to say that in the past three years the Congress has passed more constructive water legislation than in any other time of our national history. I shall mention only the most important programmes.

The Congress has enacted the *Water Resources Planning Act*, a landmark measure which places water resource planning on a river basin basis. It recognizes the fundamental fact that water does not stop at state or county or municipal boundaries, and that any planning which does not take this into consideration will be piecemeal planning—with piecemeal effect. (As an aside, may I add that water does not recognize international boundaries in its interaction with either terrain or gravity.) The Congress has launched a *Water Research Programme*, which will invest nearly $100 million a year for ten years on basic water research. This is over and above the programme to bring desalting of water into economic balance, both in North America and eleswhere in the world. The Congress has established a *Water Pollution Control Administration*, which will conduct and oversee a broad public and industrial pollution control programme. We have greatly increased the federal funds available to communities for the construction of waste treatment plants and other pollution control facilities.

At this session we have legislation before us which will coordinate attacks on water pollution *within each river basin*. To make the programme more effective, we have just transferred the Water Pollution Control Administration from the Department of Health, Education and Welfare to the Interior Department, where other river basin planning is centred. We are also considering in the Senate at this time a bill which would establish a *National Water Commission*, to be composed of distinguished citizens outside the government, who will consider all aspects of our complex and interrelated water problems and will recommend long-range policy solutions. This emphasis on long-range planning makes our discussions of the same subject here today even more timely. Again, there is pending in Congress—with hearings scheduled for some time this fall—a bill which I have introduced to reorganize our federal water resource management, and to place all agencies concerned with it in one department to be called the *Department of Natural Resources.* At the present time, a score of agencies in five departments have some kind of statutory responsibility for water.

In February, 1966, the Committee on Water Resources Research of the Federal Council for Science and Technology published a recommended programme for ten years of water research. It would cover techniques of planning, organization, and water law. The programme recognizes the need for better methods of weighing costs and benefits of water resource development. In addition, it would expand research in waste treatment, in water-consuming industrial processes, in agricultural practices in conservation of watersheds for improved yield, in desalting, weather modification, and many other fields. Altogether, it may be said simply that there is a welling up of interest in and activities concerned with water throughout the federal government, and throughout the country. Water is truly front and centre in the United States at this time in our history.

Sometimes I think we make the water problem appear more complex than it really is. There are four general categories of effort, and we must invest in all of them. The first is *conservation,* or taking care of water-producing areas. This means attention to trees and grass on the watersheds, as well as adequate flow control through systems of retention pools and reservoirs to prevent floods and soil erosion.

The second category is proper *water handling.* This includes pollution abatement, cleaning up the water courses, treatment of water for recycle, improvement in water-consuming processes. We must be able to define legitimate water requirements in order to bridle growing demand. Such disciplinary measures as metering come in this category.

The third category is the search for *new sources* of usable water. One way is the desalting of the seas and inland brackish water. Another is rain-making, or weather modification. I recently heard a most descriptive term applied to the latter: "Stimulated Atmospheric Transport."

The fourth is *water resource development,* which covers the collection and storage of surplus water, interbasin transfers, and recharging of aquifers. In this category we find the multiple-use projects for domestic and industrial water supply, irrigation, recreation, transportation, power, and wildlife support.

While redistribution systems, such as the NAWAPA concept, fall essentially in the fourth category, they play an important role in the others. Continental planning makes no sense unless we practise conservation, pollution control, and efficient utilization of water. Economic exploitation of desalting and rain-making both depend upon efficient distribution.

It will cost billions of dollars to restore and to extend the water resources of the United States over the next two or three decades. Were this a meeting of the Chamber of Commerce, I would say to you that the business to be done in the water improvement field during the last third of this century will be greater than the economic explosion of railroad building over two-thirds of the nineteenth century. For example, the NAWAPA concept has a price tag, obviously very loosely attached, of $100 billion for a 25- to 30-year construction programme. Of course this sounds like a lot of money, but it is not unprecedented. The U.S. Interstate Highway programme is a 15-year programme to cost between $45 and $50 billion.

Parsons' engineers estimate that about 48 per cent of the NAWAPA investment would be in Canada, slightly less in the United States, and about 5 per cent in Mexico. The total revenues from NAWAPA activities and services, from the sale of water and electric power, and from other charges for use of facilities, are estimated at about $4 billion a year. Annual operating expenses are estimated at less than $1 billion, leaving $3 billion for capital financing. This makes the scheme quite practical for amortization within the usual time for water projects in my country.

Most of the water revenues would come from the United States. While more than half of the power available would be generated in Canada, the United States would, in the normal course of events, provide a market for large amounts of this Canadian-generated power. More of the navigation benefits would accrue to Canada. Recreation benefits would be about evenly divided. The benefits of such a continent-spanning water collection, saving, and distribution system are very real. They would be felt throughout the continent.

The level and purity of water in the Great Lakes would be restored and sustained, and the Lakes could be used as a distribution manifold, as is proposed specifically in the expanded Kierans' Plan. The flow of water in the Columbia and the St. Lawrence would be stabilized for both power generation and navigation. We could write *finis* to destructive floods on these and other rivers. The collection and redistribution system established in the Prairie Provinces would end floods there, provide a water supply, and mesh into a nation-wide system of water transportation. The new lakes and recreation areas would make the northlands even more attractive. Canada's recreation lure is already beckoning countless thousands of Americans. Their numbers would increase and, with almost limitless stretches of new waterways, the boating boom would become continent-wide.

British Columbia would have the greatest NAWAPA investment, in storage, power, and navigation facilities. The town of Prince George would be the centre of a complex of waterworks unrivalled anywhere in the world. British Columbia would be the site also of what might be the single most controversial feature of the initial NAWAPA concept. This is the proposal to make a huge lake out of the natural defile known as the Rocky Mountain Trench, along the west side of the Canadian Rockies. Studies must be made, of course, to determine the ecological impact of such a man-made, inland, freshwater sea. If this project were judged to be too costly in terms of real estate and wilderness impact, other routes for the transfer of water could doubtless be found, but the value of such a great, useful, spectacular new lake should also be considered.

First-hand studies, including bio-environmental studies, hydrological and geological surveys, and field engineering work may reveal flaws in the NAWAPA proposal. The United States may find it more beneficial to build a great collection and storage complex in Alaska, and then ask Canada for right-of-way to transfer some of this water to the contiguous states. It has even been proposed that we might do this by a plastic pipeline which could be submerged in the Pacific Ocean. Both America and Canada must determine what we should do—and determine it fairly soon.

To help make such a determination, I introduced a resolution last summer to provide for the use of the mechanism of the International Joint Commission to investigate the NAWAPA proposal. I chose this Commission because it is an existing and qualified agency through which both countries can work. I am now beginning to have some reservations, however, about using the IJC, not because of principle but because of timing and the scope of the job. The task is broader than the Commission's charter, and there are several years of American and Canadian homework to be done merely to develop instructions for an international agency. Besides, IJC studies of pollution and on control of water levels of the Great Lakes must be speeded up because of the pressing importance of corrective action in that region. The lessons to be learned in working out joint programmes for the improvement of this shared water resource should point the way to broader programmes involving the transfer and export of more distant waters.

I predict that you will see a big change in the overall water outlook in the United States in the next ten years. I *hope* that our domestic water programmes will be so successful that America will not need to seek any of Canada's bountiful supplies. But, even so, we would be happy to join with Canada in a continent-wide conservation and development water study. Canada's investment in water resource development would extend, without limit in decades or acre-feet, the producing lifetime of your water harvest areas, and would evolve a better distribution system. Such a programme would head off more expensive Canadian investment later on. Common sense and prudence dictate that both countries keep an eye on a possible continental system as each of us designs national water resource projects. Let us make sure that while we are making up our minds about the value of a continental approach we do nothing to make it unworkable.

One final thought—the total amount of moisture in the earth's life-support envelope is fixed and constant: the number of people to use it is not. Their numbers expand; their water uses change and increase; their modes of travel, their industries, and their residences shift. Should the United States and Canada approach the solution of the problem of water supply versus water demand separately or together?

A MONSTROUS CONCEPT, A DIABOLIC THESIS

A. G. L. McNaughton, F.R.S.C.

I SHOULD LIKE to thank the Royal Society of Canada for giving me this opportunity to set forth my views on the uses of Canada's water. I should also like to thank the Society for providing a forum for discussion of the important questions of the exploitation of Canada's water and whether it should be diverted to the United States, and the related questions of the development of the resources of this country and perhaps even its survival and growth as a nation.

Canada has been endowed by Divine Providence with abundant resources which confer immense advantages upon this country. It is our responsibility to use these resources with discretion, and to treasure the more basic of them for the generations of Canadian citizens who will come after us is a paramount responsibility. Of our many resources, two are fundamental: land and water. In Canada, they are closely related, and we alienate or squander either only at our peril.

For this reason, vital and important questions are raised affecting this country's future by propositions such as that currently being touted under the somewhat pretentious name of the North American Water and Power Alliance, or NAWAPA for short. Of course this proposal is not concerned with an alliance at all: it is nothing more than an attempt by the Ralph M. Parsons Company, of Los Angeles, California, a private engineering firm, to drum up business for themselves.

A great deal of publicity has been created for these proposals in the United States and much attention has been directed to them in Canada. I feel obliged to say, therefore, that they are quite unacceptable, and to set forth the position which should be taken by Canada and the provinces. Despite some temporizing pronouncements which have been issued by distracted politicians, I believe that this position represents the view being taken by our best-informed technical and administrative officers and by responsible members of our engineering profession, who are best qualified to judge the merits and demerits of any physical arrangement of this kind.

There are similar, and indeed possibly associated schemes, being put forward in Canada by such people as Thomas Kierans of Sudbury, whose GRAND canal scheme would divert rivers flowing into James Bay, and more recently by Professor Edward Kuiper[1] of the University of Manitoba, who would reverse the flow of a large part of the Nelson and Churchill rivers flowing into Hudson Bay. The origin of the waters affected in these schemes lies for the most part in several provincial jurisdictions, except for the Red River, a small part of which may represent a re-export of some waters originating in North Dakota and Minnesota. With this one exception, these rivers are all *national* rivers of Canada—that is, they flow entirely within Canada, from source to mouth, and therefore the benefits which accrue from them belong *wholly* to Canada. Over national waters, the jurisdiction of the nation in which they are situated is supreme. Canada would be foolish indeed to recognize or permit any international character to be ascribed to these national waters, and they would assume just such a character if they were to be subjected to any international study.

Within Canada, the rights to ownership of interprovincial rivers, as between upstream and downstream provinces, is by no means clear. One might suppose that claims could be based on any of the various doctrines which may have superseded that of riparian rights. In any event, the physical jurisdiction rests largely with the particular upstream states concerned, and they have made their views quite explicit. British Columbia, Alberta, and Saskatchewan have made the clearest declarations against the sale of Canadian waters; and Quebec is too well informed and too intimately concerned over water for the public welfare to be drawn into export, especially for compensation in the form of a silly project like a canal to Knob Lake, which forms part of the Parsons scheme. An example of the position taken by provincial governments is that of Premier W. A. C. Bennett, who said that British Columbia "will sell the U.S. hydro-electric power but *not* water. Even to talk about selling it is ridiculous. You do not sell your heritage."

It should be noted that no government or government agency on this continent has commissioned any technical study of the NAWAPA scheme. Indeed, there has been very little formal government discussion on even the possibility of such studies. I have not overlooked the discussion of NAWAPA by a United States Senate subcommittee. Nor have I overlooked the fact that the United States government has not seen fit to act on a Congressional resolution to refer the NAWAPA scheme to the International Joint Commission for study.

[1]E. Kuiper, "Canadian Water Export," *Engineering Journal, 49* (1966): 13–18.

It should be noted also that the Canadian government, in referring the problem of Great Lakes levels to the IJC, expressly forbade studies of plans such as the Kierans GRAND canal scheme, involving purely national Canadian waters. At the same time, it must be noted that a joint Canada–Ontario stock-taking of northern Ontario waters is proceeding. To this must be added the fact that Quebec, where some of these rivers for diversion are located, has declined to answer an invitation to join in these federal–provincial studies.

One independent scientist who has spoken out is Trevor Lloyd, Professor of Geography at McGill University. In a paper delivered in February, 1966, Dr. Lloyd had this to say about NAWAPA: "Clearly, we have here an exercise in sophomore civil engineering which has received far greater attention than it ever deserved. It underlines the danger, all too familiar to geographers, of allowing the drawing office to replace acquaintance with the land and the people as they really are."[2]

Canada is a vast land, whose many resources are so great that we have yet to take the measure of them. We have a great deal of fresh water, but the available amount, it seems to me, tends to be frequently overstated. We have suffered in the past from permitting such overstatements to remain uncorrected, and they are being made with growing intensity in the propaganda with which we are being deluged.

Canada is a land of hundreds of thousands of lakes. These lakes are full of clear water, which has accumulated there as the glaciers receded thousands of years ago. The large surface of these lakes has a profound effect in modifying our climate from the harsh extremes of the continental effect which would prevail without their presence. But this is water in inventory; if removed it will not be replaced. Moreover, its removal could reduce the amount of rainfall and therefore reduce the supply of running water. Only the running water can be regarded as available for use, for it is only this water which is replenished by rain and snowmelt. Only this water can be regarded as perpetual and, even then, only if it is properly managed. It may come as a surprise to some, but this second kind of water, the kind we can use, is by no means as abundant as is generally supposed. In fact, our total streamflow in Canada is not limitless, as is so often imagined, but is of a similar order of magnitude to that of the United States.

The United States also has vast supplies of water in inventory, but a great proportion of theirs is underground, which means that it is situated beneath space that can be used for living. In Canada, we have much less

[2]T. Lloyd, "A Water Resource Policy for Canada," *Canadian Geographic Journal, 73* (1966): 2–17.

habitable and arable land, which means that in the future we may have to conserve this for ourselves, and in turn that we have to consider carefully before we put any more of it under water.

The NAWAPA scheme seems to be based on the premise that there are large quantities of surplus water in Canada. Any large-scale withdrawal of our water from the North raises questions which need careful analysis before any major discussions can be permitted, even in Canada.

The first of these that I would mention has recently been called to attention by H. A. Neu of the National Research Council. His advice is that a Canadian committee be formed on water, weather, and vegetation, to carry out certain studies before any system of water diversion is brought under consideration at all. Even the slightest changes may have far-reaching effects; the danger lies in the fact that if water flows were altered, the related climatic changes could affect vegetation and biological life. With decreases in local streamflow, the climate of a region could assume a more continental character—hotter during the warm months, and colder during the winter and fall. Because of temperature changes, plants might not be able to survive the heat of summer or the cold of winter. Conceivably, such changes in climate also might alter the water supply, because of a change in the régime of precipitation.

Then there is the question of permafrost, which occurs in Canada in large lenticular masses embedded in the soil at considerable depths. If these are subject to inflow of heat by flooding of the surface, the permafrost will melt and constitute a dangerous foundation upon which to impound the vast areas of storage water which have been indicated.

The NAWAPA propagandists love to talk of great quantities of water spilling unused into the Arctic Ocean. But the major sources for the scheme are hundreds of miles from the Arctic Ocean. They are in fact the rivers of the Canadian Cordillera, which provide a great series of prime power sites; rivers which form the basis of one of the world's great concentrations of the forest products industry; rivers which provide some of the finest salmon runs in the world. There are detailed plans on Canadian drawing-boards, and there are projects now under construction to harness these flows. The associated mineral and forest resources are already staked out, and the required human and financial resources are being attracted to the region. The NAWAPA promoters would move all of this out of Canada—the people, the industry, the water. It can only be described as madness to believe that Canada has surplus water in an area that is so obviously earmarked for major resource development, and where so much activity to that end is already taking place.

Of course, NAWAPA has nothing to do with the maximum development of these rivers or resources in Canada. Its purpose is to flood the valleys in Canada, and to drain off the water in regulated flow for beneficial use in the United States. But the valleys themselves are of vital importance to British Columbia, because they contain the level land which is so vitally needed for roads and railways, for industries, for people, and for agriculture. Whitehorse and Prince George would be submerged, and their land with them, as would countless miles of railway and highway. These irreplaceable assets would be destroyed in the name of trans-mountain navigation.

The grandiose concept starts with the collection of the waters of the Yukon and the Peace in the Rocky Mountain Trench, that great intramontane valley which stretches through our western Cordillera at an altitude of half a mile above sea level. It reaches from Montana to northern British Columbia, and they would put it all under water.

This scheme ignores all the plans which have been made in Canada for the use of the waters and the lands of the Rocky Mountain Trench. For example, it ignores Canadian plans to capture the waters of the Yukon River by backing them into the Atlin Lakes and thence through a head of something over two thousand feet for power in Taku Inlet. It ignores the fact that the Peace River is being harnessed for power at this very moment; it ignores the development plans which now exist for the Fraser and Thompson rivers. It seems to ignore developments which are under construction on the Columbia River, from which the United States will receive some 50 million acre-feet of Canadian water in the form of regulated flow, at a cost to the United States which is less than the cost to Canada of constructing the dams. Surely this is enough pillage in the appropriation of our waters, without further extension into the national domain.

If, in the course of development of British Columbia waters, there is water left over, the Rocky Mountain Trench is the natural reservoir for it, and the Canadian West—not the United States Northwest, or Southwest, or Midwest—is the logical beneficiary.

The natural reservoir sites of the Rocky Mountain Trench were not discovered by Parsons' engineers. The Peace River waters now being dammed up by British Columbia will be held in the Trench by structures outside it. The Trench will provide a reservoir for water of Canadian origin from the Kootenay branch of the Columbia River, to be impounded by the United States at heavy cost to Canada in terms of sacrificed opportunities, as well as in benefits which should, in equity, be payable for Canadian waters used for consumption in the United States.

Parsons' engineers did not originate the idea of pumping water over the Rocky Mountains from reservoirs in the Trench. The capture of Columbia and Kootenay river waters in the Trench, and their diversion over the Rockies, is the logical first step in development of additional water supplies for the Canadian Prairies.

Studies made or under way by the provinces of Alberta and Saskatchewan have already laid the groundwork for extensive utilization of the Saskatchewan River system. Saskatchewan studies even cover the underground water courses of this system. Tentative agreement has been reached for a joint federal-provincial inventory of the water resources of the entire Saskatchewan and Nelson river systems. This covers a network stretching from Hudson Bay and the Lake of the Woods to the Rocky Mountains. Joint Canada–Manitoba studies for extensive power development of the Nelson River, including diversion from the Churchill River, were completed early in 1966. Work on Nelson River power sites is already under way.

The Canadian Prairie region can look forward to maximum development of its agricultural potential being made possible by water for irrigation. It can also anticipate major developments in mineral, fossil, and forest resources. The logical consequence of such development will be a major petrochemical industry, metal-producing industries, pulp and paper industries—and these all call for large supplies of water from the annual flow available.

The northward course of our Prairie empire is already being staked out by prospectors and timber cruisers. It has already reached the great tributaries of the Mackenzie River system—the Peace and the Athabasca rivers. Massive lead-zinc deposits are being mined at Pine Point on Great Slave Lake, one of the huge natural balancing reservoirs of the Mackenzie system. The federal government is financing a feasibility study for a smelter at Pine Point. Mineral resources have already been staked out in the region of another great Mackenzie reservoir, Great Bear Lake.

Considering the vast potential for development of the Canadian Prairies, it seems unlikely that the waters of the Canadian Cordillera would ever reach the Great Lakes as NAWAPA proposes. What does seem possible is the re-routing of waters flowing into Hudson Bay to the Prairie region. NAWAPA, however, offers to bring western water to the Great Lakes—an offer which had rather more appeal in 1964 when the levels were low than is the case today, now that they have recovered. Here I am dealing with a matter in which I have had a close personal interest and responsibility, as Chairman of the Canadian Section of the

IJC in the flood year of 1952 and later. The proponents seem to be quite unfamiliar with the experience during the high-water of 1952, and with the very careful studies made then and subsequently.

These studies showed the sensitivity of the basin to the cumulative effects of even a short succession of years of supply only slightly above normal. The limiting factors are the great industrial and municipal developments which have taken place along the shores of the Great Lakes, and more particularly along the connecting channels, whose capacities have been formed by the rivers through long ages to accommodate natural flows. Any cumulative increase in net supply is accompanied by large sustained increases in levels, and the damage, even for very small changes in levels, is disproportionately severe. This was noted in the surveys conducted by the IJC in 1952–53, and is reflected in the damage claims made at that time—for which, even after the lapse of more than a decade, Canada is about to be sued by interests in the United States.

The costs of channel enlargements to correct this situation in high supply years would be very large, and such enlargements would accentuate the difficulties in low supply years. Moreover, the investigations showed that the time required for changes in supply to pass through the system is very long, and the relationship is very complex. Consequently, for controlled changes in the inflow to the system to stabilize levels and flows, would require an ability to predict natural supply for a period further into the future than is foreseeable. Without this ability to predict, artificial changes in supply would aggravate periodic crises and in particular increase the danger of flooding, which already causes the greatest anxiety.

In my address to the Canadian Club in Montreal in October, 1965, I referred to some of the serious legal and political implications of the NAWAPA scheme. I observed at that time that this is a monstrous concept, not only in terms of physical magnitude, but also in another and more sinister sense, in that the promoters would displace Canadian sovereignty over the national waters of Canada, and substitute therefor a diabolic thesis that *all* waters of North America become a shared resource, of which most will be drawn off for the benefit of the midwest and southwest regions of the United States, where existing desert areas will be made to bloom at the expense of development in Canada.

Evidently the NAWAPA proposal contemplates that the complete jurisdiction and control will rest with a corporation which, although it might be nominally international, would in reality be dominated by Americans, who would thereby acquire a formidable vested interest in the national waters of Canada. With this mammoth inroad into Canada's lawful rights and interests, the corporation would inevitably, in the nature of things, have to assume quasi-sovereign power to administer large areas of Canada at the expense of Canadian sovereignty.

I was very interested to hear an American, William S. Foster, editor of *The American City*, speak of the implications of water export on a CBC television programme on the politics of water, on April 11, 1966. Mr. Foster said:

> There's a great deal of risk. Offhand, at first glance, you would say that the risk is great for the southwest because the water belongs to Canada, and presumably at Canada's wish it could simply turn off the valve and the water would not be there any more. But there is a more subtle threat than that. I wonder just what would happen to the sovereignty of Canada if a nation like the United States and a nation like Mexico would suddenly say that "you no longer have the right to deny us the water even though you need it in your own industrial and agricultural development." I've often thought about that and wondered what the really long-range risks are to Canada, and I think they're considerable.

The situation in the U.S. Southwest is that any additional water which becomes available is forthwith applied to irrigation; and so if cheap Canadian water is supplied, as it is now under the Columbia River Treaty, and would be under the NAWAPA plan, it will be immediately appropriated by the irrigators. Large increases in population and investment may be anticipated, and there does not appear to be any *cheap* replacement should the Canadian water be recalled.

You will appreciate the serious probability of conflict in such a situation when I mention that the Canadian Minister of External Affairs has given assurances to the External Affairs Committee of Parliament that under the Columbia River Treaty, the Protocol, and the Sales Agreement, Canada can make use of waters of Canadian origin for consumptive purposes at any time and in conjunction with power generation in transit. When Canada does exercise this reservation, which I regard as inevitable, will the United States acquiesce in this interpretation of provisions in the Protocol agreed to by the United States Executive, but not included in the ratification by the Senate?

I believe that such a situation is much too hazardous to be left to a giant corporation dominated by United States interests. Canada faced a similar situation 25 years ago when it exported electric power to the United States on yearly permit. When under dire necessity of war we wanted it back we met a curt refusal. I do not think Canada should ever again expose herself to such an outcome, particularly over water, which is an even more sensitive matter.

To me it is obvious that if we make a bargain to divert water to the United States, we cannot ever discontinue or we shall face force to compel compliance. There is nothing in our experience to date which indicates any change in the vigour with which our American friends pursue objectives which they deem in their national interests, however much this may hurt a neighbour who has unwittingly made a careless bargain in other circumstances. Instance after instance can be cited in support of this observation, from the case of the Similkameen River after World War I to the most recent example, when the Columbia River Treaty was hailed in the Senate of the United States as having achieved one major American objective, which was to prevent Canada making best use of her waters of Canadian origin in the Basin.[3]

The imperative lesson is that we must be very careful in our discussions of vital problems related to water with the United States, and very, very careful over the bargains which we may make to ensure that the rights we think we have are admitted and confirmed beforehand.

One of the ironic things about all of this fuss regarding the export of Canada's water to the United States is that the United States has abundant supplies of water for all of its needs. What is scarce in the United States is *clean* water. This could be provided at less cost by proper administration and pollution control than by importation from Canada. In fact, I am inclined to believe that in the long run perhaps one of the most unfriendly acts that Canada could do to the United States would be to offer our water at bargain prices. Because if we did, the attack on pollution might then be postponed until the problem was no longer soluble, or the cost would be astronomical. This cost is large enough today, and it rises with every passing year at an accelerating rate.

In the foregoing, I have sought to indicate some of the perils which face Canada with respect to the commitment of our water resources at this time. We have everything to lose by hasty and ill-considered action, and we have everything to gain by waiting until the essential information is available upon which we can make our own assessment of the subject of sharing resources, and our own plans as to the course of action we shall adopt.

[3]Senate Hearings, 8 May, 1961, Udall.

General A. G. L. McNaughton, F.R.S.C.

The McNaughton-Moss Confrontation

C. E. DOLMAN, F.R.S.C.

GENERAL MCNAUGHTON had arrived well ahead of the scheduled hour, looking relaxed, in fine fettle, and obviously ready for the fray. As we chatted, he remarked how pleased he was to have this chance to revisit the Eastern Townships—"a fine part of the country, with sound traditions and excellent community spirit." He confided that he had enjoyed happy days as a schoolboy in the neighbourhood 70 years before. To Senator Moss, on the other hand, this was unfamiliar territory. Indeed, he arrived a little late, having been misdirected somehow to the city of Quebec.

The audience was worthy of the occasion—representative of all sections of the Society, expectant, and keenly attentive. The President, Dr. W. Kaye Lamb, acted as chairman of this Plenary Session and appropriately introduced each speaker in turn. The two protagonists knew each other's viewpoint from previous encounters, and did not attempt to mask their differences. But whereas the Senator's smile hardly deserted him, even when volley after volley of grape-shot was fired across his bow, the General's joviality vanished soon after he mounted the platform, and his facial expression ranged from frown to scowl. The Senator (a lawyer by profession) presented his case for diversion of surplus Canadian waters in well-reasoned, conciliatory fashion, which did him credit and earned our respect. The General's insistence upon Canada's inalienable right and obligation to retain all her waters intact in perpetuity was emphatic, at times bellicose.

The two addresses speak for themselves and need no editorial comment or embellishment. But we feel justified in drawing attention to the obvious sympathy aroused in this ostensibly hard-headed, scholarly audience by a great patriot's fervent admonitions. All our largely latent Canadianism was inspired by the vigorous forthrightness of this engineer, who was also scientist, soldier, statesman, and conservationist—surely a lesson for more "successful" politicians of so much lesser stature. These reactions became plain in the discussion period, which though fairly brief was entirely spontaneous, and yielded several observations that were relevant, remarkably candid, and on the whole free from jingoism.

No stenographic or tape recordings were taken of the discussion, so speakers will not be identified, with one exception. Perhaps the strongest point urged from the floor was a reiteration of what General McNaughton had already stressed, viz. that the Americans should halt and reverse the trend towards increasing pollution and wastage of their own previously plentiful water supplies before casting covetous eyes on Canada's alleged superabundance. Less well known, but apparently fully justified, was the contention that some American industries are shockingly extravagant in their water usage. For instance, it was pointed out that a much greater gallonage of water is involved in the production of a ton of steel in the United States than in Germany. Clearly it would be to everyone's advantage that such squandering of a vital heritage should be curbed.

Senator Moss, while readily conceding these points, stressed that educational and legislative campaigns have been and are being launched in his country to pin-point the causes, track down the culprits, and avert the extension of these avoidable water losses.

Fears of the political implications of any large-scale international water-transfer were expressed by one or two speakers. The irretrievability of such a treaty, once signed, would impose a stranglehold upon our relatively small population; and we were reminded that Canada had customarily fared badly in frontier disputes and other historic "agreements" with the United States. Oddly enough, nobody voiced any apprehension that our country had already made long-term commitments to transfer across the border huge amounts of oil and natural gas, which, unlike water, are non-renewable resources.

When the question was asked whether Canada actually had any surplus water she could afford to export, even at a fancy price (including cession of the Alaska Panhandle and Point Roberts!), General McNaughton categorically denied this possibility. The NAWAPA diversion project would entail the flooding or spoliation of vast areas of habitable and valuable land in northern British Columbia and the Yukon. To surrender this land would be a betrayal of their heritage for future generations of Canadians. At this juncture, Dr. Radforth, who had received from Senator Moss what he considered an inadequate reply to a preliminary question about the effects of NAWAPA upon Canada's northern muskeg, launched into a dissertation on this topic. His statement is reproduced below, both for its own importance and because it exemplifies how much authoritative information needs to be sought and correlated by the best-trained minds available for the task in both Canada and the United States, before the two countries should even consider embarking upon international agreements of such far-reaching nature and magnitude. Let us willingly concede that Senator Moss went to some pains to stress this necessity.

Press photographers abounded throughout the morning's session, but no picture of General McNaughton in action before the Society could be secured. However, through the kindness of Mrs. McNaughton, and by courtesy of the National Film Board of Canada, we are able to reproduce a fine likeness of the General, who died suddenly, at the age of 79, about one month after his gallant participation in the Royal Society of Canada's Symposium on "Water Resources." He was surely one of the most distinguished and versatile of our Fellows. All of us who were present on that occasion are grateful that we should have happened to be among the audience for his last public address.

NAWAPA and Muskeg

NORMAN W. RADFORTH, F.R.S.C.

SINCE 1946 I have been engaged in investigations on the environment, structure, and distribution of muskeg in the Canadian North, as well as in other areas and countries. This muskeg, a water-holding feature of our land, covers a minimum of 500,000 square miles according to conservative estimates. Its distribution coincides significantly with that marking the massive, artificially controlled water sources and systems proposed in NAWAPA, as portrayed and supported by Senator Moss.

As I attempt to comprehend NAWAPA and its implications from the scientific and engineering aspects I am aware of its boldness, the stimulus and direction it affords, and the wisdom its authors injected into the plans as detailed on the chart. While I acknowledge this with congratulations to Senator Moss, I must record on the other hand my dismay in learning that this plan has been devised without any reference to the muskeg factor which, I dare say, contains the most significant controlling agent for water supply in our North. Any system of artificial control of northern water, whether by artificial storage involving controlled level, diversion of flow, reversal of flow, change in rate of flow, or flooding—any such modification—would be devastating to the physical and mechanical constitution and physiography of the muskeg, the natural regulator of supply.

It is now widely appreciated that there are many kinds of muskeg. Each is a hidden reservoir of gravitational water, releasing this commodity to the existing "open" drainage systems in accordance with "built in" structural differentials of the organic terrain. If these differentials are to be disturbed, the seasonal or annual properties of the drainage sheds in question would be seriously modified to an unpredictable degree and our water resources drastically affected.

The muskeg factor, because it is primary, must be assessed in accordance with the water-user requirement for Canada. The muskeg is our land and it is involved in our industry and development in different fundamental ways. This assessment could be achieved in the course of lending support to and extending those investigations cited in General McNaughton's timely presentation. To endorse the NAWAPA plan as a feasible prospect would be to neglect a basic rule in design procedure. The controlling features that are significant in achieving a purpose must be recognized and incorporated in the process of affecting the design. If the NAWAPA plan is not a design but is simply a hypothesis, it has an unfortunate scientific foundation. It would seem harmful to continue to impose the NAWAPA plan on Canadians as if to elicit support and decision, and such behaviour will surely not assist us to help our neighbours elsewhere on the continent to the best of our ability.

The understanding of Senator Moss revealed in his response to my first observation is not the same as mine. The Senator's claim is that the muskeg factor (one of those problems which I think he agrees should be investigated) is perhaps significant in the Northwest but not in the Hudson Bay–James Bay Lowlands and environment. My own knowledge of the muskeg in Northern Ontario indicates that its occurrence there is likewise of the utmost importance for regulation and supply of water. Neglect of this point when final plans are implemented could devastatingly reduce biological productivity in the North as the price of converting the deserts in the South.

PART II

WATER, AN INDISPENSABLE RESOURCE

L'EAU, RESSOURCE INDISPENSABLE

Pierre Camu, M.S.R.C.

LE SEUL FAIT d'inscrire l'eau comme thème de l'une des sessions régulières de l'assemblée annuelle de la Société royale du Canada indique clairement que ses membres se préoccupent de cette grande ressource naturelle. S'en préoccupent-ils parce que c'est un sujet à la mode, qu'il est bien d'inscrire au feuilleton des débats des sujets comme la pollution de l'eau et de l'air, l'épuisement des sols, le reboisement, les richesses naturelles superflues, la crise du charbon, les ressources minières et autres sujets du genre ? J'espère que non. Que l'on ait inscrit ce sujet parce qu'il crée dans l'esprit de ses membres une inquiétude réelle à cause de la mauvaise utilisation des eaux aujourd'hui au Canada et des problèmes de plus en plus complexes qui s'y attachent, voilà, à notre avis, une excellente raison d'examiner ce sujet. Notre contribution sera modeste, concrète et, nous l'espérons, positive.

L'information géographique telle que diffusée dans nos écoles, collèges et universités est responsable de l'idée acquise et quasi indestructible de l'eau, ressource inépuisable. L'eau est abondante, on la trouve partout, il y a surabondance en certains cas, et il en a toujours été ainsi. Pourquoi s'en faire, pourquoi s'inquiéter outre mesure de l'usage que l'on en fait, du gaspillage que l'on accepte, il y aura toujours de l'eau. Voilà comment l'on raisonne. Remarquez bien que cette information géographique est exacte, qu'elle est véridique.

Examinons un instant les eaux intérieures. On nous dit qu'il y a plus de 291,571 milles carrés d'eau douce, c'est énorme, mais on nous dit aussi que cela èquivaut à huit pour cent da la superficie totale du pays. C'est plus que la superficie réunie de plusieurs contrées européenes, nous sommes à l'échelle d'un demi-continent. Les eaux des lacs et rivières se séparent et s'écoulent vers la mer par quatre grands bassins de drainage, celui de la baie d'Hudson, le plus vaste, et ceux de l'Arctique, de l'Atlantique et du Pacifique. Une petite partie du territoire, à peine dix mille milles carrés, appartient au bassin du golfe du Mexique. Pourtant, ce même pays si bien arrosé en général avec des précipitations énormes sur la côte du Pacifique et de la neige en abondance dans la vallée du

Saint-Laurent possède une zone de terre aride dans le coin sud-ouest de la Saskatchewan. Les habitants de cette partie du Canada sont les plus conscients de la valeur économique de l'eau.

La géographie nous a appris aussi que nos fleuves et rivières ont des dimensions énormes, près de 125 d'entre eux ont une longueur de plus de cent milles, un grand nombre ont une largeur moyenne d'un mille, et bien d'autres comptent un nombre incalculable de chutes et de rapides, et des débits et des comportements variés.

Les Grands Lacs sont trop connus pour qu'on s'y attarde, mentionnons la chaîne des autres grands lacs situés aux limites du bouclier canadien et des grandes plaines et vallées, comme le lac de l'Ours, des Esclaves, d'Athabaska, du Renne, de Winnipegosis et de Winnipeg. Nous avons déjà relevé il y a plusieurs années que la seule province d'Ontario comptait au delà de 25,000 lacs, et que dire du Québec. N'insistons pas, le club de chasse et de pêche, le chalet au bord du lac ou de la rivière, la maison avec vue sur le fleuve, voilà des choses typiquement, intimement canadiennes, tout comme le gel, la glace, et l'hiver.

Ce que la géographie sait mais n'a pas toujours fait connaître c'est l'importance des eaux côtières. Les gens des provinces atlantiques et du Bas du fleuve, aussi bien que ceux de la côte du Pacifique ou des postes de l'Arctique le savent, mais pas les millions d'habitants de l'intérieur. Ils ne savent pas que la côte dentelée de notre pays est la plus longue du monde, à peu près 60,000 milles, où l'on retrouve la nomenclature complètes de golfes, fjords, détroits, inlets, baies, anses, îles, presqu'îles ou péninsules. Ils ignorent trop souvent que les eaux sont salées, qu'il y a des courants et des marées qui affectent les températures et la vie organique, que le continent se prolonge par une plateforme continentale et que les limites officielles des eaux canadiennes s'étendent maintenant à douze milles en mer.

Bref, partout, les eaux intérieures ou côtières sont présentes, et il n'y a presque pas de Canadiens, à l'exception peut-être des habitants des Prairies, qui ne soient conscients de leur influence. J'oserais dire qu'on est tellement habitué a voir l'eau qu'on ne la voit plus. Ainsi, l'information géographique est exacte, on considère l'eau comme une ressource permanente et éternelle. Les savants disent qu'elle est une ressource renouvelable.

Pourtant ceux qui ont fondé ce pays en étaient plus que conscients, l'eau leur était indispensable. C'était le seul et grand moyen de communication, c'était la source d'énergie par excellence, c'était une source d'alimentation grâce à la pêche, et une source de vie inépuisable. L'information historique atteste le rôle primordial qu'a joué à travers les âges, les grands fleuves, rivières et lacs de notre pays. Le développement initial, les vagues de peuplement et les fronts de colonisation ont commencé le long des rives et bords des fleuves et des côtes pour couvrir le pays. Encore de nos jours, les plus grandes villes du pays sont également des ports de mer actifs. Dans la vie économique des municipalités, villes et régions, l'eau joue un rôle primordial. Qui n'a pas de problèmes d'aqueducs, d'égoûts, d'usines de filtration et de pompage, de réservoirs, et de distribution d'eau? Ces problèmes matériels et quotidiens rappellent à tous que l'eau est une ressource indispensable. Hélas, on ne réalise pas encore pleinement que l'eau, présente partout, n'est pas utilisée avec sagesse, qu'on la pollue et qu'elle n'a plus la qualité qu'elle avait. La consommation a augmenté considérablement avec les besoins mais le côntrole de la qualité n'a pas suivi au même rythme. On aurait dû être plus vigilant avec la multiplication des usages, on ne l'a pas été. Pourquoi en est-il ainsi? Parce qu'on n'utilise pas l'eau d'une manière tout à fait sage et rationnelle.

L'eau sert à cinq usages fondamentaux : a) à la consommation domestique, b) à des fins industrielles et agricoles, c) à la navigation, d) à la production d'énergie hydro-électrique, e) à la récréation. On pourrait ajouter, en complément, un sixième usage, celui de la pêche, mais il s'agit là d'une ressource naturelle séparée à cause de son importance.

Quand on pense à la consommation domestique courante, on pense tout de suite aux systèmes d'aqueducs et d'égoûts. N'oublions pas que la consommation industrielle est plus forte encore que la consommation domestique dans certaines villes. Il y a des procédés d'usinage qui requièrent des millions de gallons d'eau par jour, des radiateurs qui ne fonctionnent qu'à l'eau, et que dire des systèmes de protection d'incendie. En agriculture, on irrigue de plus en plus. On dépense des millions de dollars pour contrôler les crues et assurer un débit constant aux fleuves et rivières. Tout cela c'est l'aspect positif, soit celui d'assurer aux consommateurs et selon les besoins une eau pure en quantité suffisante.

Il y a également l'aspect négatif, soit l'absence de contrôle des eaux usées, d'usines d'épuration et de traitement des égoûts. Car, c'est là, à notre avis, le grand problème dans les régions peuplées du Canada, on n'a pas pensé que l'eau, que la même eau, pourrait servir encore à la ville ou à l'usine en aval. Le dernier consommateur d'en bas très souvent reçoit une eau qui n'est plus potable, qui n'est même plus qualifiée pour servir à des fins industrielles. Il y a eu pollution, il y en a de plus en plus. On s'est préoccupé d'assurer au consommateur quel qu'il soit, les quantités voulues, mais on ne s'est pas inquiété de lui fournir une eau de qualité constante. Ceci nous mène à utiliser une ressource qui, à cause des quantités requises de plus en plus grandes, ne se renouvelle plus d'elle-même. Pour restaurer la qualité de l'eau, les solutions existent, mais elles sont dispendieuses.

A ces deux premiers usages s'en ajoute un troisième, celui de la navigation. Fleuves, rivières et lacs ne sont navigables qu'à condition qu'il y ait suffisamment d'eau, c'est la première condition. Après cela, tout ce qu'on fait pour améliorer les voies navigables est la contribution des hommes. Ainsi, draguer, élargir un chenal, construire des écluses, bâtir des ports, baliser une route, installer des phares sont des raffinemments qu'apporte l'homme aux dons de la nature. La nature a été généreuse au Canada en lui procurant des grandes voies d'eau que l'on oserait qualifier d'incomparables. C'est en Finlande, je crois, qu'un proverbe dit ceci : « Quand Dieu sépara les eaux de la terre, il oublia notre pays » . Ce proverbe s'applique aussi au Canada. La nature fut généreuse et nous avons fait bon usage des voies navigables, mais en cherchant à les améliorer, surtout en élargissant et creusant le chenal principal des fleuves, on a accéléré le débit qui a provoqué une baisse de niveau de l'eau qui à son tour a eu des répercussions innombrables. Dans ce domaine comme dans les autres, on possède des solutions, mais elles coûtent cher. Citer des données statistiques ne prouverait rien. Disons qu'on a des règlements qui interdisent aux navires, gros et petits, de jeter des déchets, des ordures ou du mazout à l'eau. On surveille étroitement les navires au moyen d'hélicoptères, en général, la qualité de l'eau n'est pas affectée par le navires qui circulent sur les voies intérieures. C'est plutôt l'action de l'eau, comme l'effet des vagues qui, en lèchant les grèves et les plages, érodent les terrains riverains.

De tous les usages, celui dont on a sû tirer le plus de bénéfices sans détruire la qualité de l'eau, c'est le développement de l'énergie hydro-électrique. Des chiffres sont inutiles, on connait l'histoire de l'électricité et celle du harnachement systématique des chutes et rapides au pays. On a accompli dans ce domaine tellement de choses remarquables que le nom du Canada à l'étranger brille avec éclat. En utilisant systématiquement chaque chute (haute ou basse), chaque rapide et dénivellation substantielle, on a fait servir la même eau six, sept et même huit fois de suite, en la faisant passer par les turbines de centrales installées en aval l'une de l'autre. L'un des examples les mieux connus est l'aménagement du bassin de la Saint-Maurice. On a exploité avec intelligence en construisant des réservoirs et en accummulant des réserves d'eau au printemps, afin de les utiliser plus tard vers la fin de l'été. Les quantités comptent quand il s'agit de produire et de vendre de l'éléctricité, ce qui compte davantage c'est un débit constant, une quantité toujours la même; la qualité de l'eau est secondaire ici.

Enfin, l'eau sert à des fins récréatives. Il me suffit d'énumérer les sports nautiques à la mode, la nage, le ski aquatique, la voile, la pêche sportive, et maintenant la plongée sous-marine, pour raviver en chacun de nous des souvenirs mémorables ou nous faire penser à des projets d'évasion. Cependant, jouir des facilités qui existent n'est pas suffisant. Les heures de loisirs augmentent d'année en année, la fin-de-semaine de deux jours et les vacances annuelles payées qui s'allongent périodiquement sont universellement appliquées. La population aussi augmente, mais les lacs et rivières ne se multiplient pas. Trouver un bon site pour y construire un chalet est impossible à trouver près des grandes villes. L'accroissement du nombre de villégiateurs se traduit très souvent par un usage accru de l'eau et une augmentation de la pollution à cause d'égoûts inadéquats, voire de leur absence totale en certains cas.

La conservation de l'habitat est ainsi une chose importante à laquelle on ne pense pas. L'eau sert aussi dans le décor; je pense à certains paysages extraordinaires des Rocheuses, des Laurentides et des Cantons de l'Est, qui perdraient en valeur touristique si' l'on polluait l'eau qui les environne. On pourrait arrêter le spectacle des chutes du Niagara et transformer toute cette eau qui tombe en énergie. Mais qui perdrait ou qui gagnerait en définitive; peu importe comment on examine cet aspect de la question, on estime que le spectacle vaut plus que la production d'éléctricité. De la même manière, en plus petit, l'eau a un usage décoratif. Avant de quitter ce sujet, pensez aux jeux d'eau, aux fontaines, au site d'une exposition universelle au milieu d'un fleuve.

La pêche commerciale, qu'elle soit pratiquée en eaux intérieures, en haute-mer ou près des côtes, est une ressource renouvelable en autant que l'on respecte le cycle de la reproduction et les autres grandes lois de la Nature. Il y a des richesses dans l'eau, j'oserais dire, pure, car plus elle est polluée, moins il y a de vie.

J'ai signalé en énumérant les principaux usages de l'eau quelques problèmes spécifiques : voici maintenant une ébauche de solution d'ensemble.

Au départ, on a un besoin immédiat de meilleures données statistiques sur les eaux de surface, les eaux souterraines et sur la consommation de l'eau. Ces données s'obtiennent par une observation minutieuse et répandue et par une recherche organisée tant hydrologique, qu'hydrographique et océanographique. Tous les gouvernements doivent participer à une telle recherche et compilation des données.

En second lieu, dans l'immédiat, par une législation sévère et appliquée, que l'on impose à toutes les municipalités, cités et villes, et à toutes les grosses et petites industries qui utilisent l'eau, de construire et d'exploiter des usines de filtration des eaux usées et de traitement des égoux. La lutte à la pollution est vitale. Que l'on impose des amendes sévères à ceux qui utilisent les rivières comme dépotoirs et égoûts à ciel ouvert et ruinent du même coup un beau site ou un beau paysage.

En troisième lieu, dans l'avenir, qu'on planifie avec intelligence en prenant le bassin de drainage comme unité de base. Les deux problèmes principaux sont l'entreposage et la redistribution. En ce moment, on puise l'eau là où elle est, chaque municipalité organise son approvisionnement sans trop se préoccuper des besoins de la ville voisine. Après un certain temps, dans un pays où l'eau coule en abondance, comme au Canada, on découvre qu'on en manque. Pensons aussi à reboiser les flancs dénudés des montagnes afin de contrôler l'égouttement, accroitre l'humidité et améliorer le débit. Que de choses il reste à faire quand on pense à l'irrigation et au drainage savamment agencé afin d'intensifier la production agricole. Enfin, nous commençons seulement à construire des barrages pour emmagasiner l'eau et rétablir le milieu écologique original de certaines sections de rivières et fleuves. Je songe ici aux barrages de l'Hydro-Québec entre Beauharnois et Valleyfield sur le Saint-Laurent, exemple à imiter ailleurs. De même, de petites centrales pourraient être construites encore afin d'harnacher des sites potentiels dans les régions peuplées. On a préféré se concentrer sur les grands développements comme ceux de la Manicougan, mais avec la technique moderne, on récupère de nos jours à même les plus faibles débits.

En quatrième lieu, on peut dès maintenant solutionner les conflits de juridiction entre états et provinces quand il s'agit de développer et d'utiliser des fleuves comme le Saint-Laurent, le Columbia, ou des rivières-frontières comme l'Outaouais et la Saint-Jean. Pourquoi attendre quand on peut régler des conflits d'intérêts comme l'usage en commun d'une rivière pour la navigation, la flottaison du bois et la production d'énergie hydro-électrique ? Si vous pensez que les problèmes de terrains et de bornages sont complexes, à notre avis, rien n'égale les disputes soulevées par des droits d'eau. N'attendons pas qu'ils prennent des proportions gigantesques.

L'eau est une ressource indispensable et nous n'avons pas le choix de la gaspiller, même si la Nature nous a favorisé. Pour nous, comme pour les habitants des zones arides chez qui elle a tant de valeur, nous devrions considérer l'eau comme la première de nos richesses naturelles. Antoine de Saint-Exupéry a écrit quelque part, lors d'une escale africaine sans doute, un bref commentaire sur la valeur de l'eau que je vous rappelle en terminant : « L'eau n'a ni couleur, ni saveur, elle n'est pas nécessaire à la vie, elle est la vie » .

WATER, A PHYSICAL RESOURCE

W. M. Cameron

IN ORDER to appreciate the place of water in the range and varieties of physical resources on which mankind depends, it is important to recognize that in so far as the solar system is concerned, water holds a unique position in the physical constitution of our planet. The ever-growing literature that amplifies our previous knowledge of the planets of the solar system offers scant evidence that any other planet possesses a significant amount of water, especially in its liquid form. These revelations are disappointing for those of us who are intrigued at the implications of the possibility of life on other planets, because we would prefer that our first contact with a metabolically active organism elsewhere in the universe should be with one which depends on water as an essential component of its viability. Life (of the kind with which we are familiar) is a reflection of the peculiar properties of water that set that substance aside from substances of more orderly and mundane properties. In other words, water is the staff of life as we know it.

People who spend their lives on the solid frame of a continent find it difficult sometimes to appreciate the immensity of water which the surface of the earth displays. It is an overworked oceanographic cliché to remark that 71 per cent of the earth's surface is covered by liquid water. An observer from outer space could say that the earth is a planet covered with water, except for some segments of dry land that rise above its great expanse. But it is not only the superficial coverage that is so great. In terms of mass, water is prevalent in almost embarrassingly large quantities on our earth. Were the solid surface of the earth planed down to a smooth spheroid, in equilibrium with the force of gravity and the centrifugal force of rotation of the planet, that surface would be covered by water almost 3,000 metres deep.

The existence of large quantities of water and a continental–oceanic distribution of superficial material is not purely coincidental. A generally accepted theory[1] concerning the early history of this planet holds that its water is not derived from the condensation of some primeval atmosphere, but from a degassing of the substances of the earth's interior. In other words, the forces that have given rise to an abundance of water on the earth are those same forces that have been involved in continent building. These processes are going on even now—suggesting an effective balance over lengthy geological history of the generation of water from subterranean sources and its deposition and removal by the process of sedimentation.

It is fortunate for us that the fundamental geophysical processes which have governed the evolution of this planet have decreed that it should have continents and deep ocean basins—a distribution and coalescence of crustal material that permitted, in the dawn of planetary evolution, that peculiar environment in which life was first initiated.

I shall not dwell on the special conditions which were assumed to prevail when life originated on earth, by the synthesis of complex organic molecules from methane, ammonia, hydrogen, and water, in a reducing atmosphere under the influence of high-energy ultra-violet radiation.[2] What is significant, to my mind, is not only that there should be an abundance of water, but that the process probably took place in lagoonal conditions—conditions that could only apply in the presence of the continental–oceanic basin distribution.

Even more remarkable than the spatial distribution of water on this globe—a one-to-two ratio between continent and ocean—is the distribution of the mass of this water. The world's ocean contains somewhat more than 97 per cent of the bulk of water on the surface of the earth, and just under 3 per cent is distributed, in various forms, on the continents. Of this 3 per cent, almost four-fifths is locked in polar ice-caps and glaciers. Less than 1/100th of 1 per cent of the total water supply on the planet is contained in freshwater lakes and streams. But there is 60 times this volume in the form of groundwater. Finally, to round out the picture, the atmosphere contains a volume of water approximately equal to one-tenth of the volume contained in the world's freshwater lakes and streams.[3]

[1]W. W. Rubey, "Development of the Hydrosphere and Atmosphere with Special Reference to Probable Composition of the Early Atmosphere," from *Crust of the Earth*, ed. A. W. Poldervaart (Geological Society of America, Special Paper 62, 1955), pp. 631–50.

[2]S. L. Miller, "Production of Some Organic Compounds under Possible Primitive Earth Conditions," *J. Am. Chem. Soc. 77* (1955): 2351–61.

[3]R. L. Nace, *Water Management, Agriculture and Ground-Water Supplies*, Geological Survey Circular 1945 (Washington, D.C.: U.S. Department of the Interior, 1960).

When considering this water distribution in terms of availability, it is not enough to consider merely its distribution in various forms and relative magnitudes. Water is continuously flowing through these forms in a hydrological cycle, with various detention times in each form. On the basis of our present knowledge of the rate of flux of water from one form to another, and of the total volume of the various categories, we can calculate the relative detention time—the mean time a molecule of water is retained in a particular reservoir. For example, the detention period for the oceans is estimated at about 5,000 years, but for the atmosphere it is only 10 days. Water on this planet is cycling through a gigantic dynamic system; it is detained in some forms for only a fleeting moment, but in other forms for centuries and millennia. Its availability to man depends on the delicate balance of this cycle: scarcities and abundances are but reflections of minute fluctuations in its transfer from one form to another.

Water displays a unique combination of anomalous properties. "Liquid water is easily the most complex and ill-understood substance known to man. It is anomalous in nearly all of its physical and chemical properties. To mention a familiar example, it is a liquid at room temperature although it should be a gas like its sister compounds of higher molecular weight, hydrogen sulphide, selenide, and telluride."[4] These anomalies stem from the approximation of the relative inclination of the electron pair of the water molecule to a tetrahedral angle, and the existence of hydrogen bonds for intermolecular bonding.[5] Many of the peculiar properties of water that are so important in its influence—its relatively high specific heat, especially of vaporization and of fusion, and its maximum density in the liquid phase—stem from the existence of these bonds.

The circumstances that this substance has an unusually high dissolving power, that it is a liquid at ordinary temperatures and a gas at a relatively modest temperature interval above its fusion point, that it is present in such large quantities on the earth's surface, and that it is so intimately associated with and essential to biological processes explain its importance as a physical resource. That it is a renewable resource, renewable by natural processes inherent in the hydrological cycle, not only in quantity but in quality, explains in part the magnitude of society's dependence on it, and also mankind's past negligence and carelessness in the exploitation of natural supplies.

[4]R. A. Horne, "The Physical Chemistry and Structure of Sea Water," *Water Resources Research, 1* (1965): 263–76.

[5]D. J. G. Ives, "Some Reflections on Water," Inaugural Lecture at Birkbeck College, London (1963).

The availability of water has profoundly affected the course of social evolution. There is little doubt that prehistoric man tended to live in close proximity to lakes or streams, attracted not only by the availability of water for his own needs, but by its effect on the distribution of the game animals on which he depended.

I need not emphasize the association of the centres of development of early civilization with the deltas of large African and Asian rivers, which made possible the first management of water as a resource. By diking and irrigation this management so increased the efficiency of the ancient agriculturist that it made possible the growth of complex societies with specialized castes—artisans, priests, and soldiers—whose specializations led to both the benefits and the liabilities of civilization. Some of our earlier societies, then, were founded on a water economy—involving its use for irrigation. This dependence cannot be ignored in our present North American society, for a large proportion of the present consumption of water in the United States today is associated with agriculture.

I have referred to the importance of water in both historical and present times in what may be called the life processes. Its direct consumption in a potable form by man is of course extremely modest, for he requires but a litre or two of water per day for his metabolic well-being. The greatest consumption for his direct metabolic requirements is that associated with the production of food: hence agriculture figures largely in the demand on available water.

Society is also dependent on certain physical uses of water. First, a few words on the involvement of water in the development of power. A small but significant use of water in the early years of North American settlement was to work grist- and saw-mills to serve the growing communities. The development of hydroelectric power had its influence on the concentration of early industries near favourable water-power sources. This geographic dependence is now less intimate, as more efficient systems of long-range transmission of electrical energy have been developed. Cheap thermal electric power was not primarily dependent for its development on the availability of water in relatively pure form as a source of steam but on its use for the cheap transport of fuels. As more thermoelectric power is derived from atomic energy, the dependence will swing from reliance on water as a means of transport to its importance for cooling in the development of energy.

Although the use of water as a means of transportation is here given a broader interpretation, this is not intended to underemphasize the importance of navigable waters to an industrial development. All of us are aware of the influence upon industrial development of the great navigable waterways of North America, and although certain waterways have declined in importance for the movement of goods, this decline has generally been where those movements can be made more economically by other means. The economy of water transport of large bulk quantities of raw material is still undisputed.

Rather than developing this familiar aspect of the use of water as a means of transportation, I propose to extend the concept to a broader and less familiar facet. This is the increasing use of water as a transport mechanism in more specialized industrial activities. Industrially, water usage is steadily shifting in importance from the transport of raw materials to the transport of the by-products and the wastes of industrial processes.

The significance of this dependence is not always appreciated in our own domestic lives. The development of our vast municipal water-supply networks has not stemmed from our requirement for water for drinking purposes. Were this our only use for water we could still depend on its door-to-door delivery, as with milk and bread. But water is needed in large quantities to accept and take away our waste products. In other words, a water supply to a great city is developed primarily to feed its sewerage system, not to supply potable water.

Some parallels may be drawn between domestic and industrial uses of water. As in the domestic usage just cited, the actual consumption of water by industry in its processes is relatively modest. Certain industries, e.g. those catering to human consumption (the food and drink industries), have a large proportion of water in their products. Certain other industries ship many products in dispersion or in aqueous solutions. However, it has been estimated that only 2 per cent of the water that industry uses is consumed.[6]

A large industrial application of water is that of cooling. Those of us who do not enjoy or require air-conditioning systems might consider this as an instance in which there is no parallel between domestic and industrial usages of water. But mention should be made of the ban against air-conditioning systems invoked in the recent New York drive for water conservation. Washing, another domestic use of considerable importance, is reflected in many industrial activities, such as the textile industry. An important and growing function of water is that of transporting materials within an industrial process. The pulp and paper industry affords a striking example of this type of usage. Most of the

[6]E. P. Partridge, "Your Most Important Raw Material," Edgar Marking Lecture (Philadelphia: American Society for Testing Materials, 1957).

industrial wastes come from the use of water as a medium of transport within industry, and in washing. It is from this aspect of both domestic and industrial uses that the most far-reaching consequences derive.

The above considerations lead to an examination of the problem of water supply and demand which is in the forefront of public discussion today. The problem arises from the recognition that there is in North America a finite supply of water and a growing demand for water, stemming not only from an increasing population but from a mounting use per capita. Extrapolation of this growing demand suggests that eventually the total North American supply will be insufficient. This line of reasoning leads finally to the argument that only grandiose diversion schemes will postpone the eventual limitation of the North American economy by its water supply.

The complexity of the situation is reflected in the variety of forecasts that are made as to when demand will equal supply. There is general agreement that in the United States this will occur between 1980 and 2000. However, it must be emphasized that the forecasts assume a growing use for water according to current patterns. A United States estimate gives the following figures for water usage among the various sectors of the economy: rural use (exclusive of irrigation), 1 per cent; public supplies, 7 per cent; self-supplied industrial, 46 per cent; irrigation, 46 per cent, of which about one-quarter is lost in canals.[7]

These figures indicate that irrigation and industry together account for over 90 per cent of the total water demand. However, the figures do not reflect the estimate already alluded to, that only 2 per cent of water used by industry is actually consumed, or the fact that most of the water withdrawn for irrigation is lost to the atmosphere. If these considerations are taken into account, agriculture may be said to consume some 20 to 30 times more water than does industry.

The actual consumption of water is the all-important consideration. Water returned to the supply after use can be reused, and it is the availability of reusable water supplies that must be considered and planned. The growth of the North American economy in future will depend not so much on increasing the supply of water as on the development of more effective techniques for its use and reuse. This point emphasizes the growing tragedy of pollution—a subject foremost in the public mind, but about which I shall make only a few concluding remarks. Until recently our society has been shaped by the availability of copious supplies of water. But too often the adaptability of our rivers

[7]L. B. Leopold and W. Longbein, *A Primer on Water* (U.S. Geological Survey, 1960).

to transportation of large quantities of materials has caused them to be treated as open and inexpensive sewers. We are now facing the consequences of our past neglect.

The reduction of pollution is not easy and it is expensive. But it has been stated that it is more economical to treat a waste than to treat a polluted source into which that waste has been discharged. This economic fact is undoubtedly at the root of the German success in effectively combatting pollution in the Ruhr Valley.

The increasing alarm about the possibility of growing demands for water outstripping the available supply requires that from now on we must study not only the technical aspects of water supply and demand, but also the social and economic aspects. For example, the technical requirements of various users for water of different qualities, and the technical aspects of treating wastes before discharge, certainly require more extensive investigation. But to compare the value of water to one particular user with its value to another entails the development of economic yardsticks by which to measure competing demands. In other words, studies of water problems can no longer be considered the prerogative of the hydraulics engineer or the limnologist: they must be the concern of demographers, geographers, sociologists, economists, and even of jurists. Only through the cooperative studies of this wide range of specialists, supported by the public's acceptance of its responsibility to make decisions and take actions on the basis of those studies, can we hope to preserve the availability of our most common, yet most necessary, physical resource.

WATER RESOURCES*

J. M. Harrison, F.R.S.C.

CANADIANS are surely among the blessed, for they have inherited not only a large part of the earth, but also about one-third of its fresh water. We have been altogether too meek, however, in seeing that the quality of our abundant waters remains high. Perhaps it is because there has been so much water ready to hand that we have been laggard in the investigations and control measures required to keep it reasonably pure.

The Great Lakes of North America probably exemplify better than any other bodies of water the difficulties with which we are now faced. These lakes contain about 25 per cent of the world's supply of fresh surface waters. In the drainage basin of the Great Lakes lives a small fraction, perhaps 1 per cent, of the world's population. These people represent nations that pride themselves on being technologically the most advanced, and yet they have managed to pollute a substantial part of this great supply of fresh surface waters. We must now prove our technological and scientific capabilities by reducing the pollution and using the lakes for something other than a vast sewer system.

In this Symposium, the authors will set forth various problems of water resources. They will indicate the sort of research required on water as a physical commodity—its availability and its shortages—so that we can assess the degree of seriousness of pollution, and determine what must be done to assure adequate and suitable supplies of water. Studies and proposals that will help to provide a better basis for calculating the amount of water furnished by the atmosphere will be outlined. Clearly, biological research of several kinds is needed to answer certain of these problems, while only interdisciplinary research can provide the means of preventing further pollution and of improving the present situation.

*Chairman's Introductory Remarks to First General Symposium on "Water Resources," R.S.C., June 6, 1966.

Finally, I would like to emphasize that Canada can live by trade, as other nations do, without great sources of mineral or agricultural wealth; but we cannot live without water. Water is the indispensable medium for all people in all places. To view water as a continental resource is ideal, but I think it should be kept in mind that once an economy or community is based on imported water, that supply of water can never be cut off. There is no substitute.

PART III

THE ST. LAWRENCE, THEN AND NOW

THAT GREAT STREET: THE ST. LAWRENCE

Hilda Neatby, F.R.S.C.

THE ST. LAWRENCE has a magnificent history as the living centre of a great commercial empire, the continental road of the fur trader, the explorer, and the missionary. There is also a quieter story to be found in its more intimate relations with those who lived along its banks and who gradually learned how to get the most profit and pleasure from this splendid but reluctant and occasionally treacherous servant. The achievement of these individuals, often taken for granted, underlies the triumphs of the commercial empire.

Many writers have expatiated on the economic, the social, the strategic, and the political significance of this river, quite literally the gateway to an entire continent. From it the French created their magnificent sketch of an empire in North America, an empire extending from Newfoundland to the Rockies, and from Hudson Bay to the Gulf of Mexico. In the exploitation of that great North American staple, fur, the St. Lawrence finally emerged victorious in the long struggle with two other famous waterways, Hudson Bay and the Hudson River. The dominion, or kingdom, or federation of Canada is only a part, although a large one, of the old fur-trading kingdom created largely from the St. Lawrence.

All this and much more is familiar ground. In recent decades it has been brilliantly and meticulously set forth by those who have done so much to reinterpret our history, notably H. A. Innes and D. G. Creighton. My purpose in this paper is only to add to this great and striking picture of one of the great rivers of the world a few homely details—one could even call them housekeeping details—that have come to my attention in an examination of some of the sources of the history of the Canadian community during the thirty years which followed the conquest of the country by the British in 1760.

Although the St. Lawrence first aroused the interest of explorers as a possible road to the western sea, it was soon attracting attention because of the wealth contained within its waters. Along the whole length from the gulf up through Lake St. Peter and to the great lakes beyond, it yielded a great variety and quantity of fish. This fish was used as a trade article. It was also used by the community living along the river banks as food for man and as fodder for cattle during the long winter. Great stacks of frozen fish were piled up and were used to supplement the sometimes scanty supply of hay. The St. Lawrence from early times attracted seal fishers, although this ancient sealing differed from the modern industry that has lately caused so much discussion. The early sealers were interested in the adult seals, which they caught by means of nets stretched across the passages between the rocky shores and the nearby rocky islands. These passages were frequented by the seals in their seasonal migration. The adult seals were wanted for their oil and for their skins; the skins were not luxury furs but were sold chiefly in the colony for the making of winter moccasins.

The wealth of the St. Lawrence fisheries was, however, in no way extraordinary. The importance of the river lay in its potentialities as a road, or as Chief Justice William Smith picturesquely called it, in relation to the community, "a great street." Primarily men saw it as a means of entry to the tremendous interior of the continent. Going up from Montreal, the highest point to which a ship of any size could penetrate, traders and missionaries from the mid-seventeenth century set off for the certain privation and uncertain perils of the wilderness, intent like earlier travellers elsewhere, on gospel, gold, and glory. In the other direction, ships leaving Quebec on its massive rock opposite the Island of Orleans, at the point where the river widens into a gulf, found their way to the ocean routes which linked the colony and the missionary and fur-trading enterprise to the metropolis in Europe—to Paris before 1760, to London afterwards. As historians have pointed out, the whole economy of our country during its early history was geared to a metropolis. There were very sound economic reasons for Canadian loyalism.

The stretch of river from a few miles above Montreal to some distance below Quebec thus served a double purpose. First, it was the "great street" on which centred the economic life of the community, which by 1760 comprised perhaps 75,000 people. Secondly, it was the hinge on which turned the total operation of the fur trade, the complex relationships between the few hundreds of traders scattered over tens of thousands of miles of territory, and the few men in London who initially financed the trade, and ultimately disposed of the furs. Almost every merchant in Quebec, Montreal, and in the towns and villages between, was, directly or indirectly, involved in this double function. Immediately after the conquest and even before it was completed, traders from the colonies and the British Isles moved in. Along with Canadian associates and rivals they began the task of reorganizing, largely on free enterprise principles, and with London as the metropolis, economic operations hitherto carried on either through the French government or under very close government supervision.

The service of the river to the river community, while it may seem obvious and unexciting, presents in its details a vivid picture of the methods of satisfying the daily wants and needs of the people. From far down the river and the gulf, fish of all kinds—cod, green and dry, salmon, oysters, and eels—along with the seal skins and the seal oil to feed the lamps during the long winter evenings, went up-river to Quebec. From the country districts about Quebec there was collected the local homespun cloth, used for clothing by habitants generally and by the working classes. No doubt this cloth was made everywhere in the province, but evidence seems to show that a good deal went up-river for sale. This may be because the cloth was in demand for making bags for the shipping of grains and flour, produced in far greater quantity on the rich farming lands of the Richelieu River and the upper St. Lawrence than lower down.[1] From the district of Quebec also lime and stone for building purposes went up-river. These last commodities may have gone in smaller boats rather than in ships. From Montreal down-river went wheat, oats, peas, flour, and biscuit. Flour and biscuit were not exported much in the early part of this period, but they were used to supply the fishing stations of the lower river and the gulf. Montreal also sent apples and pears (especially the much prized pears from the orchards of the Seminary), nuts, pumpkins, wooden staves for the construction of casks and barrels, and timber for building purposes; and from Montreal and

[1]Merchants at this time were constantly preoccupied with securing suitable containers for goods that moved up and down the river or overseas by ship. Those concerned with transportation today, when the making of packages and containers of all sorts has become not only a science but an art—if a rather debased art—would find it hard to imagine the time and effort spent by their eighteenth-century predecessors in securing suitable containers. Packages had to be of a convenient size and shape for handling and for getting on and off the ships without modern mechanical aids. They had also to be secure against the rough treatment that they might receive in loading and unloading, and also the inevitable rough treatment from winds and waves, especially damaging if they had not been skilfully stowed on board. It was also desirable that the packages should be at least partially waterproof. Much use was made of casks or barrels of all sizes from the small keg to the hugest of casks; they had the great advantage that they could be rolled and otherwise manoeuvred with relative ease and with a minimum of damage. Dry-goods generally came out from Europe in trunks, probably relatively small trunks with handles. Shoes, however, were often shipped in casks, at least within the province. Wheat and other grains and flour went in casks or bags.

the upper districts came the bearskins, which seem to have been generally used throughout the province as winter blankets.

In the midst of this stretch of river the little town of Three Rivers supplied melons and tobacco, for which commodities it seems to have been famous throughout the province. Three Rivers also had a minor ship-building industry. Ships and canoes were constructed and repaired there. Everywhere on the river, no doubt, there were innumerable local exchanges which have left little trace behind them in the papers of the period. There is, however, much evidence of the brisk trade in fire-wood that was conducted by water in the neighbourhood of the cities and especially of Quebec. Many of the city houses were built with large lofty rooms and spacious windows in the fashion of the day. Exposed as they were to the bitter rigours of the northern winter, they were kept comfortable by open fire-places in every room and iron stoves in every passage. Coal not being used at all, these all had to be fed by wood. The consumption must have been enormous.

Another but related business on this mid-stretch of the river was the distribution of the commodities that came in from overseas for local consumption. It is easy for one absorbed with the needs of the fur trade to forget that even this relatively small community did demand a considerable store of luxuries and comforts from abroad. It is true that the habitant was largely self-supplying in food and in clothing. However, it seems quite clear that the habitants of Quebec, unlike the European peasants, did not manufacture their holiday clothing at home. The women of Quebec of all classes in society dressed as fashionably as their means would permit. Probably not many women of the countryside were able to afford the twenty-five yards of white silk brocade such as one merchant purchased for his wife's new dress. Perhaps few of them even managed to purchase the fashionable white silk stockings. Yet, as a small town like Terrebonne was said to rival and even surpass Quebec and Montreal in its fashionable life, costly clothing was certainly not confined to the cities, and everywhere there would be some demand also for the striped, checked, and flowered cottons, which were used both for dresses and for household hangings. Merchants took great pains to explain to their English correspondents the taste of Canadian women in these matters. The many little stores which were now appearing throughout the province would have to be supplied with these articles, and also with such things as vinegar, wine, olive oil, imported cheese, spices, sugar, molasses and, to judge from certain lists which have survived, a large and various store of drugs. The local storekeepers often acted as grain buyers in the country, extending credit on the pledge of the coming crop. Occasionally they may also have been the local innkeepers, although it seems likely that the local cabaret was a separate and rather less respectable undertaking.

Far more complicated, however, than the demands of the local trade, was the total organization of the fur trade, which also took place along the stretch of river between Quebec and Montreal. Much of the planning and labour, and much of the risk involved in transferring the pelt of the beaver from its original owner in some far western stream to the ultimate owner—perhaps Gainsborough's lovely Georgiana, Duchess of Devonshire, who, it will be recalled, enhanced her charms with a beaver hat of impressive proportions—much of this labour and risk rested on the shoulders of a handful of merchants at Quebec and Montreal. When Montreal became a common resort for ocean-going ships, the undertaking was greatly simplified. But at least for two or three decades after the conquest the great import-export centre for goods was Quebec, the chief source of canoes and tobacco essential to the trade was Three Rivers, and Montreal was the assembling place for the goods, the canoes, and the crews ready to go up-country, as well as the receiving centre for the returning crews and their cargoes. The operations at Montreal were, in the early days, complicated by the fact that all passes for canoes going up-country had to be secured from the secretary of the province down at Quebec. On these passes it was necessary to state the name of the owner of the canoe, all the items of its cargo, the names of all members of the crew, and their place of origin. Later the securing of the passes was much simplified by a provision which permitted the commander-in-chief at Montreal to issue them to the traders.

The result of these combined operations meant that there was an enormous amount of coming and going and of correspondence between Quebec, Montreal, and, to a lesser extent, Three Rivers. Travelling in winter was by sleigh and could be quick, easy, and pleasant. William Smith wrote to his wife in the fall of 1786 that he was going to buy himself a closed sleigh in which he could lie down comfortably at full length and perhaps even sleep on his journey. Trains of sleighs could be used for necessary winter freighting, especially in late winter and early spring, when goods were sent by sleigh from Quebec to Montreal to be ready for the departure of the canoes. Even in the summer, travellers and letters went by the road as being more speedy than the river. But toward the end of this period river vessels did attempt a regular passenger service. In one of the local newspapers of the 80s there is a vivid description of a passage from Montreal down to Quebec. It appears to have been one long picnic, with plenty of conversation and plenty of liquid as well as other refreshment.

From the beginning, however, nearly all the freight in summer went by river, an easier route than the indifferent dirt roads and the numerous ferries which had to be negotiated on the north shore between Quebec and Montreal. The river traffic in summer must have been impressive for the size of the community. Up and down the river would pass canoes and small boats, heavy whaling boats, little sloops and schooners with crews of only three men, and others much larger, up to the ship drawing 16 feet of water, the largest ship that could penetrate as far as Montreal. In addition to these conventional craft there were rafts of all kinds, particularly the peculiar rafts fashioned by the men who cut staves up the Richelieu and floated them in long trains down to Quebec in the spring.

But the St. Lawrence, now famous the world over for its magnificent stretches of water, its lovely islands, its shore alternating peaceful pastoral scenery with wild and wooded rocky stretches, was not to be used with impunity by the ignorant or the reckless. The whole rhythm of life in the colony had to be adapted not only to the nature of water transport, but to the whims of a particular river which could be extremely whimsical.

It had been known for many years that the St. Lawrence was an exceedingly difficult river to navigate. Not only did the ebb and flow of the tide make it all too easy for ships to become grounded unless conducted by skilled and knowledgeable pilots; the river-bed was also in some places broken by rocky shelves and ridges which at low tide came dangerously close to the surface. American and British invaders under the French régime had paid their tribute to the river by the pains they took to secure Canadians to pilot them up the gulf even as far as Quebec. Captain Cook, later the explorer of the Pacific, was employed in charting the river soon after the conquest. The Canadians themselves were under no illusion about its dangers. The Jesuits lay claim to having established the first university in Canada, because they instituted classes in hydrography for those preparing to act as pilots on the St. Lawrence. Throughout the period following the conquest, in response to petitions from merchants and others, successive ordinances were passed regulating the training, the apprenticeship, certification, and conditions of work of the pilots on whose services the whole safety of commerce depended.

In addition to this fundamental and special problem was the general problem with which all Canadians are familiar. The St. Lawrence does not provide an open winter port. All the commercial operations of the country had to be geared to the very short season from some time in May until early November. The spring ships from London might reach Quebec late in April, but they were much more likely not to arrive until the first, second, or even the third week of May.

The concern of the merchants in Quebec and Montreal was to get their goods and to distribute them to retailers throughout the country as quickly as possible. The Quebec merchants were in an advantageous position. They could clear their goods immediately, giving the customs officer a note for the amount of the duty if they had no ready money. In those early days, there being no customs buildings, the officer was only too glad to get rid of his responsibility. The Montreal merchants always tried to get the London suppliers to put their goods on ships bound for Montreal. Often this was impossible. Also, many Londoners were probably as vague about the relative positions of Quebec and Montreal as some Canadians still are about those of Australia and New Zealand. The Montreal merchant who had to receive his goods in Quebec could confide them to Quebec commission merchants, who would send them up-river for a commission of one half of one per cent, in addition, of course, to the freight charges. Montreal merchants resented this additional expense, and it seems likely that many merchants of Montreal and Quebec performed these and similar services for each other without charge. It was taken for granted that goods would be forwarded as promptly as possible. Occasionally, however, a commission merchant in Quebec, instead of sending on goods by the first boat, would keep them waiting in order to be able to send them on his own private vessel later when business should slacken.

It might also happen for a special reason that no ships were available. Ordinarily river ships would wait at Quebec in the spring for the arrival of the ocean fleet. They would then load on goods for Montreal and intermediate points and, on the return journey, would bring down wheat from the winter threshing along the Richelieu and upper St. Lawrence. This was the ideal plan. Unfortunately, it required ideal weather conditions: an early break-up in the gulf and steady winds from the northeast to bring the ocean-going ships up to Quebec. Then, especially if the northeast winds continued to favour them, the little ships could make their way up-river before the ebb of the spring floods made navigation of the Richelieu impracticable for them. When the ocean ships were long delayed, local ship-owners and captains had to make a series of agonizing reappraisals, which sometimes resulted in the schooners going up-river without a cargo in order to reach the Richelieu in time. Captains who lingered too long at Quebec might miss both the arrival of the London ships and the Richelieu flood-time. If merchants occasionally became short-tempered during the busy season, and they did, they had ample excuse.

The goods that came out in the spring then were forwarded more or less promptly from Quebec to Montreal. They would arrive too late for the great event of the spring, the dispatch of the fur-trading canoes up-country. Canoes which were to return from the upper country in the fall had to start as soon as the ice broke in the spring. Preparations for this were made in the late winter. If necessary, trains of sleighs would take goods from Quebec up to Montreal to be ready for the dispatch of the canoes as soon as the ice broke. The Quebec merchant, François Baby, was accustomed to go himself to Montreal at this time to send off his fleet of canoes to his brother and partner, Duperron Baby, in Detroit. The canoes set off in May, often to face during the journey the hideous discomfort of bitter cold rain or very light snow. They struggled up-river and along the lakes, the men sheltering at night as best they could under their canoes. Nothing could match the horror and scorn of the hardy captain of militia when he had to report that men impressed for the *corvée* (in this case the transport of goods along the lakes) were demanding tents to sleep in.

All goods for these spring canoes would have come out in the previous year by the fall ships. Seamstresses worked in the winter at making the lengths of cotton and linen into shirts, petticoats, and so on, suitable for the Indian trade. The spring ships from overseas supplied the needs of the community, and also stock for the canoes which left later in the summer. These would winter up-country, and return in the following spring.

Ships from overseas needed a return cargo if ocean rates were not to be impossibly high. There would always be available, no doubt, some furs from the winter take at the King's Posts down-river, and from the trade which came into Three Rivers. Ships could also get furs from the canoes that had wintered up-country and come down in the spring. Furs, however, took relatively little space. The returning ships would also take the staves which had been cut in the Champlain district and elsewhere during the winter, and had been brought down the river to wait for them at Quebec. Smaller ships might load up with flour and biscuit for the supply of the fishing islands and sealing stations in the gulf before returning to the colonies or Europe with a supply of fish.

A most important, and increasingly valuable, commodity on the journey back to Europe was wheat. As has been mentioned, one of the preoccupations for the owners of river schooners was to get their little ships up the St. Lawrence as early as possible in order to take advantage of the spring floods on the Richelieu. If the harvest had been plentiful the previous year and if the price in Europe was good, wheat was a welcome cargo to the various ships gathered at Quebec. A most profitable arrangement for the ship-owner and for the merchant was to fill the holds of the ships with wheat, and to pile the bundles of staves on the decks, thus making use of every possible space.

The busy exchange in the few months of spring and summer constantly provides illustrations of the embarrassment of merchants in the face of inadequate and uncertain means of transport on the river. The season was so short that ship-owners wanted to be certain of full employment during the summer. This meant that in the busiest periods there was never enough transport. A merchant in Montreal might well be faced with an acute shortage of some commodity urgently demanded by his customers. He would write frantically to Quebec, telling his correspondent there to get it up to him in any way he could, though fully aware that want of shipping might make this impossible. Meanwhile he might be communicating with Three Rivers, on the chance of there being a surplus there which he could secure, or he would be going about the town of Montreal to see what he could get from his fellow merchants. Evidence of a considerable variety in prices even between Montreal and Three Rivers confirms the impression of a serious transport problem. Sometimes a merchant would have on his hands a large quantity of wheat which he must send down immediately if he would catch the ships before they left for Europe, and which in any case he would wish to get rid of for want of a suitable place to store it. Again he would encounter the problem of shipping. The owners of the river schooners had a sellers' market and knew how to make the most of it.

However, ship-owners, many of whom were merchants, had their own troubles. Having secured a schooner, their next task was to get a reliable crew, and this was often difficult. Too many competent captains were illiterate and therefore incapable of handling bills of lading. One merchant, for example, writes to another asking if he knows of any capable man who can read and write, and who would be willing to serve on his schooner and help the captain, who cannot read, with the paper work. Sometimes the captain and crew were unsatisfactory in other ways. Montreal merchants learned to count carefully the bundles of dried cod that came up to Montreal, because it was entirely possible that the crew might have been living at their expense on the journey from Quebec. It was more important still to make sure not only that the casks of wine were full, but that the contents were wine and not wine and water. An ingenious captain might draw off quantities of the wine for the refreshment of himself and possibly of his crew, compensating at least in weight by adding water.

The ship-owner also had to meet special hazards such as might occur in war. It is true that the vastly increased needs of transport in war-time might enable him to make large profits; but then his ship might be taken over by the government, with unfortunate results. One ship-owner complained that his boat had been conscripted and used to convey goods up to Montreal. On the way back it became grounded in Lake St. Peter. He was not able to get it free until the following spring, when he found it much damaged. The total compensation that he could obtain from the government was £45, the rental agreed on for the month that the ship was in service.

It is quite clear to any reader of mercantile correspondence that what was needed in order to make the best use of the short season and all shipping available was ample and secure storage space. Given such a provision the goods could always be ready and waiting for the ships and their crews, which could thus be maintained in constant employment. Failing storage facilities, one might find, for example, that a ship would arrive in the spring in the Richelieu River ready to take on a whole cargo of wheat, and would have to wait impatiently while the grain merchant hurried round to the homes of all the habitants, who were storing it in their granaries, trying to persuade them to leave their farm work in order to bring it as quickly as possible to the wharf. In fact the province was very poorly supplied with storehouses. It is true that the stone houses along St. Paul's Street often had ample, well-constructed, dry stone-lined vaults, which were used by merchants for storing the furs that came down from the upper country, and the woollen goods that might be waiting to go up. There were, however, far too few of these vaults, and from time to time furs and woollens were damaged by damp, moths, or rats.

Much bigger in every way was the problem of storing wheat. Not only were granaries needed at the regular pick-up points along the Richelieu and St. Lawrence rivers; larger ones were needed at Montreal, and most of all they were needed at Quebec, where the wheat was gathered to await shipment overseas. Gradually, as the wheat trade grew, the province did become equipped with suitable granaries, but this was a work of time. The whole wheat trade was built up empirically in the post-conquest era. Before 1760 there had been not much free enterprise, as the government was likely at any time to take the wheat at a fixed price from the habitants or other owners. Peace and security, the growth of population, and possibly the influence of Englishmen interested in farming who bought up some of the seigneuries, appear to have sent wheat production up rapidly. The difficulty was, however, that until a trade was regularly established with Europe (and this trade depended on the uncertain fluctuation of European prices), it was not worth while to invest in granaries. Yet without the granaries it was almost impossible to have a regular trade at all. What was needed, as in any new enterprise, was faith and capital. Fortunately the merchants, although they had little capital, had much faith, but their real trials, their risks, and their losses during these experimental beginnings are vividly recorded in their letters.

The merchants of Quebec during this period have been criticized as narrow-minded bigots, unfriendly to Canadians and anxious to domineer over them. These charges are partly true. It should be remembered, however, that Canadians worked with English in this trade and that all of them displayed a perseverance, a courage, and a tenacity which in themselves inspire respect, if they do not quite atone for the want of other virtues. The wheat trade was patiently and courageously built up by the Quebec merchants and the Montreal merchants associating themselves with local shopkeepers, with individual buyers, with operators of the river schooners and of the ocean ships, and with the London correspondents who ultimately disposed of the shipments. Like the timber trade which followed it, the wheat trade was absolutely dependent on the river. Furs, if necessary, could have gone down from Montreal to Quebec overland in the winter. With wheat and wood this was impossible.

The most complicated problem encountered by the merchants in using the river I have left to the end. This was important in itself, and was also curiously interwoven with a mass of potentially conflicting interests: merchant and merchant, Canadian and English, official and private person, army and civilian. This problem is the obvious one of wharves. It is easy to speak of a river road while forgetting the great question of access and egress. In order to use the river the tiniest boat had to have a beach or a landing stage. The larger ships were proportionately more exacting in their requirements. Montreal merchants who dealt only with canoes, boats, and the smaller ships seem to have settled their problem without much trouble. They had enough room along their waterfront for the building of wharves. Quebec, with many more ships, and larger ones, all huddled in the relatively short space running from the foot of Cape Diamond to the mouth of the St. Charles River, gave much trouble before any satisfactory arrangements could be made.

Early in Governor Murray's régime, a natural conflict of interest between local and provincial trade appeared. Merchants and others at Quebec asked for concessions of the available space in order to build wharves, and a number were granted. Serious trouble broke out, however, when the Council was asked to consider disposing of the stretch of beach customarily reserved for the vendors of fire-wood, who were accustomed to put in their boats anywhere, stack up their piles of wood, and make sales on the spot to private purchasers. No fees were charged for this privilege. The merchants who wished to secure a grant of this beach, or part of it, apparently urged that space could be left for the wood lot, and that even if all land were taken, the service through a regular wharf would be more efficient. They may have had in mind that wholesalers could take over the fire-wood and pass it on at retail to purchasers. They argued, reasonably perhaps, that it was wrong to retain valuable land for one purpose only. The retort was obvious. Little boats carrying fire-wood which would suffer no material damage from wetting or rough handling needed no expensive facilities. Construction of wharves would be certain to send up the price.

The issue lay between the general body of consumers and the small group of merchants. It also lay, to a considerable extent, between English and Canadians. The promoters of wharves had to win in the end. Time was on their side. Meanwhile it is interesting to note, even in this minor matter, the alignment of the conservative forces standing ostensibly for community interests, against English "improvers"—in this instance each being so much in the right that only a very imaginative and sympathetic compromise could have satisfied both. The information on the working out of this particular problem is fragmentary, but a wharf was erected on this place eventually.

A long and bitter controversy involving mercantile rivalry, the interests of government, and the privileges of the army developed over the one large and adequately constructed wharf which dated from the French régime. The King's Wharf at Quebec was situated up-river at the place where the beach begins to narrow to a point below Cape Diamond. It was an irregular quadrilateral, pierced from the river side by a long narrow slip for the construction and repair of ships. At the lower end of the wharf as the river flowed was the *cul de sac*, a kind of inlet sheltered from above by the wharf as it projected into the river. Here ships were stored in winter, and here, during the busy season, they crowded together, waiting to unload.

Unfortunately, this wharf, perhaps damaged during the siege, had fallen partially into ruin, and not for ten years after 1760 could arrangements be made for its adequate repair and maintenance. It was crown property, but for some years after the conquest the province yielded practically no crown revenue. Governors met necessary expenditures by drawing bills on the British treasury, with the encouraging assurance that if the British authorities found their expenses unnecessary, the amount of the bills would come out of their own pockets. There was no money for public works except for defence.

Thomas Ainslie, a merchant, and a friend of Governor Murray, who had appointed him collector of customs in 1763, made some use of the wharf and the buildings on it in his official duties. Realizing its potential value he offered to repair and lease it. His fellow-merchants immediately petitioned against the lease, offering to raise £2,000 for the repair of the wharf rather than see it in private hands. This was probably an empty gesture intended to prevent the customs collector (by his office unpopular, as the merchants were vigorously protesting the customs duties) from extending his commercial advantages.

However, it was clear that the wharf could be put into full service only through private enterprise. Lieutenant-Governor Carleton, who arrived in 1766, passed over Ainslie. Ainslie was Murray's friend, and Carleton, always suspicious of officials, often with justification, thought his personal fees too high. There was a sharp tussle between other firms tendering for the lease. Accusations of undue influence, and of spying into private papers with a view to undercutting bids, were rather freely bandied about. Eventually the lease went to the firm of Johnston and Purss, after much bargaining about the upkeep of the wharf, the fees that might be charged to ships tying up at the wharf or moored in the *cul de sac*, and on all goods landed. There were precise specifications on repair and upkeep, apart from the obvious repairs that had to be made immediately to the wharf itself. The wharf was to be surrounded on the landward side by a heavy stone wall pierced by two gates; the slip in the centre was to be maintained, and the whole frontage on the river and on the *cul de sac* was to be faced with heavy timbers. In addition the river bottom in front of the wharf and in the *cul de sac* was to be kept clear of stones.

In return for this, and for a rental of five shillings a year, the lessees could charge dues on all ships tying at the wharf or moored in the *cul de sac*. They could also charge specified rates (over which there was much haggling) on every tun, pipe, butt, barrel, cask, or quarter-cask containing brandy, rum, wine, or sugar, and on other goods and containers in proportion. "King's Ships," however, were to be free of charge. There was inevitably a brisk debate on "King's Ships," the lessees insisting that contractors carrying government stores were not to claim exemption as King's Ships.

And so at last, after ten years, on the eve of Carleton's departure for Britain in 1770, the lease was signed, and the wharf—the only adequate wharf in the city—was on the way to being rendered serviceable. The merchants complained that Quebec, of all cities in North America, was the worst provided with wharves—and yet in five years it was to become not only the main entry to the continental fur-trading country but an essential base of operations in the American Revolutionary war.

There is nothing in this story of the mid-stretch of the river to compare with the great epic of the inland fur trade. Yet the historian, charged in a sense to do justice to all, must pay tribute to the energy, the ingenuity, the endurance, and the ceaseless toil of innumerable men —from the wealthy, or at least ambitious, merchants through traders, shopkeepers, and agents, through captains, sailors, boatmen, and pilots, to the humblest habitant negotiating the rapids on his rickety raft to get his staves down to Quebec. By their efforts local industry and trade were stimulated and coordinated to serve the fur trade, and to cut down freight rates by ensuring that the great ships need not always return to Europe with empty holds. But for them, that "great street," the lovely but captious and treacherous St. Lawrence, could not have been forced to provide the essential link that joined the great inland fur country to its metropolis overseas.

NOTE ON SOURCES

The information for this article has been gathered piecemeal from a variety of sources, going all the way from official or semi-official reports on economic matters to the most casual references in personal letters. The dispatches to and from the Colonial Office (C.O. 42), often carrying interesting enclosures, have been useful. The minutes of the Legislative and Executive Councils of the province, and the accompanying collections of papers filed in the Council office (S. series), contain important material. Most fruitful for colourful detail, however, are the collections of business and personal correspondence (Baby Letters, Jacobs Papers, Lindsay-Morrison Papers, etc.). All these collections are available in the Public Archives of Canada.

LE RÔLE DU QUÉBEC DANS LE TRAFIC MARITIME AU CANADA

Benoît Brouillette, M.S.R.C.

D'AUCUNS seront surpris d'apprendre que la province de Québec se place au premier rang pour le commerce maritime du Canada. Les ports québécois manipulent, à eux seuls, le tiers des cargaisons transportées par eau, soit 81.1 millions de tonnes de marchandises sur 235.0 millions en 1964[1] (voir tableau I). L'examen de ces données illustre du premier coup d'œil que c'est dans le commerce maritime international que le Québec l'emporte sur les autres régions du Canada. Ses ports chargent à destination des pays étrangers la moitié des cargaisons totales, soit 41 millions de tonnes sur 83 millions en 1964, et les mêmes ports reçoivent de l'étranger 29.2 pour cent des marchandises entrées au Canada par les voies d'eau, n'étant en cela dépassés que par les ports ontariens des Grands-Lacs avec 47.2 pour cent du trafic total. En ce qui concerne le cabotage, c'est-à-dire le trafic intérieur entre ports canadiens, le Québec occupe, pour les marchandises déchargées, encore le premier rang avec le tiers du volume total, tandis que pour les expéditions, les ports de l'Ontario et de la Côte du Pacifique dépassent largement ceux de notre province.

LES PRINCIPAUX PORTS DU QUÉBEC

Le Québec possède, sur les rives du Saint-Laurent, une dizaine de ports importants dont le trafic global dépasse un million de tonnes (voir le tableau II). Celui de Montréal manipule, à lui seul, le quart du volume total, soint plus de 21 millions de tonnes. Ce tonnage le place

[1]Données extraites des cinq fascicules du Shipping Report (Ottawa: Bureau Fédéral de la Statistique, 1964).

au premier rang des ports canadiens[2], en avant de son rival du Pacifique, Vancouver, dont le commerce, cependant, est beaucoup moins bien équilibré. Les deux ports suivants, Sept-Iles et Port-Cartier, n'exercent qu'une fonction unique, celle d'expédier le minerai de fer de leur hinterland. Les autres ports, Baie-Comeau, Québec, Trois-Rivères et Sorel, ont d'abord un rôle régional qui est renforcé par leur commerce de transit des céréales grâce aux élévateurs dont ils sont dotés. Enfin, Port-Alfred importe la bauxite des Guyanes et l'alumine de la Jamaïque pour les fonderies d'aluminium; Contrecœur est un lieu de transit du minerai de fer importé d'outremer; Havre-Saint-Pierre ne fait qu'expédier vers Sorel l'ilménite du lac Allard. Notre classification des ports repose sur le trafic des marchandises, sur les cargaisons transportées dans les navires, et non pas sur le tonnage de jauge des navires que fréquentent les ports. Ce dernier critère, d'une aburdité évidente, était autrefois celui qu'utilisait l'annuaire du Canada, et qui faisait de Montréal, en 1954 par exemple, un port deux fois moindre que Vancouver et légèrement inférieur à Victoria.

LA NATURE ET LA VALEUR DES MARCHANDISES EXPORTÉES PAR EAU

Jusqu'à présent, on ne pouvait estimer l'importance du trafic maritime que selon le volume des marchandises ainsi transportées, comme on peut le voir sur les tableaux I et II. Afin de pousser l'analyse plus loin, il conviendrait de connaître la nature des denrées et surtout leur valeur. L'absence de données statistiques avait empêché de considérer cet aspect jusqu'ici, mais voici qu'une nouvelle publication[3] du Bureau Fédéral de la Statistique nous permet de connaître au moins la valeur des marchandises exportées par eau du Québec[4]. La période couverte par ce document qui, espérons-le, sera publié annuellement, n'est encore que des trois derniers trimestres de 1963. Toutefois, cette période correspond à la saison de navigation presque entière, car, d'après les relevés men-

[2]Montreal se place au 11e rang parmi les ports de l'Amérique du Nord en 1963, sur un pied d'égalité avec Chicago, très loin derrière New-York (105 millions de tonnes).

[3]*Trade of Canada: Exports by Mode of Transport, April 1 to December 31, 1963* (Ottawa: Bureau Fédéral de la Statistique, 1965).

[4]Voir aussi : « Destination des expéditions des produits manufacturés du Québec » , *Statistique* vol. IV no 2 (Bureau de la Statistique du Québec, 1965), pp. x–xvi. Etude fort intéressante, mais limitée aux articles manufacturés dans le Québec, excluant donc le commerce de transit ainsi que les matières premières exportées à l'état brut. Elle n'indique pas non plus les moyens de transport utilisés.

TABLEAU I

REPARTITION GÉOGRAPHIQUE DU TRAFIC MARITIME DU CANADA EN 1964
(Volume du commerce en milliers de tonnes de 2,000 livres)

	Maritimes et T.-N., Côte de l'Atlantique		Québec, St-Laurent		Ontario, Grands-Lacs		Manitoba et Terr. N.-O., Baie d'Hudson		Colombie Britannique, Côte du Pacifique		Canada
	Vol.	%	Vol.	%	Vol.	%	Vol.	%	Vol.	%	(Vol.)
a) *Commerce international*											
Chargements	11,837.4	14.2	41,636.5	49.8	10,396.9	12.5	653.4	0.8	18,986.5	22.7	83,510.7
Déchargements	8,323.8	17.5	13,851.5	29.2	22,437.0	47.2	37.8	0.1	2,928.2	6.1	47,578.3
Sous-total	20,161.2	15.3	55,488.0	42.4	32,833.9	25.1	691.2	0.5	21,914.7	16.7	131,089.0
b) *Commerce intérieur* (*cabotage*)											
Chargements	7,029.3	13.5	8,383.0	16.1	21,434.9	41.2	20.5	0.1	15,129.7	29.1	51,997.4
Déchargements	5,692.7	11.0	17,230.8	33.2	13,870.3	26.7	42.7	0.1	15,028.3	29.0	51,864.8
Sous-total	12,722.0	12.2	25,613.8	24.6	35,305.2	34.0	63.2	0.1	30,158.0	29.1	103,862.2
TOTAL	32,883.2	13.9	81,101.8	34.9	68,139.1	28.9	754.4	0.3	52,072.7	22.0	234,951.2

TABLEAU II

LES PRINCIPAUX PORTS DU QUÉBEC EN 1964
(Cargaisons en milliers de tonnes de 2,000 livres)

	Commerce international		Commerce intérieur		Commerce total, 1964
	Sorties (exports)	Entrées (imports)	Sorties	Entrées	
Montréal	5,548.0	6,431.8	4,250.0	5,333.1	21,562.9
Sept-Iles	15,685.4	421.8	308.5	183.3	16,599.0
Port-Cartier	10,138.4	65.5	11.1	9.4	10,224.4
Baie-Comeau	3,763.3	1,739.9	278.5	2,523.7	8,305.6
Québec	1,688.5	840.6	187.2	3,372.0	6,068.3
Trois-Rivières	1,882.5	1,083.5	27.8	1,553.8	4,547.6
Sorel	1,679.7	307.3	77.5	2,295.0	4,359.5
Port-Alfred	453.8	2,340.4	18.0	500.4	3,312.6
Havre-Saint-Pierre			1,363.2	8.4	1,371.6
Contrecœur	403.2	509.7		88.5	1,001.4
Autres ports	393.5	111.0	1,859.8	1,363.2	3,748.9
TOTAL	41,636.5	13,851.5	8,383.0	17,230.8	81,101.8

suels du trafic maritime, moins de 63,000 tonnes de cargaisons auraient été chargées à destination des pays étrangers à Québec et Trois-Rivières entre janvier et mars (aucune statistique mensuelle n'est publiée sur le port de Baie-Comeau). Donc sur un volume total d'environ 32 millions de tonnes en 1963, les cargaisons exportées durant le premier trimestre (janvier-mars) sont pratiquement négligeables.

A l'aide de ces données inédites, nous avons pu établir le tableau III qui ne manquera de suprendre même les spécialistes du commerce extérieur. Premier sujet d'étonnement : jamais on n'avait encore révélé l'origine des denrées exportées par zones économiques du Canada. On sait maintenant que 34.5 pour cent des exportations canadiennes sont passées par le Québec durant les neuf derniers mois de 1963, soit pour une valeur de $1,847,882,000 sur un total de $5,355,566,000. Or presque les trois quarts de ces marchandises sont sorties du Québec par la voie maritime (72.7%), ce qui revient à dire que les 32 millions de tonnes sont estimées à un milliard et un tiers de dollars, le reste des exportations s'acheminant vers les Etats-Unis par le rail (15.3%), par la route (8.2%), ou vers tous les autres clients étrangers par l'avion (3.5%). Notre tableau révèle la nature des merchandises exportées par le Québec. Le principal groupe est celui des matériaux fabriqués, c'est-à-dire des produits semi-manufacturés, dont le Québec exporte pour une valeur de 678.8 millions, soit 28 pour cent du total canadien. Ces marchandises pondéreuses s'acheminent principalement par eau (60%) et par le rail (35.3%). Trois d'entre elles constituent à elles seules les deux tiers du groupe : le papier à imprimer, l'aluminium en lingot, et le cuivre, toutes issues des grandes industries du Québec. Le papier dont la valeur dépasse 200 millions quitte le Québec moitié par eau, moitié par le rail (moins d'un dixième prend la route). En fait, cependant, le Québec vend encore plus de papier à l'étranger, car il en passe en transit par l'Ontario en direction de Detroit et de Chicago. On observe le même phénomène pour les lingots d'aluminium, dont le Québec est le seul producteur du Canada oriental. La province en exporte pour une valuer de 126 millions (70% par eau), mais il en passe par l'Ontario pour 55 millions et par les provinces maritimes pour 10 millions. A propos du cuivre cependant, la situation diffère, car le principal producteur est l'Ontario (Sudbury), quoique la raffinerie de Montréal-Est ait la plus forte capacité du pays.

Après le groupe de matériaux fabriqués vient celui des matières premières (matériaux bruts) dont le Québec exporte pour une valeur de 483.4 millions de dollars, soit 43 pour cent du total canadien. Pondéreux par définition, ces produits sortent du Québec par les voies maritimes à raison de 90 pour cent. Or, ce sont presque uniquement des minerais non traités : d'abord le minerai de fer (188.3 millions) qui, de Sept-Iles et de Port-Cartier, s'oriente vers les ports américains des Grands-Lacs et de la côte de l'Atlantique et vers les ports européens; puis le minerai du nickel ontarien (86.6 millions) destiné surtout à l'Angleterre et à la Norvège; l'amiante des Cantons de l'Est qui gagne l'étranger, l'Europe, l'Asie, l'Océanie par eau, et les Etats-Unis par le rail. Il en sort pour 81.2 millions par le Québec et 27 millions par l'Ontario.

Les exportations de produits alimentaires atteignent une valeur presque égale à celle du groupe précédent, soit 457.6 milions, 40 pour cent des exportation canadiennes, et elles s'acheminent par eau en majeure partie (89.0%). Une denrée domine largement l'ensemble du groupe : les céréales, dont la valeur exportée du Québec s'élève à 321.5 millions. Il s'agit évidemment du blé de la prairie canadienne transbordé aux ports du Saint-Laurent. Le second produit alimentaire est la farine avec une valeur de 23 millions seulement, suivie par les boissons alcooliques (20 millions), les produits laitiers (15.8 millions), le tabac (14.5 millions), et les fourrures (12 millions).

Le quatrième groupe de produits exportés par le Québec est celui des articles manufacturés, dont notre province expédie 37 pour cent du total du pays, soit pour une valeur de 221.9 millions. Dans ce cas les modes de transport diffèrent des groupes précédents. La voie maritime demeure encore la plus importante, mais avec 42.2 pour cent seulement.

TABLEAU III

VALEUR DES EXPORTATIONS DU QUÉBEC ET DU CANADA SELON LES MODES DE TRANSPORT, 1er AVRIL À 31 DÉCEMBRE 1963

	Modes de transport										Valeur totale	
Groupes de marchandises	Bateau ($1000)	%	Camion ($1000)	%	Train ($1000)	%	Avion ($1000)	%	Autres ($1000)	%	($1000)	% rég-ional
I. *Animaux vivants*												
Québec	569	27.5	1,173	56.7	14	0.7	312	15.1			2,068	0.1
% du Canada	74.3		4.7		0.6		27.0				7.0	
Autres régions	196	0.7	23,801	87.1	2,491	9.1	848	3.1			27,336	0.8
Canada	765	2.5	24,974	85.2	2,505	8.5	1,160	3.8			29,404	0.5
II. *Aliments, breuvages*												
Québec	406,551	88.9	36,568	8.0	13,853	3.0	642	0.1	25		457,639	24.8
% du Canada	43.6		22.7		22.1		69.5		83.3		39.6	
Autres régions	525,618	75.2	124,482	17.8	48,788	6.9	281	0.1	5		699,174	19.9
Canada	932,169	80.6	161,050	13.9	62,641	5.4	923	0.1	30		1,156,813	21.6
III. *Matériaux bruts*												
Québec	436,226	90.4	15,319	3.1	25,489	5.2	6,304	1.3	20		483,358	26.2
% du Canada	65.1		39.3		14.1		54.3				43.0	
Autres régions	233,668	36.4	23,948	3.7	155,428	24.2	5,294	0.8	224,002	34.9	642,340	18.3
Canada	669,894	59.5	39,267	3.5	180,917	16.0	11,598	1.0	224,022	20.0	1,125,698	21.1

TABLEAU III

VALEUR DES EXPORTATIONS DU QUÉBEC ET DU CANADA SELON LES MODES DE TRANSPORT, 1er AVRIL À 31 DÉCEMBRE 1963 *(continued)*

Groupes de marchandises	Modes de transport										Valeur totale	
	Bateau ($1000)	%	Camion ($1000)	%	Train ($1000)	%	Avion ($1000)	%	Autres ($1000)	%	($1000)	% rég-ional
IV. *Matériaux fabriqués, non comestibles*												
Québec	406,257	59.9	43,732	6.4	225,763	33.3	2,207	0.3	724	0.1	678,683	36.7
% du Canada	36.6		21.6		21.1		32.7		2.2		28.0	
Autres régions	704,065	40.3	161,258	9.2	846,860	48.4	4,470	0.3	30,927	1.8	1,747,640	49.9
Canada	1,110,322	45.7	204,990	8.5	1,072,623	44.2	6,737	0.3	31,651	1.3	2,426,323	45.3
V. *Produits finis, non comestibles*												
Québec	93,489	42.2	54,804	24.7	16,086	7.2	55,743	25.2	1,745	0.7	221,862	12.0
% du Canada	63.4		25.0		13.0		54.1		34.0		37.0	
Autres régions	54,066	14.4	163,664	43.5	108,504	28.8	46,921	12.4	3,391	0.9	376,551	10.7
Canada	147,555	25.0	218,468	36.4	124,590	20.7	102,664	17.1	5,136	0.8	598,413	11.2
VI. *Transactions spéciales*												
Québec	171	4.0	442	10.4	122	2.6	169	4.1	3,368	78.9	4,272	0.2
% du Canada	21.4		10.0		20.3		17.8		28.0		17.2	
Autres régions	625	4.2	3,983	27.2	475	3.2	952	6.5	8,608	58.9	14,643	0.4
Canada	796	4.2	4,425	23.3	597	3.2	1,121	6.0	11,976	63.3	18,915	0.3
TOTAL												
Québec	1,343,258	72.7	152,038	8.2	281,327	15.3	65,377	3.5	5,882	0.3	1,847,882	
% du Canada	47.0		22.3		19.5		52.6		2.1		34.5	
Autres régions	1,518,243	43.3	501,136	14.3	1,162,546	33.2	58,826	1.6	266,933	7.6	3,507,684	
Canada	2,861,501	53.4	653,174	12.2	1,443,873	27.0	124,203	2.3	272,815	5.1	5,355,566	

C'est l'avion que vient ensuite avec 25.2 pour cent, puis la route avec 24.7 pour cent, tandis que le rail ne prend que 7.2 pour cent.

Parmi les nombreuses marchandises du groupe, ce sont les véhicules de transport et leurs accessoires que se placent au premier rang des exportations du Québec, avec l'avion en premier lieu (37.3 millions). La voie des airs (16.1 millions) est tout indiquée pour les appareils fabriqués surtout à Montréal; les pièces d'avion (16.4 millions) s'acheminent hors du Québec par la route. Les navires chargent le matériel roulant de chemin de fer (15.1 millions), les véhicules routiers et les pièces de navires. Les machines de toute nature viennent ensuite avec 33 millions de dollars, dont 22.3 quittent le Québec par eau et 6.1 par la route; puis ce sont des appareils de mesure et autres instruments scientifiques qui, sous un faible poids et dotés d'une grande valeur, s'acheminent surtout par la voie des airs, soit 22.1 millions sur une valeur totale de 30.9 millions. Les vêtements eux-mêmes préfèrent l'avion (5.1 millions sur 9.2), ainsi que les machines de bureau (3.8 sur 8.9 millions). Quant aux articles servant aux télécommunications, le Québec les exporte surtout par la route (10.4 millions sur 18.7) et plus par le train (3.4) et l'avion (3.2) que par la voie maritime (1.6).

Quelque fastidieuses que soient les énumérations faites ci-dessus, elles illustrent un aspect du commerce extérieur québécois qui se fait, répétons-le, aux trois-quarts par eau. Or ce commerce s'établit en valeur à deux milliards de dollars par année. Il reste maintenant pour compléter le tableau à connaître les importations du Québec. Souhaitons que le Bureau Fédéral de la Statistique commence à publier les données statistiques qui s'y rapportent selon les mêmes rubriques.

Les données pour 1964, publiées depuis que nous avons présenté notre communication, confirment les tendances observées. En effet, les exportations du Québec se sont élevées durant les douze mois de 1964 à deux milliards 810 millions de dollars, soit 34 pour cent du total canadien. Plus des deux tiers, 68.9 pour cent, se sont acheminées par eau, 13.7 pour cent par le rail, 9.6 pour cent par la route et, chose exceptionnelle, 7.4 pour cent par la voie des airs. Le trafic maritime du Québec continue donc de jouer un rôle capital dans l'économie non seulement de la province mais du Canada entier.

PART IV

THE GREAT LAKES: UNIQUE FEATURES AND PECULIAR PROBLEMS

THE UNIQUENESS OF THE GREAT LAKES

A. D. Misener, F.R.S.C.

MY TIME is short and my subject is vast, so I shall attempt no more than to awaken your interest and perhaps stretch your imagination. From other contributors you will have an opportunity to learn more of the behaviour of the Great Lakes.

Considered in the context of "Water Resources," the Great Lakes system is unique. The sheer size of the system is, of course, the most obvious of its unique characteristics. There are other drainage basins of comparable size in the world, but in none is one-third of such a huge area occupied by the lakes themselves. This fact alone poses some unique problems for the hydrologist and the meteorologist, as others will indicate. One example will have to suffice here. To the meteorologist the Lakes present this mesoscale feature: their size is such that at any given time there is one and only one "weather system" over each of them. Hence, if he is studying the air–water interactions in Lake Huron, his observations are not complicated by the fact that there was a tornado in Idaho two days before. In the ocean, his observations would be complicated by the swells from a major disturbance that far away.

Likewise with respect to volume, the magnitude of the Lakes gives them uniqueness that relates not simply to their dimensions, but also to their behaviour. The measurements and dimensions you can find in encyclopaedias and atlases. From these data, simple calculations should convince you that the Great Lakes are a series of enormous reservoirs connected by gentle trickles flowing in at one end and out at the other. This may sound ludicrous to admirers of the "mighty St. Lawrence" or the "majestic Niagara," or to those who have watched the navy of commerce battling the swiftly flowing St. Clair at Sarnia; so let me provide a small example.

We have heard much of the poor state of health of Lake Erie—the smallest and shallowest of the larger lakes—a mere pond compared to Lake Superior. If we were to attempt to give this sick lake a replacement-transfusion of good clean water from Lake Huron (cutting off all contamination from Detroit, Windsor, Sarnia, and Port Huron) and if we could so arrange it that this flushing out by pure water would proceed as a steady front down the lake without eddies and backwaters, it would take roughly 3 to 3½ years to complete the transfusion.

But the uniqueness of the Great Lakes is not confined to their physical make-up and behaviour. To say nothing of their biological problems and potentials, they pose a unique problem also, for example, for the student of constitutional law. The present welter of "authorities" having overlapping and sometimes conflicting jurisdictions with respect to the Lakes is totally inadequate to deal with the newly emerging problems of the region—problems that did not exist when these authorities were constituted. How does one legally and constitutionally replace them by an effective and acceptable group?

Again, the Lakes are unique in that, as a water resource, they are of concern to a much larger segment of the population than that inhabiting their immediate vicinity. Our colleagues from the west, both in Canada and the United States, have a vital interest in the decisions that are made about the utilization of the waters of the Lakes.

In passing, it should be pointed out that the whole vast volume of these waters is not available for use, except by shipping and for diluting sewage. The only water we "use up" is roughly the amount that enters and leaves annually. The Lakes are indeed tremendous reservoirs upon which to draw in times of shortage, and in which to store surpluses; but the average annual usage must equal the average annual net flow into them. This fact puts in new perspective many of the grandiose schemes for diverting water into and out of the Lakes.

The greatest problem involving the Great Lakes is that of making wise, workable, and far-reaching decisions about their management and use. The bases of these decisions must rest on an intensive and comprehensive study in human ecology. The scientific disciplines represented in Section III of this Society, given the wherewithal, can ascertain the facts of the Lakes' behaviour, and can predict what would or would not be feasible as regards their management. But the sociologists, economists, lawyers, and politicians must study them to determine what *should* be done—what parts of which lakes should be used for which purposes and to what extent. In other words, this unique system might well attract and absorb all the diverse interests represented in the Royal Society of Canada.

One can cite here an example of immediate concern, Lake St. Clair. Long a prolific producer of reed beds, the habitat of ducks and other waterfowl, in recent years it has been used increasingly to satisfy the desires of those who wish to enjoy its waters by boating on them. Boat propellors cut off the reeds, which float up and foul the beaches to the annoyance of all. A decision must be made—either to keep the lake for reeds and the duck hunters by banning boats, or to clear the reeds and promote the pleasure of the boaters and water skiers. A most unattractive decision for a politician to have to face! I suspect the boaters influence more voters.

Of course it is not always man that wins the outcome. As expressed by Ogden Nash in his *Terse Verse* (which I hesitate to quote before real Canadian poets):

The hunter crouches in his blind
'Neath camouflage of every kind,
And conjures up a quacking noise
To lend allure to his decoys.
This grown-up man, with pluck and luck
Is hoping to outwit a duck.

To sum up, multiple use of waters of the Lakes is inevitable. Decisions regarding their use must be based on socio-economic values, and sensible decisions can only be based on scientific knowledge of their characteristics and behaviour. The Great Lakes present a unique and truly interdisciplinary problem for all sections of this Society. It is to be hoped that we will not permit the necessary decisions to be made by people governed by emotion and in ignorance of the facts.

UNIQUE RESEARCH OPPORTUNITIES AFFORDED BY THE GREAT LAKES

David C. Chandler

In the past decade, research on the Great Lakes has grown from that done by a handful of investigators representing four or five organizations, to the present efforts of several hundreds, working for at least fifty organizations. The studies range from individual projects to multidisciplinary programmes backed by several sponsors. Some of these activities have taken on the proportions of crash programmes—of course with the usual results.

In the light of the great interest now being focused on the Great Lakes, it should be profitable to consider some of the natural characteristics of these lakes that make them unique. In so doing we may find ways of utilizing the lakes for new approaches to the solution of major problems in the aquatic sciences, and to the development of methods, equipment, and general facilities that are more effective than the conventional ones now used on oceans or small lakes.

According to geographers, the mid-continent of North America is a geographic phenomenon. The interior of no other continent possesses a combination of natural resources so favourable to human utilization, nor is the interior of any other continent so completely and effectively occupied by man. Other continents have a dry, desert-like interior. Hence it follows that the people of the world live mostly beside the sea except in the heart of North America, where tremendous water resources are centred, conspicuously represented by the Great Lakes.

By a chance of nature, through glaciation, three major river systems with their included large lakes were formed, extending in an almost straight line from northwestern Canada through the northeastern United States. These are the Mackenzie drainage basin, containing the Athabasca, Great Slave, and Great Bear Lakes; the Nelson drainage basin, containing Lakes Winnipegosis and Winnipeg; and the St. Lawrence drainage basin, containing Lakes Superior, Michigan, Huron, Erie, and

Ontario. These are among the world's largest lakes, and their combined volume constitutes over 50 per cent of the surface fresh water of the North American continent.

By virtue of their location, size, and general characteristics these lakes afford unique opportunities for a great variety of studies. However, the intent of this paper is to call attention only to the more conspicuous opportunities afforded by the St. Lawrence–Great Lakes region, making no attempt at completeness or detail.

REGIONAL ENVIRONMENTAL STUDIES

The St. Lawrence–Great Lakes region provides the essential features for a model study relating to the enhancement of the human environment. It is a physiographic unit dominated by the largest single mass of fresh water on the earth's surface, and is in the path of the most rapid industrial and urban development in the United States and Canada. This offers an exciting study of the interrelations and interactions of the social, political, and economic aspects of the region along with the scientific management and exploitation of its tremendous freshwater resources.

These lakes also lend themselves uniquely as a model for studies in international resource management, since they are a huge natural resource of great economic importance to both Canada and the United States. Probably no two other countries share a resource of this magnitude and also have so much technical knowledge as well as similar political and economic philosophies and a long record of friendly and successful cooperation.

SCIENTIFIC INVESTIGATIONS

Aquatic scientists employ different scales of study in their attempts to understand the physical, chemical, and biological phenomena and processes in bodies of water, and the interactions between these waters and their atmospheric and geologic boundaries. In the size-series of water bodies from small lakes to oceans, the Great Lakes represent the mesoscale aquatic system; and it is their mesoscale characteristics that give rise to unique research opportunities.

Contributing also to the uniqueness of these lakes is their possession of both lacustrine and oceanic characteristics, which may be summarized as follows:

Lacustrine characteristics:

(i) Inlets and outlets (flow-through).

(ii) Low salt content.
(iii) Freshwater biota.
(iv) Seiches rather than tides.
(v) Definite boundaries (land-locked).
(vi) A single weather system at a given time.

Oceanic characteristics:

(i) Visible effects of Coriolis force.
(ii) Distribution of upwelling and sinking according to relationship of current-stream lines and the shore.
(iii) Presence of distinct water masses.
(iv) Modifying effect on weather.
(v) Thermal cycle with essentially one period of stratification.

The Great Lakes as a mesoscale aquatic system are subject to essentially the same physical, chemical, biological, meteorological, and geological régimes as the oceans, but in addition they possess definite boundaries and have a single weather system over them at a given time. Furthermore, the Great Lakes drainage basin is a discrete physiographic unit within which exist integrated social, political, and economic régimes directly dependent upon the lakes.

These combinations of characteristics afford unusual opportunities for miscellaneous studies of the following kinds:

1. *Interactions between air and water.* Lake Michigan, for example, subserves a unique laboratory function in the study of weather modifications by water. Situated transverse to the movement of air masses and weather from west to east, this lake is large enough to produce clean-cut modifying effects upon the weather crossing it, yet is not so large that separate weather systems can exist over it at the same time. Its land-locked nature allows it to be surrounded by weather stations, a condition that cannot be achieved adequately for oceans. A similar case might be made for the study of such phenomena as precipitation and evaporation on the Great Lakes.

2. *Wind-to-wave relations.* These studies may be made under simplified conditions, because of the absence of wave-trains or swells from other distant weather systems. Open-water fetches of 50 to 300 miles are common on the Great Lakes.

3. *Water masses.* The origin, characteristics, and fate of water masses can be studied under mesoscale conditions. These masses lend themselves to studies of lake circulation, and of phyto-zooplankton development and interrelationships. The growth, reproduction, and seasonal abundance vary for a given plankton species in different water masses.

4. *Synoptic surveys.* It is feasible to make a single-day multiple-ship survey of an entire lake, since ports are numerous, the maximum breadth

is less than 185 miles, and numerous vessels are available for charter.

5. *Effects of land drainage on water quality.* Rivers entering the lakes are relatively small, but large enough to encompass a wide variety of land-use practices within a single drainage basin. Also, the lakes are large enough to receive the river discharge without an entire lake being affected.

6. *Statistical studies of commercial fish catches.* Records of commercial catches of Great Lakes fish are continuous and complete since 1867. These records make possible unusual studies in population dynamics, and in population and species changes due to environmental changes and fishing pressure.

7. *Invasion of marine species.* Marine species are entering the Great Lakes and some have become firmly established in Lake Superior, 1,000 miles from the sea. Examples include the sea lamprey, *Petromyzon marinus*; alewife, *Alosa pseudoharengus*; smelt, *Osmerus mordax*; a polycheate, *Manayunkia erienensis*; and a copepod, *Eurytemora affinis.* Studies of such species will contribute pertinent information on the rates and mechanisms of adaptation of marine organisms to fresh water.

8. *Eutrophication.* The nature and rate of natural and artificial eutrophication can be studied effectively on the Great Lakes, since each lake is distinctive in respect of the geochemical conditions in its drainage basin, and of the degrees of urbanization and industrialization. There is a wide spectrum of eutrophication conditions, from advanced stages in Lake Erie to a minimum in Lake Superior.

9. *Effects of multiple basins.* The flow-through characteristics of the lakes makes it possible to follow downstream the water originating in the upper lakes, for purposes of determining changes in biological and chemical characteristics. These lakes, although connected and subjected to the same meteorological conditions, exhibit individual physical, chemical, and biological characteristics.

10. *Ice cover.* The formation, structure, extent, break-ups, and energy relations of the ice cover vary with each lake, because of differences in latitude, lake morphometry, and orientation to prevailing winds. Records of ice may be obtained from shore stations, planes, or satellites. The relation of ice to lake navigation adds an applied aspect to an otherwise theoretical problem.

EDUCATION AND TRAINING

In the fields of limnology and oceanography, the basic problems, methods, and procedures and much of the equipment are identical, and in many instances a person trained in one becomes professionally employed in the other. Since the Great Lakes are intermediate in the total size-series of the world's water bodies, and possess both lacustrine and oceanic characteristics, they are uniquely suited for the education and training of aquatic scientists. The overlap of several disciplines in Great Lakes studies provides a natural common ground and needed meeting-place for limnology and oceanography that can and should be utilized to the benefit of both.

Within the Great Lakes region are at least 20 universities with established programmes in the aquatic sciences involving curricula, scientific personnel, and a great diversity of teaching and research facilities. Research vessels suitable for training purposes are operated by several universities in the region. In addition to giving students shipboard experience with oceanographic equipment and procedures, this arrangement has the unique feature of dealing with a complete aquatic system in an interdisciplinary manner. Such an approach is not possible on either small lakes or oceans.

ENGINEERING AND DEVELOPMENT

Surface Vessels

The conduct of research on the Great Lakes requires equipment, instruments, and procedures very similar to those needed for oceanographic studies. Nevertheless essential differences do exist between these two environments in regard to, for example, distances, sea state, and number of accessible ports. Most oceanographic cruises are from a few weeks to several months in length, while on the Great Lakes cruises are from one to several days. In these differences lie opportunities for exploring new concepts of the construction and operation of research vessels. Conventional vessels can be successfully used on the Great Lakes, but other designs may well be more efficient and economical for the pursuit of investigations thereon. The construction of a vessel with some of the combined characteristics of the conventional ship and the "boat truck," or off-shore drilling vessels, offers some interesting possibilities. Using the conventional "Vee" hull, it should be possible to construct a vessel with space for general uncommitted laboratory work, portable vans or pods, and with deck area adequate for standard shipboard activities, plus that required to accommodate a 5 to 7 ton submersible vehicle. Such a surface ship would serve the multiple purpose of a research vessel, of a support vessel for submersibles and diving equipment, and of student training.

Again, the Great Lakes afford a good place to try out the use of hydrofoils and various kinds of airplanes for a rapid coverage of lake-surface conditions.

Submersibles and Man-in-the-Sea Project

One objective of the United States National Oceanographic research programme is man's complete utilization of the ocean's tremendous resources. This encompasses the harvesting and management of all the usable products, the understanding of the ocean's characteristics, processes, and phenomena and their potential application to man's welfare, and the ultimate occupancy of the ocean as a place for man to live and enjoy. This thinking has led to the concept of the Sea Grant College, a plan to establish institutions charged with the responsibility of developing and implementing this idea through ocean engineering, basic marine research, and educational programmes in the marine sciences. In recognition of the role of the Great Lakes in the aquatic sciences, one Sea Grant College is planned for the region. It is generally agreed that these lakes have a significant contribution to make in the areas of instrumentation and marine engineering.

Water 500 feet or greater in depth is accessible in several parts of the Great Lakes within a distance of 20 miles or less from shore. Numerous deep-water ports exist on all the lakes, and within the immediate region are work and research ships, diversified industry, supply and engineering companies, and the intellectual and technical resources of numerous universities. In no other place in the world does this combination of conditions and facilities exist within so small an area. These conditions are highly favourable for the development and testing of instruments, fixed platforms, research submarines, and various aspects of the "Man-in-the-Sea" project. The economy of time and money is evident.

Instrumentation of Commercial Vessels to Obtain Scientific Data

Application of the concept of "Ships of Opportunity," or Neptune Projects, to commercial vessels in the Great Lakes has some promising possibilities. One hundred or more vessels, freighters, ferries, and fishing vessels may be on the lakes on any given day during the navigation season. Most of them operate on a scheduled predetermined course. With proper instrumentation, a synoptic coverage of any one lake, or possibly of all the lakes, could be done on a daily basis. In addition to giving lake-wide coverage (impossible with research vessels) this would be a means of collecting valuable routine survey data, while freeing research vessels for specialized duties. Technology is now available for collecting various kinds of physical, chemical, and biological data from a ship under way at speeds up to 18 to 20 knots. The operators of commercial vessels are apparently receptive to this idea.

Other examples, equally important, might be cited to illustrate the uniqueness of the Great Lakes for various kinds of studies. If each investigator of the Great Lakes were to identify and delineate the unique characteristics of these lakes with respect to his own research interest, this might well result in far more meaningful programmes of studies.

ENVIRONMENTAL CONTROL IN THE GREAT LAKES–ST. LAWRENCE REGION OF NORTH AMERICA

E. G. Pleva

THE GREAT LAKES, with their great discharge river the St. Lawrence, comprise the most economically significant body of water or water system in North America and perhaps in the entire world. More than 36 million North Americans live in the Great Lakes–St. Lawrence drainage basin: over 25 million in the United States and 11 million in Canada. Many millions more are directly affected by what happens to these lakes and the waters in them or discharging from them. We have estimated that by 1985 the population of the drainage basin will increase to 57 million human beings, of whom about 19 million will reside in Canada. During this period, in other words, an annual increase in population of approximately one million is indicated.

The most important industrial and urban agglomeration in Canada parallels the axis of the lower Great Lakes and the St. Lawrence River. A map of Canada shows that a relatively straight line may be drawn from Quebec City through Montreal, Kingston, Toronto, London, to Windsor, approximately 700 miles long. If one visualizes a belt 50 miles wide (25 miles on each side of the imaginary line) running its entire length, the belt or corridor would be 35,000 square miles in area. Although this comprises less than 1 per cent of the total area of Canada, this corridor is an extremely important part of the country; for it contains approximately three-fifths of Canada's population, four-fifths of the industrial activity as measured by the value of manufactured goods, and one-third of the commercial agriculture as measured by the value of products sold off the farm. One of Canada's railway champions, Alexander Galt, named this corridor over a century ago. When arguing for a railway to run from the salt water of the St. Lawrence estuary to the heart of the continent in Chicago, he said: "This railway will serve the Grand Trunk of North America."

Obviously Canada has an exceedingly large stake in the maintenance and improvement of the quality of the environment in the Great Lakes–St. Lawrence drainage basin. Yet in this area, the quality of the surface waters, rivers, and lakes, and even that of the groundwater, is decreasing from year to year. There is general agreement that pollution by municipal and industrial wastes is the main cause of this deterioration.

The physical map of North America shows a natural unity of the Great Lakes–St. Lawrence drainage basin: it is one system. However, a political map displays a pattern of fragmentation. This natural unit is shared by the United States and Canada: by the nine states of Minnesota, Wisconsin, Illinois, Indiana, Michigan, Ohio, Pennsylvania, New York, and Vermont; and by the two provinces of Ontario and Quebec. It is generally realized that the local government units of a century ago are inadequate to meet the problems of today's expanding urban areas; but it is not so well known that historically evolved state and provincial boundaries are great obstacles to dealing with large environmental problems. A governor can speak only for his state; a premier can refer only to things being done in his province. There is no unitary system or approach for dealing with the basic problems of this great drainage basin. Ohio cannot speak to Ontario except through the State Department and the Department of External Affairs. This process can take forty years.

Lake Erie, the most critical part of the system, may be regarded as illustrating the complexities involved in trying to reach a unitary basis in the environmental planning of a region fragmented into many political jurisdictions. Every major magazine, newspaper syndicate, and television network seems to have provided a "horror story" on Lake Erie in the past year. The *New York Herald Tribune* invented a new word in its article on Lake Erie—*lacocide*, the death of a lake.

The International Joint Commission, established as a consequence of the 1909 Treaty, has certain obligations and procedural practices. It should be studied as a model for a working framework of some "authority" more closely related to the problems of 1967. The treaty works well and the IJC has a commendable record of activities, but it must be pointed out that the great deterioration of the Great Lakes and St. Lawrence River has taken place since 1909—the period when the IJC was operative. Clearly something has been lacking.

Ontario has excellent water resources legislation in the Water Resources Commission Act. Ohio, likewise, has excellent water legislation. But even if Ontario and Ohio were able to work together, what happens when a substantial portion of the pollution of Lake Erie comes from industrial wastes originating in Michigan? Presumably this is where federal and international cooperation should take over. However, in both Canada and the United States, water is a natural resource that comes basically under the control of the provinces and the states. Here is a very serious dilemma that must be resolved without delay.

Many scientific conferences have been called in the past few years to deal with the problems of the Great Lakes and their alleviation. But the conferences always come up against the hard facts of fragmented political jurisdiction and the absence of any operational mechanism able to produce a unitary approach. No one is so naïve as to believe in some cumbersome centralized political remedy. History has given us our fragments of states and provinces and we must work within this framework.

The recently passed United States Water Quality Act of 1965 (P.L. 89–234), although geared to the cooperative and coordinated efforts of the three levels of government—federal, state, and local—recognizes the comprehensive scope of water resources problems when they transcend boundary lines. Perhaps an arrangement may be worked out by the United States and Canada whereby the five states of Ohio, Michigan, Indiana, Pennsylvania, and New York (operating under the Water Quality Act) could cooperate with Ontario (operating under the Ontario Water Resources Commission Act) to deal positively with the improvement of Lake Erie.

There are some who claim emphatically that more research and more education are needed. These needs are acknowledged, but the most urgent necessity now is to develop the means whereby unitary programmes may be undertaken by fragmented political units. While further research is necessary, we actually lack today the practical means of applying the knowledge we already have.

In the absence of working machinery to deal with regional water resources problems on a regional basis, many proposals involving massive adjustments of the continental water budget are being given great publicity. North America's future may include major water diversion and water transmission projects, but the immediate challenge is to control pollution, the great destroyer of water in the Great Lakes–St. Lawrence basin. This economic region is fortunate in its store of fresh water. But the usage of this water is limited by pollution, and the limitation has now reached critical proportions.

There are several positive consequences to a successful programme in water management and pollution abatement. Water is the most planning-sensitive factor in determining the pattern of new urban growth and the redevelopment of old urban areas. As already indicated, the management of water resources in Ontario is and always has been a provincial responsibility. The Ontario Water Resources Commission Act merely establishes procedures whereby the province exercises its responsibilities. Ontario will double in population in the next quarter-century. All this growth will be in the urban sector. The proper management of water resources, including the supply and distribution as well as the treatment of wastes, will be a major element in developing the kinds of urban patterns that could be a credit to a civilized technology and a humane people.

CONCLUSIONS

1. The Great Lakes–St. Lawrence region of North America is one of the world's most important industrial and urban areas.
2. Its water resources are abundant but are being limited in utility by pollution. The seriousness of the condition is increasing.
3. A unitary programme on water management and pollution abatement has been difficult to achieve owing to the political fragmentation of the drainage basin.
4. The most critical area in the system, Lake Erie, may be dealt with on a unitary basis provided that Canada and the United States were to enable Ontario and the five states of New York, Pennsylvania, Ohio, Michigan, and Indiana to work together under the terms of recent existing legislation. The working out of such an agreement would take a high degree of statesmanship. Perhaps the principal decision-makers should convene upon an island in Lake Erie and stay in session until a working agreement is reached.
5. The planning and management of water resources may be the most important factor in achieving a civilized pattern of land uses in rapidly developing urban areas. Decision-makers must find courage for compromise between potentially competitive uses for water.
6. The people of the region, through research and education, must become more adequately informed in preparation for the decisions that will lead to prudent and rational management of water resources. This knowledge is necessary in order that simple panaceas for water resources problems may be evaluated critically in all their implications, and that projects which are bold in scale and novel in purpose may be appraised intelligently by the taxpayers.
7. Finally, the regional inhabitants must accept and be prepared to underwrite the considerable costs involved in effective water management works.

THERMAL RÉGIME AND CIRCULATION IN THE GREAT LAKES

G. K. Rodgers

DETERMINATION of the lake-wide circulation patterns and temperature structure within the Great Lakes constitutes a basic problem in the physics of these lakes. Research has recently advanced our knowledge of these questions significantly, but is still seeking answers which were first sought many years ago.

One of the earliest contributions to these studies was a report by Harrington (1895) on surface circulation based on drift bottle returns —a paper often quoted as the classic study for this region. Another pioneer was Freeman (1926), who made a contribution to the study of evaporation, a vitally important factor in thermal processes in the Lakes.

Following the Second World War, work on the Lakes was stimulated first by changes in the commercial fisheries, later by concern over water levels, and most recently by evidence of detrimental pollution.

One field of current research received an initial stimulus in the 1940's, when the seasonal changes of temperature structure in Lake Michigan were described by Church (1942, 1945), who was the first to make extensive use of the bathythermograph in the Great Lakes. In 1952, Millar published charts showing the patterns of average surface temperature for each month for all the Great Lakes. Since then the work has been intensified to such an extent that it is not feasible to record here all the contributions that have been made. However, in the course of the studies of currents and temperatures, two techniques have been applied most extensively. The first is the execution of synoptic or quasi-synoptic surveys over a complete lake, involving a series of sampling stations at which temperatures are measured from the surface to the bottom of the lake (Ayers *et al.* 1956; Rodgers and Anderson 1963). The second technique utilizes recording current meters and thermographs, moored in the lakes for long periods of time at a number of locations and depths in each lake (Verber 1965).

Two areas of work seem to be underdeveloped at this time. First, direct observation of the history of individual masses of water is required. Ideally, natural tracers would be useful for tracking this flow, but few seem to be available; hence artificial ones may be required. A partial solution to this requirement may be the tracking of drogues (drift anchors with a marker float) over periods of two days or more. Long periods of tracking are required, because it has already been found in the records from fixed meters that large periodic fluctuations in currents with periods of 15 to 20 hours are common. Drogues are not ideal "tracers," since it is uncertain to what degree they stay with a given body of water, particularly when strong vertical motion is present.

The second underdeveloped area is in the field of theoretical studies. These are urgently needed to provide a framework for the descriptive work which has already been completed.

In the following discussion, the relation between circulation and water temperatures is first explored in a general way, and then attention is focussed on a particular temperature and circulation phenomenon only recently recognized in the Great Lakes.

GEOSTROPHIC FLOW AND TEMPERATURE STRUCTURE

Geostrophic flow is the steady motion of a fluid under the influence of pressure and the earth's rotation. Under certain assumptions the pressure field can be determined from the density distribution. Therefore currents may be computed from the density structure in a lake, and since density differences in the Great Lakes are determined primarily by temperature and pressure, determination of the temperature structure may provide an estimate of the current. This technique, used for many years in oceanography, has been adapted for fresh water by Ayers (1956), who has used it in Lake Huron (Ayers *et al.* 1956) and Lake Michigan (Ayers *et al.* 1958).

To the optimistic, at this point in our understanding of lake-wide circulation, the appearance of consistent patterns in the distribution of temperature in summer suggests that some "permanent" circulation patterns may be reflected in the density distribution. On the other hand, the observation of strong temperature fluctuations (Mortimer 1963) indicates that a number of the assumptions in the development of the geostrophic theory may not be valid for the Lakes. Yet this is a potentially powerful method of determining circulation, because at present it is much easier to obtain a series of temperature profiles than to measure currents. But a full-scale test of the validity of the technique is still awaited.

In any case, the dynamic height method will probably be limited to use in relatively deep water. In shallow waters the lower boundary will interfere, and near-shore waters in some areas are of higher turbidity and anomalous chemical composition—conditions which introduce complex factors into the computation of fluid density.

HEAT ADVECTION AND CIRCULATION

Circulation can sometimes be inferred from changes in the heat content of a volume of water: in other words, by using water temperature as a tracer. Temperature is not a conservative property. However, if something is known about the heat flux across the air–water interface, changes in heat content of a volume of water may be interpreted as the result of the inflow and outflow of water with respect to that particular volume, after adjustment has been made for the heat flux at the surface. An example easily visualized is the case at the mouth of a river, where water flowing from the river is either colder or warmer than the lake into which it is flowing. At certain times the Niagara River water within Lake Ontario can be identified in this manner (Rodgers 1966).

On a lake-wide scale, the detail which one can expect to glean from this type of analysis is restricted. The limitations result from the long time it takes to sample a lake, compared with the period of the large temperature fluctuations noted above. A final point must be made about deriving a quantitative measure of the circulation from the change in heat content. In order that circulation may be inferred from changes in the heat content of a volume of water, the difference in temperature between water flowing into and out of the volume is required. When dealing with the volume of water in the middle of a large lake, the values used for these temperatures usually have to be inferred from other considerations. The extent to which this technique may be used will be illustrated in the phenomenon described below.

A SYNOPTIC SURVEY PROGRAMME

In 1958, a synoptic survey programme was initiated under the direction of Dr. D. V. Anderson of the Ontario Department of Lands and Forests, which has been continued by the Great Lakes Institute of the

University of Toronto from 1960 to the present. The basic plan of the programme was to carry out a survey of a lake once each month throughout the year. Each survey involved 60 or more observation stations, and required about three days to complete, working 24 hours each day with a single large ship. Several types of observations have been made, including the collection of chemical data, biological and geological sampling, as well as temperature measurements.

From this series of surveys, seasonal temperature patterns have been established. The data for Lake Ontario are particularly complete, because the survey vessel C.C.G.S. "Porte Dauphine" is permitted to operate in winter after the commercial navigation season closes. Lake Ontario, unlike the other Great Lakes, is relatively free of ice during the winter. Another advantage of Lake Ontario is that the great depths found there are comparable to those found in the deep Great Lakes; yet its smaller size makes adequate sampling possible in a shorter period of time.

For these reasons, the following remarks apply mainly to Lake Ontario, where the results of the surveys described above have led to recognition of a particular temperature and circulation feature called the "thermal bar," which will be described in more detail.

THE SEASONAL TEMPERATURE PATTERN

The customary seasonal sequence of temperature profiles reveals the classical picture of a dimictic lake of the temperate zone (Fig. 1). In a dimictic lake there are two periods of stratification: one of strong stratification in summer, and one of weak stratification in winter. These periods are separated by times when the water column is relatively uniform in temperature in spring and fall, the temperature being close to the temperature of the maximum density of water (approximately 4° C). The temperatures at 200 metres in the lake are between 3° and 5° C throughout the year.

From the temperature data at all depths in each survey the average temperature or heat content can be computed. The sequence of surveys provides an estimate of changes in heat content, and the first physical problem is to account for these changes. This has been done for Lake Ontario (Rodgers and Anderson 1961). The results of computations based on land data, empirical equations, and climatological data for meteorological parameters and surface water temperatures were confirmed by observed changes of heat content in the lake. The results, however, must be viewed as monthly trends and not as indicative of

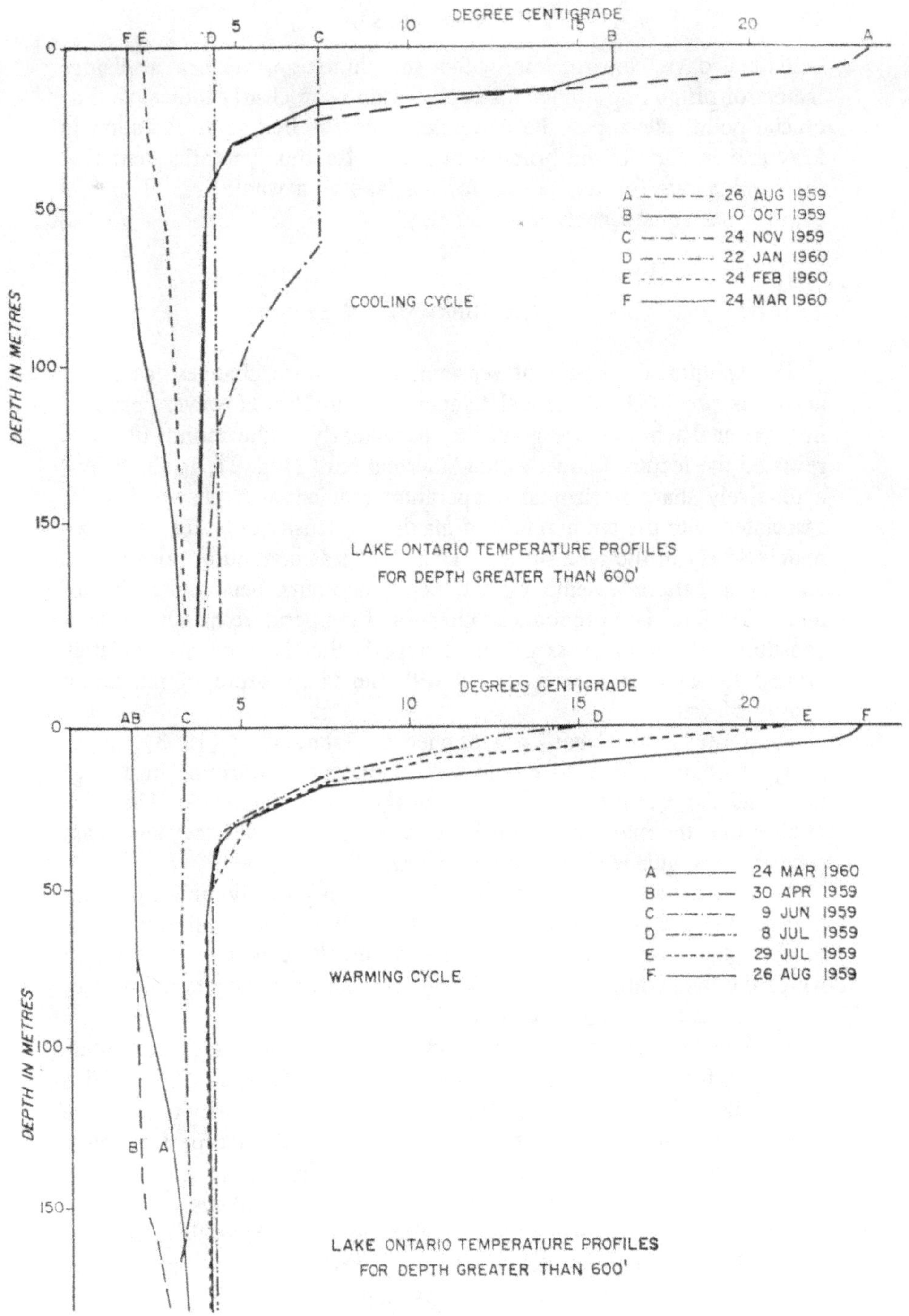
DEGREE CENTIGRADE
5
10
15
20
F E
D
C
B
A
0
50
100
150
DEPTH IN METRES
A 26 AUG 1959
B 10 OCT 1959
C 24 NOV 1959
D 22 JAN 1960
E 24 FEB 1960
F 24 MAR 1960
COOLING CYCLE
LAKE ONTARIO TEMPERATURE PROFILES
FOR DEPTH GREATER THAN 600'
DEGREES CENTIGRADE
5
10
15
20
AB
C
D
E
F
0
50
100
150
DEPTH IN METRES
A 24 MAR 1960
B 30 APR 1959
C 9 JUN 1959
D 8 JUL 1959
E 29 JUL 1959
F 26 AUG 1959
WARMING CYCLE
B
A
LAKE ONTARIO TEMPERATURE PROFILES
FOR DEPTH GREATER THAN 600'

FIGURE 1

individual days. Nevertheless, within this limitation, the heat exchange factors of prime importance for each season were clearly indicated. The crucial point relevant to the discussion below is that solar radiation in May and in June is the prime heat source for those months, and that the heating rate for this period for the lake as a whole is 500 to 550 calories per square centimetre per day.

THE THERMAL BAR

The traditional picture of seasonal temperature changes, as noted above, is provided by vertical temperature profiles. However, patterns in horizontal temperature gradients, particularly in the month of June, revealed the feature known as the "thermal bar" (Fig. 2). In the "bar," a relatively sharp horizontal temperature gradient was observed to be associated with the temperature of maximum density of water (approximately 4° C) at the lake surface. This band was continuous around the lake in a pattern resembling the depth contours beneath. It is not unusual to find such pronounced changes of temperature in a lake: what constitutes the uniqueness of this change is that it extends completely around the lake and is associated with the temperature of maximum density of water.

The term "thermal bar" was applied by Tikhomirov (1963), in his study of Lake Ladoga, to this feature of the spring warming in a large lake, and (to a less marked extent) of the fall cooling cycle. The term implies that thermal characteristics may act as a barrier to water mass exchange, as will be demonstrated below.

As winter passes, the lake has temperatures nearly uniform, both horizontally and vertically, at 2° or 3° C. With heating, shallower waters reach higher temperatures more quickly, and the condition develops in which the temperatures of mid-lake and of near-shore waters are respectively less than and higher than 4° C.

In 1965, the lake was sampled for temperature at three-week intervals from the end of April to the end of June (Rodgers 1966). This survey showed the progress of the thermal bar, from its beginning close to shore until its disappearance in mid-lake in the latter part of June. The relationship to depth was indicated clearly by surface isotherms (a line of constant temperature). From this series of surveys it was also possible to infer a feature of the lake circulation, on the basis of changes in the heat content as described in a previous section. It appears that changes of heat content (approximately 600 calories per square centimetre per day) before the bar arrives in the mid-lake region can be

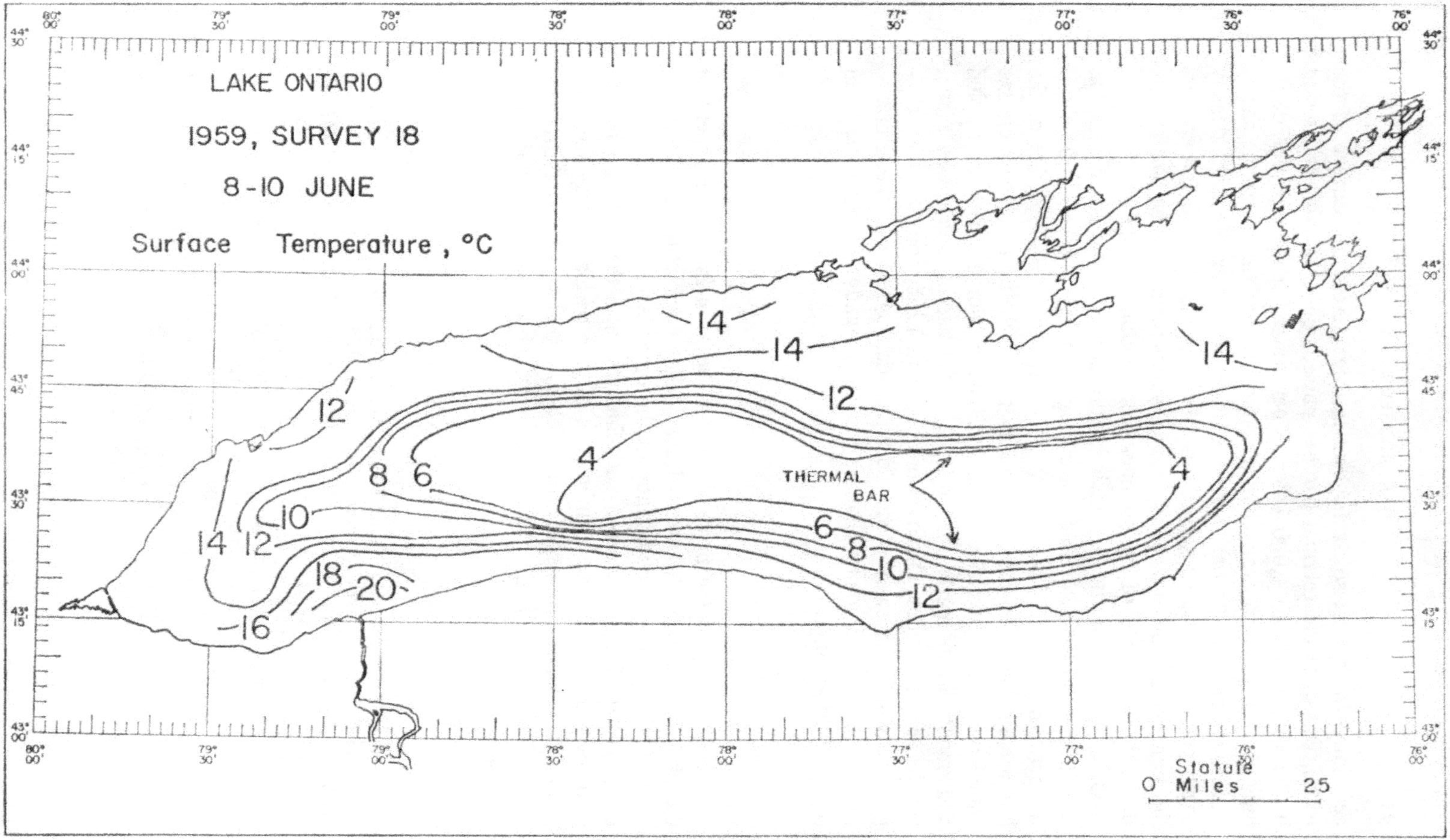
LAKE ONTARIO
1959, SURVEY 18
8-10 JUNE
Surface Temperature, °C
THERMAL BAR
Statute Miles
0
25
14
12
10
8
6
4
16
18
20

Figure 2

accounted for almost solely by heat transfer across the surface of the water. But once the thermal bar has passed, the heat content rises at higher rates (800 to 1,000 calories per square centimetre per day), indicating an influx of warm surface water from areas nearer the shore. This illustrates the "barrier" nature of the thermal bar. Since the density of surface waters is greatest at the bar (approximately 4° C), it appears that convergence takes place there, and waters formed in the bar become the cold lower layer of the summer stratification period.

Other aspects of the bar include turbidity and colour changes, as well as marked gradients in surface roughness associated with the sharp temperature change at the bar. Warm waters on the shore side of the bar are greener, browner, and more turbid than the colder, clearer waters on the mid-lake side of the bar. The division between the rippled and smooth water marks the presence of the bar in such a way that it can be seen for miles. Observations made in 1966, considered in conjunction with a review of some older records, suggest that the temperature, turbidity, and colour changes can vary greatly in magnitude from one year to another.

CONCLUSION

The discovery of the thermal bar has been an interesting aspect of the physics of one of the Great Lakes. Theoretical study of the bar is called for, as well as examination of the other large lakes in the Great Lakes system for its presence and characteristics there. Nowhere else in the world is there such a unique set of lake basins of large size, and of differing shapes and depths, in which to examine the variety of ways in which the thermal bar occurs, and in which to put the theories outlined above to the test.

REFERENCES

AYERS, J. C. (1956), "A Dynamic Height Method for the Determination of Currents in Deep Lakes," *Limnol. Oceanog. 1*: 150–61.

AYERS, J. C., ANDERSON, D. V., CHANDLER, D. C., and LAUFF, G. H. (1956), *Currents and Water Masses of Lake Huron*, Ontario Dept. Lands and Forests, Div. of Res., Maple, Ont., Res. Rep. No. 35.

AYERS, J. C., CHANDLER, D. C., LAUFF, G. H., POWERS, C. F., and HENSON, E. B. (1958), *Currents and Water Masses of Lake Michigan*, Great Lakes Res. Div., Univ. of Michigan, Publ. No. 3.

CHURCH, P. E. (1942), *The Annual Temperature Cycle in Lake Michigan, Part I*, Inst. Meteorology, Univ. of Chicago, Misc. Rept. 4.

——— (1945), *The Annual Temperature Cycle in Lake Michigan, Part II*, Inst. of Meteorology, Univ. of Chicago, Misc. Rept. 18.

FREEMAN, J. R. (1926), *Regulation of Elevation and Discharge of the Great Lakes* (The Sanitary District of Chicago, Ill.), pp. 1–548.

HARRINGTON, M. W. (1895), *Surface Currents of the Great Lakes*, U.S. Dept. of Agric. Weather Bur. Bull. B. (rev. ed.), pp. 1–14.

MILLAR, F. G. (1952), "Surface Temperatures of the Great Lakes," *J. Fish. Res. Bd. Can. 9*: 329–76.

MORTIMER, C. H. (1963), "Frontiers in Physical Limnology, with Particular Reference to Long Waves in Rotating Basins," *Proc. 6th Conf. on Great Lakes Res.*, Great Lakes Res. Div., Univ. of Michigan, Publ. No. 10, pp. 6–42.

RODGERS, G. K. (1966), "The Thermal Bar in Lake Ontario, 1965," *Proc. 9th Conf. on Great Lakes Res.* (in press).

RODGERS, G. K. and ANDERSON, D. V. (1961), "A Preliminary Study of the Energy Budget of Lake Ontario," *J. Fish. Res. Bd. Can. 18*: 617–35.

——— (1963), "The Thermal Structure of Lake Ontario," *Proc. 6th Conf. on Great Lakes Res.*, Great Lakes Res. Div., Univ. of Michigan, Publ. No. 10, pp. 59–69.

TIKHOMIROV, A. I. (1963), "The Thermal Bar of Lake Ladoga," *Bull.* (Izvestiya) *All-Union Geogr. Soc. 95*: 134–42.

VERBER, J. L. (1965), "Current Profiles to Depth in Lake Michigan," *Proc. 8th Conf. on Great Lakes Res.*, Great Lakes Res. Div., Univ. of Michigan, Publ. No. 13, pp. 364–71.

METEOROLOGICAL PROBLEMS ON THE GREAT LAKES

T. L. Richards

THE PROBLEMS of the meteorologist active in Great Lakes research are too numerous and too varied to be adequately described in a short review. Here it is only possible to outline some of the major topics and to select just one of these for more detailed discussion. For those wishing to investigate more fully a specific facet of the field, a selected bibliography is appended.

Meteorological problems associated with the Great Lakes may be divided into two distinct categories: those associated with the effects of the lakes on the weather and, conversely, those dealing with the effects of meteorological factors on the lakes themselves. These may be further subdivided by defining the particular meteorological parameter or parameters involved.

THE EFFECTS OF LAKES ON WEATHER

If this review were to be directed exclusively to the meteorologist it would no doubt dwell on the first-noted category, for it is well known that the nearly 100,000 square miles of water making up the Great Lakes system have a powerful influence on the weather, not only over the water but also over thousands of square miles of the surrounding land areas.

Moderating Influence on Temperature and Humidity

That the lakes have a moderating influence on the temperature régime of the nearby land is an economic, as well as a meteorological fact of life. A prime example is that in the early spring and the fall, the generally ice-free lakes moderate the air temperatures over nearby land, and reduce frost hazards to such a degree that tobacco may be grown commercially as far north as the Bruce Peninsula. The reverse cooling effect of the lakes in the summer is also well known and economically beneficial—witness the many thriving summer resorts along the almost 3,000 miles of Canadian shoreline.

In this connection, the lake-breeze régime of the Great Lakes is a most interesting field of study, but merely to review recent investigations would entail a full-fledged paper. Suffice it to state that progress has been made in defining the boundary conditions and many of the mechanisms of the lake breeze, and that the resulting reports have made a real contribution to the literature.

In addition to moderating air temperatures, the lakes also influence the humidity of the air over the nearby land regions by contributing tons of moisture to the atmosphere. For example, evaporation from the surface of Lake Erie averages three feet over its 10,000 square mile area in a single year. Of course, what the atmosphere gains in water vapour the lakes lose in water. This converse effect will be dealt with in more detail later.

Areal Distribution of Precipitation

The lakes also play a major role in influencing the areal distribution of precipitation. Convective day-time showers and thunderstorms are more likely to form over the relatively warmer land areas in the summer, and in the winter cold winds crossing the comparatively warm lakes cause the so-called "lake-effect snowstorms." As Canadians we are well aware of the resultant snow-belt areas in the highlands south and east of Lake Huron and Georgian Bay, where a winter's snow-fall averages 120 inches at Durham as compared to only about 45 inches in the Toronto area.

This is another intriguing lake phenomenon that is being intensively investigated with the aid of radar, aircraft, and mesoscale networks. Recent studies have sorted out the role of the lakes in the formation of these storms and have also made extensive progress in defining some of the mechanisms involved.

THE EFFECTS OF METEOROLOGICAL FACTORS ON THE LAKES

As noted at the outset there is a second category of meteorological problems associated with the Great Lakes—those involving the effects of meteorological factors on the lakes themselves. These problems concern not only the meteorologist, but also a large variety of scientists, including the hydrologist, the physical limnologist, and the engineer. In view of this broader area of scientific interest and because the meteorological implications may not be quite as well known, the major emphasis will be placed on this second category.

Wind and Wind Effects

The effect of winds on the waters of the Great Lakes is tremendous. Waves as high as 22 feet (on Lake Superior) are confirmed in the literature, there are verbal reports of 30- to 40-foot crests, and there is one persistent story of wave damage to a building on top of a 90-foot cliff. A cooperative study correlating measured wave heights with wind speed is currently in progress and should establish a reliable "wave climatology" for the Great Lakes. These large waves can, of course, be a menace to navigation, and together with currents (which in the Great Lakes appear to be mainly wind-driven) can cause damaging shore erosion. Strong winds can also pile up water at one end of a lake. This wind set-up is particularly evident on a shallow and elongated body of water such as Lake Erie, and has been known to increase the lake level at Buffalo by more than 8 feet. When the wind stress is withdrawn, the lake "sloshes" back and forth with a regular period as it regains its equilibrium. This oscillation of the water mass is known as a seiche. The study of the set-up and the resulting seiche is of particular importance for water supply forecasts for hydroelectric establishments, and some excellent physical and statistical work has been done in this area.

Despite the recognized importance of wind and wind-effects, one of the major problems still confronting the Great Lakes meteorologist is that of describing precisely the wind field over a large lake. Because of reduced friction over water, lake winds tend to be stronger than simultaneously observed winds over land. A recent study based on observations from the research vessel C.C.G.S. "Porte Dauphine" has confirmed that this difference is accentuated or reduced depending on whether the surface temperature of the lake tends to make the lower levels of the atmosphere unstable or stable.

A further wind problem concerns the relationship between the wind speed as determined or estimated for some anemometer level above the lake and the actual stress on the water surface. The recent use of specially designed meteorological equipment on lake towers and research vessels has helped to define more clearly this relationship, which has also been found to be a function of the effect of the surface water temperature on the atmospheric stability over the lake.

Ice

There is no need to stress the importance of being able to understand and eventually to predict the formation, movement, and dissipation of ice on the Great Lakes. If the lakes are to be used for winter navigation the implications are obvious. Even if navigation is not in question, the extent to which the lakes are ice-covered profoundly affects the exchanges that take place between lake and atmosphere during the winter, and thus is of utmost importance in making evaporation estimates. The physical factors associated with ice formation and the winter energy balance are difficult to evaluate, and involve a host of meteorological factors including temperature, humidity, wind, cloud cover, radiation, evaporation, condensation, and even stability of the atmosphere.

Fortunately, since 1960 the Meteorological Branch has conducted regular ice reconnaissance of the Great Lakes, and these surveys have led to an improved understanding of the meteorological factors affecting ice cover. One study has found a relatively simple relationship between ice cover and two meteorological factors, namely, the severity of the winter and the temperature régime of the previous summer. Of course, each lake has its own ice-cover characteristics, dependent upon its geographic location and physical features.

Lake Levels

One of the more complex and scientifically intriguing problems associated with the Great Lakes is that of the large fluctuations in water levels and the role of the meteorological factors that influence them. Very high levels and very low levels are of such economic importance that the governments of Canada and the United States, spurred by the record-breaking low levels of 1964, instructed the International Joint Commission to study the various factors which effect these fluctuations and to determine whether it would be practicable to bring about a more beneficial range of stage by means of regulating works.

The most dramatic feature of the recent low levels was the lowering of Lake Huron–Michigan (one lake, hydraulically speaking) by 5.5 feet in just 12 years. However, this need not have occasioned surprise, since 105 years of records reveal that the range of stage between highest and lowest mean monthly levels has been 6.5 feet in both Lake Ontario and Lake Huron–Michigan, 5.4 feet in Lake Erie, and 4.1 feet in Lake Superior.

Although some of the changes in the levels of the Great Lakes are no doubt due to such man-made alterations as diversions or channel deepenings, and to such physical factors as geological tilting or scouring of river outlets, it is recognized that these effects are comparatively small, and it is generally conceded that the major variations in levels are due to meteorological factors.

METEOROLOGICAL FACTORS AFFECTING LAKE LEVELS

The Problem

The crux of the problem of varying lake levels is the balance between precipitation and evaporation in the Great Lakes basin. Each year about 31 inches of precipitation, varying by as much as ±20 per cent, falls on the basin. Of the precipitation that falls on the land areas, a large portion is lost through evaporation or evapo-transpiration, some is held in underground storage, and the remainder (estimated at about 30 per cent) eventually finds its way into the lakes. It is the balance of these meteorological gains and losses, plus the smaller effects of man-made and geological changes, that is responsible for the variations in the Great Lakes levels and the eventual outflow through the St. Lawrence.

There are three main types of variations of Great Lakes levels, defined according to the length of the period of the fluctuations.

Short Period

The shortest of the variations is the seiche, which is measured in terms of minutes or a few hours. The previously mentioned wind-induced seiche is the most common, although the phenomenon may also be induced by rapid changes in atmospheric pressure. Very infrequently the two types will coincide, causing a surge such as the famous 10-foot "tidal wave" that resulted in seven drownings in Lake Michigan in June 1954. The seiche is, however, a local variation of short duration which does not change the actual volume of the water or the long-term levels.

The Annual Cycle

The most regular of the Great Lakes water-level variations is the annual cycle. Usually this cycle moves from low water in the late winter to high water in the summer, with the amplitudes differing from lake to lake and varying from year to year. On the average, Lake Ontario's rise and fall of 1.8 feet is the greatest and Lake Huron–Michigan's 1.1 feet is the least.

The annual cycle is predominantly a meteorologically induced phenomenon. Rising water levels come in the spring and early summer: (i) after the snow-melt and spring floods, (ii) when precipitation is at its greatest, (iii) when groundwater levels are highest, and (iv) when evaporation rates are lowest (due to the low water temperatures). By contrast, falling water levels come in the fall and winter: (i) when evoporation rates are highest, (ii) when groundwater levels are lowest, (iii) when precipitation is at its lightest, and (iv) when most of the winter's precipitation on the watershed is locked up as snow.

Long-Term Variations

As noted earlier, the annual rises and falls are not of regular amplitudes, mainly because of fluctuations in precipitation and evaporation. The net result is that the hydrographs of all the lakes show large, long-period fluctuations upon which the annual and short-term variations are superimposed. It is evident from the record that there is no definite pattern to these long-term variations, for periods have varied anywhere from 3 to 20 years.

Trends

In addition to the variations just discussed, the hydrographs for Lake Huron–Michigan, in particular, show a definite downward trend of water levels during the past 105 years. Although there have been suggestions of a slight trend downward in precipitation, it has been assumed that since the other lakes have not been noticeably affected, the major portion of the Lake Huron–Michigan trend is due to such man-made changes as the deepening of the ship's channel in the St. Clair River.

THE ROLE OF PRECIPITATION IN LAKE-LEVEL VARIATIONS

Since precipitation is the source of the earth's freshwater supply, it is only natural to seek a relationship between the levels of the Great Lakes and the precipitation falling on the basin. To prove that a relationship does exist we need only to be reminded that the recent low-water crisis followed three years of below-normal precipitation.

While there is a fairly adequate coverage of precipitation-observing stations on land, there has been no continuous measurement over the water areas. It is a somewhat controversial matter whether measurements of precipitation taken over land are really representative of the precipitation falling on the lakes themselves. A number of investigations have been undertaken which compare observations at island sites to simultaneous overland measurements, and most of these agree that the annual precipitation measurements over water are 5 to 10 per cent less than the corresponding measurements over land. This deficiency has a seasonal variation and is largest in the summer. However, the matter of uniform exposure of the gauges is so critical that the problem is still largely unresolved. The importance of such a deficiency, if it does exist, may be best understood in the light of estimates that a 10 per cent reduction in precipitation over the water areas of the Great Lakes would result in a reduction of outflow in the St. Lawrence River of 21,000 cubic feet per second.

From observations taken at land stations, the Meteorological Branch prepares every month an estimate of the average precipitation on the Canadian portions of each of the drainage areas. The areal averages are combined with similar figures from the United States to produce average precipitation values for each of the watersheds of the Great Lakes, and to date these have also been considered representative of over-lake precipitation as well. Based on these figures, the average annual precipitation for the entire basin is 31.1 inches, the lowest average being 29.3 for the Lake Superior basin, and the highest being 34.2 for Lake Ontario. More important than these average amounts is the fact that the year-to-year figures vary by as much as ±20 per cent (i.e. ±6 inches).

The effect of even a small annual variation is made apparent by estimates that a persistent reduction of just one inch in the annual precipitation on the Lake Huron–Michigan watershed would eventually decrease the lake level by almost one foot. But it must be emphasized that the effect of precipitation on lake-level variations is not instantaneous. A reduction of one inch in annual rainfall would result in a drop in Lake Huron–Michigan of only 0.35 foot after one year, 0.58 foot after two years, 0.72 foot after three years, and 0.92 foot after six years.

A statistical study of the same lake suggests that the present water levels are influenced 9 per cent by this year's precipitation, 37 per cent by last year's, 34 per cent by that of two years ago, and 20 per cent by that of three years ago.

THE ROLE OF EVAPORATION IN LAKE-LEVEL VARIATIONS

Although relatively little is known about evaporation from the Great Lakes, significant progress has been made in this field in recent years. While standard evaporation pan data may be representative of losses from very small water bodies, other approaches are necessary to estimate monthly and annual losses from the Great Lakes. Three basic methods have been used, each requiring its own set of hydrologic or meteorological data, and each having its own merits and short-comings.

(i) *Water budget.* This is based on a simplified equation: Inflow + Precipitation = Outflow + Evaporation. A serious short-coming in this method is that inflow and outflow figures are very large compared to those for evaporation. As a result a 1 per cent error in the large flows of influent and effluent rivers may introduce errors up to 25 per cent in evaporation estimates.

(ii) *Energy budget.* An accounting of the energy gains and losses in a lake. Though scientifically sound, this method is infrequently used because of a scarcity of year-round surveys of water temperature to depth, required for evaluation of the heat storage term.

(iii) *Mass transfer equation.* This method is most popular because it requires observations of only three factors, viz. wind speed, the humidity of the air, and the surface water temperature of the lake. New techniques developed from data obtained by the research vessel C.C.G.S. "Porte Dauphine" have recently led to a better use of the formula, and to improved estimates of monthly and annual evaporation. One serious drawback, however, is that the equation currently employed was developed for a small lake in a climatic region quite different from that of the Great Lakes. While the results obtained appear reasonable, the equation should be checked for its validity in Great Lakes studies. This would involve a very large research project for which preliminary planning has begun.

All three methods have been used to assess evaporation from each of the lakes, and results for average annual and monthly losses are reasonably compatible. On the basis of a number of studies, annual losses of 28–32 inches from Lake Ontario and 32–36 inches from Lake Erie appear valid. The few studies which have been conducted on Lake Huron–Michigan and Lake Superior indicate losses of 21–27 inches and 13–21 inches, respectively.

Only recently has there been an attempt to produce month-to-month and year-to-year estimates of evaporation. Two independent preliminary investigations have both indicated that variations in losses from one year to another are often large, and may reach as much as ±40 per cent of the average annual evaporation, i.e. twice as large as the variations in annual precipitation.

FUTURE REQUIREMENTS

Some of the more important meteorological problems associated with the Great Lakes have been briefly outlined. The variations in lake levels, particularly as they are related to meteorological factors, have been reviewed in more detail, and it is apparent that substantial progress has been made in understanding the complex relationships involved. But further scientific action is evidently required, and the remainder of this report will indicate some proposals for future undertakings and some of the steps already under way.

Precipitation

To improve the estimates of basin precipitation, the Meteorological Branch is establishing a more extensive network of observing stations on islands and about the perimeter of the lakes. In addition, studies are being conducted to establish the optimum size of precipitation network required for lake-level investigations and regulation. When established, all data, historical and future, will be standardized.

A solution to the problem of estimating over-lake precipitation may also be forthcoming from the more powerful weather radar recently installed in the Great Lakes area, and in more sophisticated radar data analysis techniques currently being developed.

Evaporation

To improve estimates of evaporation losses from the lakes, one of the main requirements is for continuous water-temperature observations. In cooperation with other Canadian and United States agencies, the Meteorological Branch is establishing a network of water-temperature recorders in the Great Lakes. To extend these observations to all parts of the lakes and to complement the surveys of research vessels, the Branch last year acquired an airborne radiation thermometer. After a comprehensive and successful field test programme, it has been established that this aerial survey technique, when properly employed, will measure surface-water temperatures to an accuracy of $\pm 1.0°$ C at flying heights up to 1,000 feet. As a result of the evaluation the Branch has established regular aerial temperature surveys of each of the lakes.

A better understanding of the wind field over each lake would also improve evaporation estimates. As indicated earlier, scientific headway has been made in this area, but much more work is required. A breakthrough may come from data being collected by the extensive buoy-observing programmes currently in progress.

With further regard to the evaluation of evaporation losses, there have been recent suggestions from both Canada and the United States that an international study be undertaken of the water balance of the atmosphere as it passes over one of the Great Lakes. Such a project—an International Field Year on the Great Lakes—has now been proposed as part of the International Hydrologic Decade. This large and complex undertaking would contribute greatly to establishing valid evaporation formulae for the Great Lakes.

Forecasts of Lake-Level Variations

Lacking long-range forecasts (of a year or more) of the meteorological factors influencing lake-level variations, the evident lag between the precipitation régime and the lake-level régime should be exploited. Several such statistical studies are now in progress and some of these are making use of very large computers. One such computer study undertaken by the Meteorological Branch was a cross-spectral analysis of Lake Huron–Michigan water levels and basin precipitation. Although considered to be only a pilot project, some of the results are most interesting. A point of major importance indicated by the study is that 70 per cent of the variance in lake levels is related to basin precipitation. Preliminary results also showed a lag between precipitation and water levels—not in terms of a fixed number of months or years, but of the order of one-quarter of the current precipitation cycle. If a lag of this order can be confirmed, a preliminary water-level forecast scheme will be programmed and tested.

CONCLUSION

Although the reported progress has been most gratifying, it must be acknowledged that there is still much to be done. In order to assess fully the effects of man-made changes on Great Lakes water levels, to plan regulatory works to best advantage, and to provide effective operating procedures for these works, we must have as complete an understanding of the problems as possible. Such an understanding of water-level variations, and indeed of all the physical problems on the Great Lakes, will require a concentrated and well-directed effort in an expanded programme of research in hydrology, physical limnology, and meteorology.

BIBLIOGRAPHY

Lake Levels

BRUNK, IVAN W. (1960), "Precipitation and the Levels of Lakes Michigan and HURON," *Great Lakes Res. Div., Univ. of Michigan, Pub. 4*, pp. 145–50.

DECOOKE, B. G. (1961), "Forecasting Great Lakes Levels," *Great Lakes Res. Div., Univ. of Michigan, Pub. 7*, pp. 79–84.

GOVERNMENT OF CANADA (1964–65), *Minutes of Proceedings and Evidence, Standing Committee on Mines, Forests and Waters Respecting the Subject-Matter of Water Levels of the Great Lakes Systems.*

LAIDLY, W. T. (1962), "Regimen of the Great Lakes and Fluctuations of Lake Levels," in *Great Lakes Basin*, Amer. Assoc. Advan. Sci., Pub. 71, pp. 91–105.

MORTON, F. I. and ROSENBERG, H. B. (1959), "Hydrology of Lake Ontario," *Proc. A.S.C.E., 85, J. Hyd. Div.*, pp. 1–29.

MULLER, F. B., GERVAIS, J. G., and SHAW, R. W. (1965), *The Effect of Basin Precipitation on the Level of Lake Michigan–Huron*, Met. Branch CIR-4264, TEC-576.

PROVINCE OF ONTARIO (1953), *Report of the Select Committee of the Ontario Legislature on Lake Levels of the Great Lakes.*

RICHARDS, T. L. (1965), *Meteorological Factors Affecting Great Lakes Water Levels*, Met. Branch CIR-4186, TEC-556.

Evaporation and Precipitation

BLUST, F. and DECOOKE, B. G. (1960), "Comparison of Precipitation on Islands of Lake Michigan with Precipitation on Perimeter of the Lake," *Geo. Res. 65* (No. 5): 1565–72.

BRUCE, J. P. and RODGERS, G. K. (1962), "Water Balance of the Great Lakes System," in *Great Lakes Basin*, Amer. Assoc. Advan. Sci., Pub. 71, pp. 41–69.

DERECKI, J. A. (1964), "Variation of Lake Erie Evaporation and Its Causes," *Great Lakes Res. Div., Univ. of Michigan, Pub. 11*, pp. 217–27.

RICHARDS, T. L. (1964), "Recent Developments in the Field of Great Lakes Evaporation," *Verh. Internat. Verein Limnol. 15*: 247–56.

RICHARDS, T. L. and RODGERS, G. K. (1964), "An Investigation of the Extremes of Annual and Monthly Evaporation from Lake Ontario," *Great Lakes Res. Div., Univ. of Michigan, Pub. 11*, pp. 283–93.

Lake Winds and Wind-Effects

GILLIES, D. K. A. (1959), "Winds and Water Level on Lake Erie," *Symposium on Great Lakes*, R.M.S. Canadian Branch, Vol. 9, No. 1, pp. 12–18.

HUNT, I. A. (1958), "Winds, Wind Set-ups and Seiches on Lake Erie," Paper presented at Second National Conference in Applied Meteorology, A.M.S.

LEMIRE, F. (1961), *Winds on the Great Lakes,* Met. Branch, CIR-3560, TEC-380.

PLATZMAN, G. W., IRISH, S. M., and HUGHES, L. A. (1965), "The Prediction of Surges in the Southern Basin of Lake Michigan," *Monthly Weather Rev. 93* (No. 5): 275–96.

PLATZMAN, G. W. and RAO, D. B. (1963), "The 14-Hour Period of Lake Erie," *Great Lakes Res. Div., Univ. of Michigan, Pub. 10,* pp. 231–4.

RICHARDS, T. L., DRAGERT, H., and MCINTYRE, D. R. (1966), "The Influence of Atmospheric Stability and Over-Water Fetch on Winds over the Great Lakes," *Monthly Weather Rev.* (in press).

Lake-Effect Snow

MCVEHIL, G. E. and PEACE, R. L. (1965), "Some Studies of Lake Effect Snowfall from Lake Erie," *Great Lakes Res. Div., Univ. of Michigan, Pub. 13,* pp. 262–272.

RICHARDS, T. L. and DERCO, V. S. (1963), "The Role of Lake Effect Storms in the Distribution of Snowfall in Southern Ontario," *Proc. 1963 East. Snow Conf., Quebec City,* pp. 61–85.

THOMAS, M. K. (1964), "A Survey of Great Lakes Snowfall," *Great Lakes Res. Div., Univ. of Michigan, 11,* pp. 294–310.

Ice

HEAP, J. A. (1963), "Some Characteristics of Winter Ice Cover of Lake Michigan, 1962–63," *Great Lakes Res. Div., Univ. of Michigan, Pub. 10,* pp. 216–18.

RICHARDS, T. L. (1964), "The Meteorological Aspects of Ice Cover on the Great Lakes," *Monthly Weather Rev. 92* (No. 6): 297–302.

Lake Breeze

MOROZ, W. J. and HEWSON. E. W. (1965), *The Lake Breeze Circulation along the Shoreline of a Large Lake,* Tech. Rept., Univ. of Michigan, Dept. of Meteorology and Oceanography, Nov. 1965.

MUNN, R. E. and RICHARDS, T. L. (1964), "The Lake-Breeze, a Survey of the Literature and Some Application to the Great Lakes," *Great Lakes Res. Div., Univ. of Michigan, Pub. 11,* pp. 253–266.

POND, G. R. (1964), *The Moderating Effect of Lake Huron on Shoreline Temperatures,* Met. Branch, CIR–4016, TEC–514.

Miscellaneous

BRUCE, J. P. (1963), "Meteorological Factors Affecting the Freshwater Environment," *Great Lakes Res. Div., Univ. of Michigan, Pub. 10,* pp. 140–19.

RICHARDS, T. L. and MASSEY, D. G. (1966), *An Evaluation of the Infra-red Thermometer as an Airborne Indicator of Surface Water Temperatures,* Met. Branch, CIR–4354, TEC–592.

PART V

PHYSICO-MATHEMATICAL STUDIES OF WATER

METEOROLOGY AND WATER RESOURCES

J. P. Bruce

THIS BRIEF PRESENTATION is based on two main premises. The first is that the major scientific water problem facing Canada today is a realistic assessment of the magnitude of our water resources and their variations in space and time. Such knowledge is required both for the development of our own resources and also to permit international negotiations from a position of knowledge and strength. If this contention be accepted, we must then place a high priority on surveying available or potentially usable water resources, and on developing the techniques for predicting their variability.

The second main premise is that meteorological knowledge and research can aid greatly in surveying water resources and in developing the basic understanding of the interrelationship of components of the hydrologic cycle. Such understanding is necessary for the prediction of future floods, droughts, and water availability. The influence of the atmosphere on the land phase of the hydrologic cycle is obvious when you consider that the source of all fresh water is precipitation, and that the main loss of water from the earth's surface is through evaporation to the atmosphere. Atmospheric water vapour is the most mobile part of the hydrologic cycle, and while the total amount of water in the atmosphere at any one time is smaller than in most other parts of the cycle, the total water vapour flux over periods of weeks or months is tremendous. For example, it has been calculated that in an average July week about 15 million acre-feet of water passes over Arizona in the form of water vapour—an amount about equal to the annual flow of the Colorado River.

When planning regional surveys of surface water resources, the value of meteorological data in generalizing and extending the results of streamflow and water level measurements has sometimes been overlooked. Substantial improvements in correlations between short-term streamflow records of a river and longer streamflow records in the region can be achieved by incorporating precipitation data for the basins concerned. Precipitation and evaporation data can be combined to yield estimates of water yields from ungauged areas. Water resources surveys begun recently in Canada have recognized the importance of meteorological data. For example, in the joint federal-provincial study of the rivers and lakes of Northern Ontario, the Meteorological Branch is installing 12 long-duration digital precipitation recorders, and is assisting in evaporation determination by lake surface-water temperature surveys, using airborne infra-red radiation thermometers.

It has been estimated by the hydrologist assigned to the United States Office of Science and Technology that about 10 billion dollars per year is spent in the U.S.A. on river, lake, and drainage structures, designed wholly or partly on the basis of precipitation data. Such structures include highway culverts, storm sewer systems, and dams, large and small. In Canada, using the usual economic conversion factor, the figure must be of the order of three-quarters of a billion dollars per year. Yet the Canadian scientists working in this field have simply not provided, to the extent needed, either the basic data or the techniques for analysing such data as are applicable to Canadian conditions, to permit engineers to select optimum design criteria for these structures. To give a few examples among very many: there are no tables or maps to allow engineers to make reliable estimates of evaporation losses from reservoirs; comprehensive studies of the magnitude and frequency of floods have been done only for certain portions of the country; rainfall intensity–frequency maps for drainage design are still based on pitifully skimpy amounts of rain intensity data; reliable methods for estimating run-off from ungauged streams, particularly during snow-melt periods, are simply not available; and we have only the most rudimentary knowledge of the far-reaching effects of changing land-use patterns on the water balance and streamflow of Canadian basins.

Fortunately, however, an increasing interest has been developing in hydrology, hydrometeorology, and hydrogeology in the past six or seven years, stimulated in part by an increasing awareness of the value and importance of Canada's water resources. In 1965, a further impetus to hydrologic research was given by the launching of the International Hydrologic Decade, sponsored by United Nations agencies, principally UNESCO, the World Meteorological Organization, and the Food and Agriculture Organization. The Canadian programme for the IHD is a truly cooperative one that involves both provincial and federal agencies and at least eight of our universities. Meteorologists have been called upon to participate to a greater or less extent in some 50 individual research projects. A number of these involve studies of small drainage basins, which are known as representative or experimental basins.

Thirty representative basins have been or are being instrumented in various parts of Canada to serve two main purposes. The first is to provide a basic understanding of the relationships between the various parts of the hydrologic cycle. All basins are being instrumented for measurement of precipitation, evaporation, snow cover, run-off, soil moisture, and groundwater movements and fluctuations. The basins are selected to be representative of the main climatic, soils, and geological zones of Canada. It is anticipated that, by using data from these Canadian basins and from other basins in all parts of the world, some general hydrologic relationships and equations can be developed by computer technique. Such relationships would allow prediction of the hydrologic régime of small ungauged river basins, if the climatic and soils conditions were known, thus permitting reliable design criteria to be selected by engineers.

The second purpose of representative basins is to provide an outdoor laboratory or framework for intensive study of some particular aspect of hydrology. For example, in the North Nashwaaksis basin near Fredericton, the University of New Brunswick is undertaking studies of the energy balance of a melting snow pack in a small plot in the centre of the basin. The concept is that the plot data can be extrapolated, for development of snow-melt estimation techniques on a larger natural basin, by conducting the plot studies within the heavily instrumented representative basin.

Experimental basins are established to determine the effects of some change in ground cover on the hydrologic régime. Work in the United States and Europe demonstrated, more than a decade ago, the feasibility of increasing run-off from forested watersheds by as much as 25 to 30 per cent by cutting trees, either completely, or in various patterns of strips and blocks. At the same time flood frequencies and sediment loads were increased. The problem is to change the land cover to obtain the benefit of increased water yield without undue penalties in floods and sediment transport. The streamflow changes are caused by changes in evapo-transpiration losses, in rainfall interception by vegetation, in snow deposition patterns, in snow shading and melting, and in soil porosity. These changes are thus mainly microclimatic, and meteorological specialists are required to evaluate them. The microclimatic changes in turn result in altered amounts and timing of run-off and groundwater recharge. In spite of critical land and water management problems in many parts of Canada, no experimentation to determine the applicability of results obtained abroad to Canadian climate and soil conditions had been undertaken until very recently.

In 1962, the Eastern Rockies Forest Conservation Board, with its need to manage the large forested source region of the vital South Saskatchewan River, instigated the first comprehensive research of this kind in Canada. A number of federal and provincial agencies are participating in the East Slopes (Alberta) Watershed Research Project. The cooperative research team includes specialists in meteorology, in streamflow measurement, groundwater, forestry, and soils. They are investigating the natural hydrologic régime and the potential improvements that could be made in three small basins in the headwaters of the South Saskatchewan River. Each of the three experimental basins is in one of the main vegetation zones of the region, Marmot Creek basin in spruce-fir, Streeter basin in aspen-grassland, and Deer Creek basin in lodgepole pine. As part of Canada's programme for the International Hydrologic Decade, similar studies are being launched in other provinces, such as the effects of logging in British Columbia and Quebec, and the hydrologic influence of urban development in Ontario.

Much of the important research under way or planned in this country's IHD programme involves meteorological instruments and knowledge. A few examples will illustrate the range of these projects. Ontario Hydro and the Meteorological Branch are collaborating on a study of the energy balance of the Niagara River above the hydro intakes at the Falls, to improve methods of predicting ice formation, which seriously affects power production. British Columbia Water Resources Service and the Meteorological Branch are planning a study of the influence of elevation, aspect, and exposure on precipitation and temperature at high-elevation water-source regions, by instrumenting mountain transects across major ranges. Applications in hydrology of remote sensing instruments, such as airborne infra-red radiation thermometers for surface-water temperatures, and weather satellite data for snow and ice cover, will be evaluated and exploited.

One of the most interesting projects is a proposed International Field Year on one of the Great Lakes. The concept is to launch a joint Canada–U.S. study of the water and energy balance of one of the Great Lakes, of the water balance of the atmosphere over the lake, and of the lake circulation. The atmospheric water balance study will involve measuring and computing the horizontal flux divergence of water vapour over the lake and the precipitation deposition from the air over the lake.

When combined with the results of other studies, it should be possible for the first time to determine accurately the evaporation from and precipitation onto the lake each month, and to use these fundamental determinations to calibrate simpler, more empirical techniques for routine computation of lake-surface evaporation and precipitation. A better understanding of these dominant terms in the water balance of the Lakes will be of great importance in understanding and predicting lake-level fluctuations. Of course, many surface-water and groundwater studies with little or no meteorological component are also being undertaken during the Decade.

This is an exciting period for those involved in various aspects of hydrologic research. First, because this field of research is undergoing a long-overdue expansion of effort in this country and, secondly, because these new efforts in Canada recognize the interdisciplinary nature of hydrology. The studies are truly cooperative, involving specialists from many disciplines, including engineers, meteorologists, geologists, foresters, agriculturists, and physicists. There are grounds for expecting that by the end of the Decade we will have achieved a far more reliable inventory of Canadian water resources and their variations. We must also by then have provided the data and developed the techniques to allow our engineers to base their designs of drainage, river, and lake structures on reliable predictions of the future hydrologic behaviour of the water bodies involved. These problems are major challenges to the few scientists working in this field. To ensure the future well-being of Canada's citizens, the challenges must be met.

L'ASPECT MATHÉMATIQUE DE L'OCÉANOGRAPHIE

Paul H. LeBlond

L'ÉTUDE de la mer jouit depuis quelques années d'une popularité et d'une publicité croissantes, stimulées sans doute par les efforts considérables entrepris en ce domaine par les grands pays maritimes. Parallèlement aux travaux de recherches, les articles de vulgarisation se sont multipliés, plusieurs expéditions océanographiques ont pris à leur bord des équipes de cinéastes et les tentatives d'adaptation de la vie humaine au milieu sous-marin fascinent l'imagination populaire.

L'océanographie théorique, aussi appelée océanographie physique analytique, est cependant restée en marge de ce processus de diffusion populaire. Il est vrai que, tant par la compréhension qualitative de l'hydrodynamique qu'elle requiert que par le langage mathématique en lequel elle s'exprime, cette branche de l'étude de la mer se prête peu facilement à la vulgarisation. Ajoutons tout de suite que je n'ai pas l'intention de combler ici cette lacune: je me propose seulement de présenter de façon générale le problème qui en est l'objet et d'attirer l'attention sur les difficultés auxquelles il y faut faire face.

L'océanographie théorique a pour but d'expliquer, à la lumière des principes fondamentaux de la dynamique des fluides, la distribution dans l'espace et dans le temps des courants marins et des champs de température, de salinité et des autres caractéristiques de l'eau de mer. Le problème central de l'océanographie se présente donc sous la forme d'un modèle mathématique dont la solution, sujette aux conditions-limites appropriées, permettra de synthétiser les données expérimentales et de comprendre à fond les mécanismes qui régissent la circulation océanique. On voit que tout espoir de prédiction logique et ultimement de contrôle du milieu marin dépend du succès de cette analyse. Nous examinerons maintenant de plus près le modèle mathématique en question: il sera ensuite plus facile d'apprécier la nature des difficultés qui s'opposent à la réalisation de cet ambitieux programme.

Une des hypothèses de base est que l'eau de mer est un fluide Newtonien, c'est-à-dire que la tension visqueuse y est proportionelle au taux de déformation. Nombre d'expériences de laboratoire confirment la justesse de cette hypothèse. Pour un fluide quelconque on a, sous forme tensorielle et dans un système de coordonnées tournant avec la terre, les équations suivantes, exprimant la conservation de la masse et du mouvement:

$$(1) \qquad \frac{\partial \rho}{\partial t} + \frac{\partial}{\partial x_j}(\rho u_j) = 0,$$

$$(2) \qquad \frac{\partial \rho u_i}{\partial t} + \frac{\partial}{\partial x_j}\{\rho u_i u_j + p\delta_{ij} - \tau_{ij}\} = -\rho g \delta_{i3} - 2\rho\epsilon_{ijk}\,\Omega_j\,u_k + f_i.$$

Les coordonnées spatiales et temporelles y sont (x_i, t). p denote la pression (dynes/cm^2), ρ la densité (g/cm^3), u_i la vélocité en direction de la coordonnée x_i (cm/sec), g l'accélération due à la gravité (cm/sec^2), Ω la vitesse angulaire de rotation de la terre (radians/sec), et f_i les forces extérieures (dynes/cm^3) agissant sur l'unité de volume du fluide.

Pour la tension visqueuse on a plus expressément pour un fluide Newtonien

$$\tau_{ij} = \mu\left(\frac{\partial u_i}{\partial x_j} + \frac{\partial u_j}{\partial x_i}\right) + \lambda\delta_{ij}\frac{\partial u_k}{\partial x_k}.$$

μ et λ sont des coefficients de viscosité. Pour un gas monoatomique parfait $-\lambda/\mu = \frac{2}{3}$, mais des valeurs beaucoup plus élevées ont été trouvées pour la valeur de ce rapport dans des liquides.

Les relations thermodynamiques qu'il faut ajouter aux équations ci-dessus peuvent être présentées sous forme d'équations de conservation de l'énergie et du sel:

$$(3) \qquad \frac{\partial}{\partial t}(\rho c_v T) + \frac{\partial}{\partial x_j}\left(\rho c_v u_j T - k\frac{\partial T}{\partial x_j}\right) + p\frac{\partial u_j}{\partial x_j} = Q + \Phi,$$

$$(4) \qquad \frac{\partial \rho S}{\partial t} + \frac{\partial}{\partial x_j}(\rho S u_j) - \rho\frac{\partial}{\partial x_j}\left(m\frac{\partial S}{\partial x_j}\right) = \Sigma.$$

T et S y sont la température (C°) et la salinité (g/kg) dotés respectivement de coefficients de conduction et de diffusion molécular k (dynes/sec/C°) et m (cm^2/sec). Q et Σ répresentent les sources de chaleur et de sel, et Φ l'acquisition de chaleur résultant de la transformation d'énergie cinétique en énergie calorique par l'action irréversible de la friction moléculaire. c_v est la capacité thermique à volume constant (cm^2/sec^2/C°). L'équation (3) est aussi appelée équation de la chaleur.

Il faut de plus ajouter à ces équations de conservation une relation entre la densité et les autres variables thermodynamiques : une équation constitutive que nous nous contenterons d'exprimer par

$$\rho = \rho(p, T, S). \tag{5}$$

Ces cinq équations forment un système complet dont la solution, satisfaisant des conditions appropriées aux limites, doit déterminer les variables u_i, p, ρ, S et T en fonction du temps et de l'espace.

Notons avant d'aller plus loin que ces relations sont d'ordre phénoménologique, étant fondées sur des données expérimentales (fluide Newtonien) ou thermodynamiques et non sur une théorie de l'état liquide. Elles n'ont donc d'application pratique que dans le domaine de conditions (qui comprend les situations océanographiques) où ces données de base sont valides. Sous la forme donnée plus haut la conduction de chaleur se fait selon la loi de Fourier $\left(\frac{\partial}{\partial x_j} k \frac{\partial T}{\partial x_j}\right)$ et la diffusion du sel selon la loi de Ficks $\left(\frac{\partial}{\partial x_i} m \frac{\partial S}{\partial x_j}\right)$. Toutes-deux sont expérimentalement justifiables, quoiqu'on puisse ajouter à cette dernière des termes de forme semblable pour tenir compte de l'influence des gradients de pression et de température sur la diffusion du sel : $\frac{\partial}{\partial x_j} m' \frac{\partial p}{\partial x_j}$, $\frac{\partial}{\partial x_j} m'' \frac{\partial T}{\partial x_j}$. La forme présentée est toutefois celle couramment utilisée (Eckart 1962).

Des recherches intensives sur les propriétés de l'eau de mer, en cours en plusieurs laboratoires, fournissent graduellement des données qui permettront éventuellement d'en déterminer de façon précise les coefficients thermodynamiques. L'incertitude résultant de notre ignorance partielle de la façon dont ρ, c_v, k et m dépendent des variables thermodynamiques p, S et T sera donc, on peut l'espérer, bientôt éliminée.

Ce surcroît d'information n'en laissera pas moins intacte une des difficultés essentielles du problème. On sait que le mouvement d'un fluide se présente sous deux régimes fort différents selon la valeur prise par un paramètre sans dimensions, le nombre de Reynolds ($R = U_0 L_0 \rho/\mu$, où U_0 et L_0 sont une vitesse et une longueur caractéristiques de l'écoulement). Pour une certaine valeur critique de ce paramètre (R_c, disons) l'écoulement passe en effet du régime laminaire au régime turbulent, et les forces non-linéaires d'inertie l'emportent sur les tensions visqueuses. Le caractère de l'écoulement s'en trouve radicalement modifié, toute régularité y semble disparaître et le mouvement ne devient prévisible que de façon statistique. L'analyse et la description de l'écoulement turbulent sont un des derniers grands problèmes de la physique classique et font depuis quelques années l'objet de recherches intensives. Or c'est précisément à ce problème qu'il faut faire face en océanographie. En effet, en dépit des vitesses généralement assez faibles des courants océaniques, les étendues qu'ils couvrent sont assez vastes (L_0 très grand) pour porter le paramètre $U_0L_0\rho/\mu$ bien au-dessus de la valeur critique R_c.

Il semble donc opportun de transformer le système d'équations ci-haut en la forme introduite d'abord par Reynolds pour étudier le mouvement turbulent. On se représentera l'écoulement comme consistant d'une partie moyenne sur laquelle se superposent des fluctuations turbulentes aléatoires : $u_i = U_i + u_i^*$. La moyenne est prise de telle sorte que $u_i = U_i$ et que, par conséquent, $u_i^* = 0$. Si l'on prend la moyenne arithmétique d'un grand nombre d'écoulements turbulents dans des situations identiques (moyenne des ensembles) on peut justifier, du moins de façon conceptuelle, une telle division des variables. Cependant, du fait que le spectre des variations temporelles des conditions océaniques s'étend jusqu'aux périodes géologiques, et que des situations identiques ne se reproduisent pour ainsi dire jamais, on ne peut baser en pratique cette division des champs sur une moyenne des ensembles. La moyenne temporelle (ou spatiale) qu'on se voit forcé d'utiliser laisse donc toujours de côté, parce qu'opérée sur un intervalle fini, les variations de période plus longue que cet intervalle. Certaines conditions (Lumley et Panofsky 1964) doivent être satisfaites pour que cette moyenne soit équivalente à une moyenne d'ensembles et donne des résultats qui caractérisent de façon générale le phénomène physique étudié, et non d'abord l'intervalle choisi. Il est évident par exemple qu'une moyenne faite seulement durant les mois d'automne de l'énergie de mouvement contenue dans les ouragans ne sera réellement pas représentative de la répartition générale de cette énergie lorsque considérée sur une période de plusieurs années. Avant de comparer les résultats de l'analyse théorique et ceux des observations on aura donc soin de s'assurer de la compatibilité des moyennes prises de chaque côté.

Il est, de plus, souvent avantageux d'introduire des valeurs-étalons, c'est-à-dire des longueurs L_{0i}, vitesses U_{0i}, température T_0, etc. caractéristiques, à l'aide desquelles on peut définir pour l'écoulement moyen des variables sans dimensions : $t' = t/\tau$, $x_i' = x_i/L_{0i}$, $U_i' = U_i/U_{0i}$, $T' = T/T_0$, etc. Ces valeurs-étalons sont bien entendu typiques d'une situation donnée et leur introduction suppose une certaine connaissance qualitative du problème étudié. On se sert maintenant des valeurs-étalons et des variables sans dimensions pour écrire les équations ci-haut sous une forme non-dimensionelle où, à condition que les valeurs-étalons soient correctement définies, le rôle joué par chaque terme est determiné seulement par la grandeur du coefficient sans dimensions qui l'affecte.

Les équations de l'écoulement moyen prennent la forme non-dimensionelle (on a laissé tomber les primes)

$$(1') \qquad \left(\rho \frac{\partial U_j}{\partial x_j}\right) + M^2 \left(\frac{\partial \rho}{\partial t} + U_j \frac{\partial \rho}{\partial x_j}\right) = 0$$

où M, le nombre de Mach (encore appelé nombre de Sarrau) est le rapport de la vitesse étalon, U_0, à la vitesse du son, c : $M = U_0/c$.

$$(2') \qquad S_t \left(\rho \frac{\partial U_i}{\partial t}\right) + \left(\rho U_j \frac{\partial U_i}{\partial x_j}\right) + C \left(\frac{\partial p}{\partial x_i}\right) + \frac{1}{F_1} (\rho g \delta_{i3})$$

$$+ \frac{1}{F_2} (f_i) + \frac{1}{R_0} (2\rho \epsilon_{ijk} \Omega_j U_k) + \frac{\overline{u_0{}^{*2}}}{U_0^2} \left(\rho \frac{\partial}{\partial x_j} \overline{u_i{}^* u_j{}^*}\right)$$

$$- \frac{1}{R} \left(\frac{\partial^2 U_i}{\partial x_1{}^2} + \frac{L_{01}^2}{L_{02}^2} \frac{\partial^2 U_i}{\partial x_2{}^2} + \frac{L_{01}^2}{L_{03}^2} \frac{\partial^2 U_i}{\partial x_3{}^2}\right)$$

$$+ \frac{\mu + \lambda}{\mu} \frac{M^2}{R} \left(\frac{1}{\rho} \frac{\partial \rho}{\partial t} + \frac{U_j}{\rho} \frac{\partial \rho}{\partial x_j}\right) = 0,$$

où $S_t = L_0/U_0\tau$ est le nombre de Stroudhal, rapport entre l'accélération locale et l'accélération advective non-linéaire,

$C = P_0/\rho_0 U_0^2$ est le coefficient de pression, rapport entre les forces de pression et les forces non-linéaires d'advection,

$F_1 = U_0^2/gL_0$ est le nombre de Froude habituel, rapport entre les forces non-linéaires d'advection et celle de la gravité,

$F_2 = \rho_0\, U_0^2/f_0\, L_0$ est un second nombre de Froude, défini par rapport aux forces autres que celle de la gravité,

$R_0 = U_0/\Omega_0\, L_0$ est le nombre de Rossby, rapport entre les forces non-linéaires d'advection et la force de Coriolis,

$R = U_0\, L_0\, \rho_0/\mu$ est le nombre de Reynolds, rapport entre les forces non-linéaires d'advection et les tensions visqueuses,

$\overline{u_0{}^{*2}}/U_0^2$ est le rapport des intensités respectives des parties turbulentes et moyennes de l'écoulement.

On a encore

$$(3') \qquad S_t \left(\rho \frac{\partial c_v T}{\partial t}\right) + \left(\rho U_j \frac{\partial c_v T}{\partial x_j}\right) - CEM^2 \left(\frac{1}{\rho} \frac{\partial \rho}{\partial t} + \frac{U_j}{\rho} \frac{\partial \rho}{\partial x_j}\right)$$

$$-\frac{P_1}{R}\left(\frac{\partial}{\partial x_1}k\frac{\partial T}{\partial x_1}+\frac{L_{01}^2}{L_{02}^2}\frac{\partial}{\partial x_2}k\frac{\partial T}{\partial x_2}+\frac{L_{01}^2}{L_{03}^2}\frac{\partial}{\partial x_3}k\frac{\partial T}{\partial x_3}\right)$$

$$+\frac{\overline{u_0{}^*T_0{}^*}}{U_0\,T_0}\left(\rho\frac{\partial}{\partial x_j}c_v\,\overline{T^*u_j{}^*}\right)=Q',$$

$$(4')\quad S_t\left(\rho\frac{\partial S}{\partial t}\right)+\left(\rho U_j\frac{\partial S}{\partial x_j}\right)+\frac{\overline{u_0{}^*S_0{}^*}}{U_0\,S_0}\left(\rho\frac{\partial}{\partial x_j}\overline{S^*u_j{}^*}\right)$$

$$-\frac{P_2}{R}\left(\frac{\partial}{\partial x_1}m\frac{\partial S}{\partial x_1}+\frac{L_{01}^2}{L_{02}^2}\frac{\partial}{\partial x_2}m\frac{\partial S}{\partial x_2}+\frac{L_{01}^2}{L_{03}^2}\frac{\partial}{\partial x_3}m\frac{\partial S}{\partial x_3}\right)=\Sigma',$$

$$(5')\quad \frac{\rho}{\rho_0}=\frac{\rho}{\rho_0}\left(C,\frac{T}{T_0},\frac{S}{S_0}\right),$$

où $E = U_0^2/c_vT_0$ est le rapport entre l'énergie de mouvement et l'énergie calorique interne du fluide,

$P_1 = k/c_v\,\mu$ et

$P_2 = m\rho_0/\mu$ sont des nombres de Prandtl, représentant respectivement les rapport entre les coefficients de diffusion moleculaire de chaleur et de sel et celui de l'impulsion,

$Q' = (Q + \Phi)/\tau\rho_0\,c_vT_0$ est le rapport entre l'apport net de chaleur par unité de temps et le contenu calorique du fluide,

$\Sigma' = \Sigma/\tau S_0\,\rho_0$ est le rapport entre l'apport de sel par unité de temps et le contenu en sel du fluide.

Les termes des équations (1′) à (5′) contenus entre parenthèses ne renferment que des variables sans dimensions. Il est souvent possible de choisir les valeurs-étalons de telle sorte que tous ces termes soient au plus de l'ordre de grandeur de l'unité. Etant donné que le choix des valeurs-étalons, à l'aide d'hypothèses physiques appropriées, détermine de plus la valeur des coefficients S_t, C, M, F_1, F_2, R_o, R, . . ., on a donc en main un moyen de réduire de façon rationelle la complexité des équations. On peut alors en effet ne retenir que les termes affectés des plus grands coefficients. Que l'on ne s'intéresse par exemple qu'aux écoulements stationaires : le nombre de Stroudhal, S_t, devient zéro, et l'on peut laisser de côté tous les termes affectés de ce coefficient. De même si, comme dans les études de circulation générale océanique, on ne s'intéresse pas directement aux ondes sonores, on peut poser $M = 0$. Nous reviendrons sur ce point.

L'influence des fluctuations turbulentes ne s'exerce dans les équations de l'écoulement moyen qu'à travers un seul terme supplémentaire dans chacune des équations (2′), (3′) et (4′). On a dans les équations du mouvement les tensions de Reynolds $\partial(\rho\overline{u_i{}^*u_j{}^*})/\partial x_j$, et dans les équations de la chaleur et du sel un terme représentant l'échange turbulent : $\partial(\rho c_v \overline{u_j{}^*T^*})/\partial x_j$ et $\partial(\rho \overline{u_j{}^*S^*})/\partial x_j$ respectivement. Quoique ces termes supplémentaires jouent un rôle d'une certaine façon analogue à celui de la diffusion moléculaire, on n'en peut déterminer la forme exacte que par la solution d'un système d'équations régissant le mouvement turbulent. Ces dernières équations s'obtiennent par différence en retranchant des équations complètes celles décrivant l'écoulement moyen; elles contiennent de plus des gradients de variables moyennes. Les deux systèmes sont donc interdépendants, et on ne peut résoudre l'un sans l'autre. Ceci ne facilite pas les choses : si les équations de l'écoulement moyen sont compliquées, celles de l'écoulement turbulent le sont plus encore.

Afin de désengrener les deux systèmes on a souvent recours à une hypothèse due à Boussinesq. Se basant sur la nature dispersive des fluctuations turbulentes, on suppose que la tension de Reynolds produit une diffusion analogue à celle des échanges moléculaires, et l'on écrit

$$\overline{u_i{}^*u_j{}^*} = -\frac{\mu_t}{\rho}\frac{\partial U_i}{\partial x_j}.$$

μ_t est une « viscosité turbulente », d'habitude beaucoup plus grande que son équivalent moléculaire. On pose de même pour la diffusion turbulente de la chaleur et du sel :

$$\overline{u_j{}^*T^*} = -\frac{k_t}{\rho c_v}\frac{\partial T}{\partial x_j}, \qquad \overline{u_j{}^*S^*} = -m_t\frac{\partial S}{\partial x_j}.$$

Ce subterfuge est cependant basé sur une analogie physique fort grossière et, bien qu'approprié à l'étude de mouvements étendus sur de vastes régions océaniques, où la forme exacte des mécanismes de diffusion n'est pas importante, il n'en masque pas moins la nature réelle des échanges turbulents et ne peut se prêter à des études plus détaillées. Les systèmes dont la structure dépend intimement de la forme des échanges turbulents (c'est le cas de la couche limite atmosphérique, par exemple) ne peuvent donc pas être analysés de cette façon.

Même après avoir ainsi séparé les équations de l'écoulement moyen de celles du mouvement turbulent, on n'en reste pas moins avec un problème fort compliqué à résoudre. Le système (1′) à (5′) d'équations différentielles partielles est encore plus ou moins non-linéaire, et doit de plus satisfaire à un ensemble approprié de conditions aux limites. Pour prédire sans ambiguité la distribution spatio-temporelle des variables océanographiques il faut spécifier, à partir d'un instant initial, les valeurs de ces variables et d'un nombre suffisant de leurs dérivées sur les parois (fond, surface, littoraux) du bassin océanique. Si l'on considère la complexité géométrique des fonds et littoraux, la variabilité des forces (surtout météorologiques) qui agissent en surface et la diversité des sources de sel et de chaleur, on voit que, même si on disposait d'une solution générale pratique des équations du mouvement moyen, on ne pourrait procéder que de façon numérique.

Les météorologistes, qui ont à faire face à un problème semblable, procèdent en effet de cette façon et réussissent par l'intégration numérique à produire des pronostics assez justes des conditions atmosphériques générales pour des périodes de quelques jours. Par suite de certaines différences qualitatives entre la circulation de l'atmosphère et celle des océans, et surtout par suite de l'absence d'un treillis assez serré de points d'observation, cette méthode ne peut encore être appliquée en océanographie.

N'oublions pas non plus que la possibilité d'une intégration numérique, soit-elle basée sur des séries d'observations aussi justes et aussi détaillées qu'on le veuille, ne saurait reléguer à l'arrière-plan la recherche théorique. Une solution numérique ne peut en effet nous renseigner d'une manière qualitative (si ce n'est d'une façon empirique) sur l'importance relative des divers mécanismes physiques qui régissent l'écoulement.

Devant l'impossibilité actuelle de résoudre exactement le mouvement océanique, même après l'introduction de coefficients de « viscosité » et de « diffusion turbulente », on en revient à analyser des cas particuliers, dans l'espoir d'acquérir une connaissance suffisante des parties pour en venir à comprendre le tout. Selon les hypothèses physiques choisies et les valeurs prises comme étalons, on tire du système (1′) à (5′) divers systèmes d'équations simplifiées. Deux examples classiques illustrent bien cette méthode.

Courants géostrophiques. Il s'agit d'un écoulement stationnaire de très faible intensité dans un fluide incompressible. On suppose donc S_t et M très petits. On laisse de plus de côté l'influence des échanges turbulents et des forces extérieures autres que celle de la gravité. F_2 et R_t seront donc très grands (R_t est un nombre de Reynolds défini selon μ_t). On obtient le système simplifié

$$\frac{\partial U_j}{\partial x_j} = 0,$$

$$2\rho\epsilon_{ijk}\,\Omega_j\,U_k = -\frac{\partial p}{\partial x_i} + g\rho\delta_{i3},$$

$$\rho = \rho(x_i).$$

Si l'on néglige de plus la composante verticale de la force de Coriolis on a tout simplement un champ hydrostatique de pression, dont les gradients horizontaux sont balancés par la force de Coriolis agissant sur un écoulement horizontal, lequel est alors dit géostrophique. Ce type d'écoulement correspond assez bien aux courants océaniques lents, loin des côtes. Les équations simplifiées ci-dessus sont à la base de la méthode dynamique, utilisée de façon routinière pour calculer le champ de vitesses, à partir d'observations portant sur le champ de densité.

Spirale d'Ekman. Il s'agit dans ce cas d'une analyse simplifiée de l'écoulement moyen produit par l'action d'un vent uniforme et stationnaire soufflant à la surface d'un fluide visqueux. On prend S_t et M très petits et F_2 très grand. Par suite de l'uniformité spatiale du vent les longueurs-étalons dans le plan horizontal sont infinies. La pression est donc hydrostatique et la balance horizontale des forces se fait entre les tensions de Reynolds et la force de Coriolis. On a expressément le système

$$2\Omega U_2 = \frac{\partial p}{\partial x_1}, \qquad 2\Omega U_1 = -\frac{\partial p}{\partial x_2},$$

$$\rho g = -\frac{\partial p}{\partial x_3},$$

$$\frac{\partial U_1}{\partial x_1} + \frac{\partial U_2}{\partial x_2} + \frac{\partial U_3}{\partial x_3} = 0,$$

$$U_3 = 0 \quad \text{sur } x_3 = 0,$$

$$U_1 = U_2 = U_3 = 0 \quad \text{pour } x_3 = -\infty .$$

A la surface du fluide s'exerce une tension T_v, due à l'action du vent. On trouve comme solution de ce système l'écoulement connu sous le nom de spirale d'Ekman. Le vecteur de vitesse a une intensité maximum à la surface, orienté à 45° à droite (hémisphère nord) de la direction du vent. L'intensité de la vitesse diminue exponentiellement en profondeur, en même temps que son orientation change linéairement vers la droite (hémisphère nord). Le transport total de fluide est perpendiculaire et (dans l'hémisphère nord) à droite de la direction du vent. Ce modèle donne une explication simple des phénomènes de remontée d'eaux profondes dues à un système de vents soufflant parallèlement à une côte. On trouvera d'amples détails sur les courants géostrophiques et sur la spirale d'Ekman dans Lacombe (1965) par exemple.

On a de cette façon obtenu des solutions détaillées d'une foule de phénomènes correspondants à divers choix de conditions simplificatrices et de conditions aux limites. Ces solutions correspondent souvent assez bien aux observations. Il faut cependant se garder d'en appliquer les résultats à des situations où les hypothèses de base ne sont plus valides. Un courant, par exemple, ne peut être en balance géostrophique au contact d'un littoral, vu que les tensions turbulentes et visqueuses y deviennent importantes.

Malgré les succès remportés par cette méthode d'analyse et la justesse avec laquelle des modèles ainsi simplifiés expliquent nombre de phénomènes océanographiques, le cœur du problème n'en demeure pas moins à peine touché. On ne trouve en effet jamais dans l'océan de situations correspondant exactement à l'un ou à l'autre de ces modèles simplifiés. On y découvre plutôt un mélange, en diverses proportions, de plusieurs types de mouvement. Souvent, bien entendu, un type donné contribuera de façon dominante à l'écoulement total, et la solution simplifiée qui lui correspond représentera une approximation assez juste de la situation. Etant donné cependant l'absence de linéarité des équations, on ne peut décrire exactement une situation en superposant des solutions correspondant aux divers phénomènes en lesquels on peut la disséquer. Une somme de solutions d'un système non-linéaire n'est en général pas une solution de ce système. Dans le cas où un type de mouvement l'emporte de beaucoup sur les autres on peut, il est vrai, améliorer la qualité de l'approximation en se servant de la méthode des perturbations. De façon plus générale, pourtant, on ne peut parvenir à une compréhension profonde d'un système non-linéaire qu'en le considérant comme un tout différent de la somme de ses parties.

On saisira peut-être mieux les implications de l'absence de linéarité si l'on considère qu'à travers les termes non-linéaires se produit une interaction continue entre les divers types d'écoulements. Tout transfert d'énergie entre différents types de mouvements se fait par l'intermédiaire de termes non-linéaires de l'écoulement moyen ou des termes représentant les échanges turbulents. On constate que si l'on se contente de considérer un système non-linéaire simplement comme la somme de ses parties, on n'en peut obtenir qu'une représentation quasi-statique. Cette façon d'envisager le problème suppose en effet que la répartition de l'énergie entre les divers types de mouvements qu'on peut y déceler demeure stationnaire.

Plusieurs chercheurs (on trouvera une longue bibliographie dans Hasselmann, 1966) se sont depuis quelques années attaqués, à l'aide de la méthode des perturbations, au problème des interactions faibles, surtout entre divers types d'ondes d'une part et les courants ou le relief sous-marin d'autre part. (Une interaction peut être dite faible si l'énergie de chacun des types d'écoulements, caractérisés par des périodes-étalons finies, τ_i, qui y prennent part ne change que par une petite fraction au cours du plus long des τ_i.) Ces recherches ont donné des résultats précieux qui ont de beaucoup étendu notre connaissance de ces phénomènes.

Mais la méthode des perturbations ne s'applique qu'à des échanges d'énergie relativement lents, et il existe dans l'océan des zones de courants très intenses (tels le Gulf Stream, ou le Kuroshio) où il se produit certainement des interactions rapides et violentes. Que ces interactions fortes n'aient cours qu'en des régions relativement restreintes n'en diminue pas leur importance, puisque leur influence peut être propagée à de grandes distances en aval. Il semble y avoir peu de doutes que nombre de situations sont intimement contrôlées par de telles interactions. Le rôle précis qu'elles jouent dans la circulation océanique générale ne pourra toutefois être déterminé que par des recherches plus approfondies. Ces recherches se heurtent pour le moment à des difficultés mathématiques considérables, et profiteront énormément de tout progrès réalisé dans la théorie des équations différentielles partielles non-linéaires.

On comprendra finalement mieux l'importance pratique de ces recherches sur les interactions fortes entre divers types d'écoulements si l'on considère la possibilité future d'exercer un certain contrôle sur la circulation océanique. Tout mécanisme efficace de contrôle d'un système de haute énergie doit comporter un élement d'amplification. Il est en effet fort inélegant, et certainement très peu économique, de modifier un système de façon brutale, en y injectant des quantités d'énergie comparables à son énergie totale. On doit donc s'efforcer de découvrir un mécanisme catalytique qui, une fois déclenché, tirera du système lui-même l'énergie nécessaire pour effectuer les modifications désirées. La recherche de ce catalyste nous amène donc à étudier la stabilité du système devant divers types d'interactions. Il n'est évidemment pas suffisant d'établir de façon qualitative des critères de stabilité : on doit de plus s'assurer que les changements d'état ainsi provoqués correspondent aux modifications qu'on veut produire. D'où la nécessité de s'attaquer vigoureusement à l'étude des équations du mouvement sous leur forme non-linéaire avant de se lancer aveuglement dans des projets de contrôle océanographique de grande envergure.

On doit donc s'attendre à ce que plusieurs années de recherches approfondies soient encore nécessaires avant qu'on aie suffisamment démelé l'écheveau des interactions fortes pour songer à s'attaquer à de grands projets de génie océanique. Il faudra bien entendu continuer à s'attaquer au problème sous plusieurs angles à la fois. Les résultats d'observations de plus en plus détaillées ainsi que des expériences, soit de laboratoire, soit numériques, devront continuer à guider et à inspirer les recherches théoriques qui sont à la base de notre compréhension de ces phénomènes.

REFERENCES

ECKART, C. (1962), "The Equations of Motion of Sea Water," *The Sea, Ideas and Observations*, Vol. I, ed. by M. N. Hill (New York: Interscience Publishers).

HASSELMANN, K. (1966), "Feynman Diagrams and Interaction Rules of Wave–Wave Scattering Processes," *Revs. Geophys.* 4: 1–32.

LACOMBE, H. (1965), *Cours d'océanographie physique.* (Paris: Gauthier-Villars).

LUMLEY, J. L. et PANOFSKY, H. A. (1964), *The Structure of Atmospheric Turbulence* (New York: Interscience Publishers).

ESTIMATES OF GROUNDWATER RECHARGE ON THE PRAIRIES

P. Meyboom

THE QUANTITY of water passing through any arc of the hydrologic cycle can be evaluated by the so-called hydrologic equation, which simply states that $I - O = \Delta S$, where I is inflow into a region during a given period, O is outflow from that region during the same period, and ΔS is the change in storage within the region. The hydrologic equation (which is essentially a form of the continuity equation) is the central concept of hydrology.

In hydrogeology, the hydrologic equation is generally referred to as the groundwater balance or groundwater budget, in which case it is written as $R - D = \Delta S$, where R is recharge to the groundwater system, D is discharge from the groundwater system, and ΔS is the change in storage within the system. For sufficiently long periods, under undisturbed conditions, ΔS becomes insignificantly small and it is therefore often said that recharge equals discharge.

Recharge makes groundwater a renewable resource, and groundwater management should be based on the knowledge of rates of natural (and possible artificial) recharge.

In the initial stages of development of a groundwater reservoir, some water must be withdrawn from storage in order to attain an equilibrium between recharge and artificial discharge. This stage will be characterized by dropping water levels. Once the equilibrium has been reached, there should be no further withdrawal from storage and water levels should remain stable. Following this line of thought, Thomas and Leopold (1964) visualized the ultimate stage of development as one in which "the aggregate pumping has reached a steady state after inducing all possible recharge and eliminating as much as possible of the natural discharge." This amount of "aggregate pumping" corresponds closely with Todd's concept of "safe yield," which he defined as "the amount of water which can be withdrawn from a groundwater basin annually without producing an undesired effect in quantity or quality (see Todd 1959, p. 200).

During the Third Canadian Hydrology Symposium, held at Calgary in 1962, Professor Kuiper asked the assembly whether groundwater supplies on the Canadian Prairies are such that they can contribute up to 1,000 cubic feet per second (cfs) to the future water demands; or whether the groundwater contribution will be insignificant, say less than 100 cfs. Mollard (1965) estimated that the present groundwater use in southern Saskatchewan amounts to 50 million gallons per day (mgd), or approximately 90 cfs, of which 14 mgd are derived from concentrated exploitation around population centres that cover less than 3 per cent of the area considered. From these estimates he concluded that theoretically there should be another 486 mgd (900 cfs) available in the remaining 97,200 square miles of Saskatchewan. These quantities are well within Professor Kuiper's requirement for a "significant contribution" to the Prairie's water demands some 20 to 30 years from now.

Groundwater development on the Canadian Prairies has not been hampered by the absence of suitable reservoirs. The search for aquifers during the past 30 years has been successful in many places, regardless of whether there was a demand for domestic, municipal, or industrial supplies. Precise testing techniques have been employed to determine the hydraulic characteristics of these aquifers, but the rate and even the mechanism of groundwater replenishment on the Prairies are still poorly understood. Moreover, Staple *et al.* (1960) presented evidence that groundwater recharge on the Prairies may be rare and quantitatively insignificant. They noticed from soil-moisture measurements that in early spring of such years as 1951, 1952, 1953, and 1955, some moisture passed below the root zone, but they concluded that the "losses" were exceptional and that the amount of water involved was probably small.

Much of the present hydrogeological research on the Prairies pertains directly or indirectly to the question whether groundwater is indeed a renewable resource. This problem can be approached in two ways: either by computing the amount of groundwater flow from a mathematical model of the flow system[1] or by solving the groundwater balance directly from field measurements. Direct solution of the groundwater balance requires measurements either at the recharge

[1]The term flow system is used in the sense of Tóth (1962) as being "a set of flow lines in which any two flow lines adjacent at one point of the flow region remain adjacent through the whole region, and that can be intersected anywhere by an uninterrupted surface across which flow takes place in one direction only."

end of the flow system or at the discharge end. This is the reason why the configuration of the flow system has to be known fairly well before meaningful measurements can be made. Flow systems of various magnitudes have been described and a definite methodology has been developed for the prairie region to recognize and analyse them (Toth 1962; Meyboom 1962; Freeze 1966).

This paper discusses how groundwater flow systems can be measured and how these measurements are being used to solve the hydrologic equation with respect to groundwater replenishment on the Prairies.

A GROUNDWATER BALANCE INFERRED FROM CALCULATIONS ON DISCHARGE

Patterns of Groundwater Flow in the Arm River Drainage Basin

The Arm River drainage basin in south-central Saskatchewan (Fig. 1) will be taken as the first example of how a groundwater balance can be estimated. The drainage pattern in this part of Saskatchewan is a lobate one, made up of a number of parallel streams which originated either as meltwater channels (Arm River) or as spillways (Qu'Appelle River and Last Mountain Lake) (Christiansen 1961).

Geologically, the area is made up of nearly horizontal Cretaceous strata overlain by till. The bed-rock strata belong to the Bearpaw Formation, which consists of marine shale with some sandy intervals in its lower part. Two members of the Bearpaw Formation are relevant to this discussion: the Snakebite Member, which comprises 250 feet of soft grey bentonitic shale; and the Beechy Member, which consists of an upper shale (120 feet), a middle sandstone (35 to 50 feet), and a lower shale (200 feet). In the bed-rock of the Arm River basin we encounter 370 feet of shale, being the combined Snakebite Member and the upper Beechy shale, overlying the middle Beechy sandstone.

The flow system within this geologic framework can be deduced from piezometer cross-sections. A piezometer is a small-diameter pipe which has been placed in the ground in such a way that the water level in the pipe is a measure of the total hydraulic head at the very point in the flow field where the piezometer ends. Three or four piezometers at one location, terminating at different depths, form a piezometer nest, whereas a line of piezometer nests constitutes a piezometer cross-section. As each piezometer records the value of total head at a particular depth, a piezometric cross-section yields a series of potential values in a vertical plane through the flow field.

Lines of equal head can be drawn between the observed values, and using the rules laid down by van Everdingen (1963) a two-dimensional project of the flow system can be constructed.

Piezometer cross-sections through the Arm River drainage basin

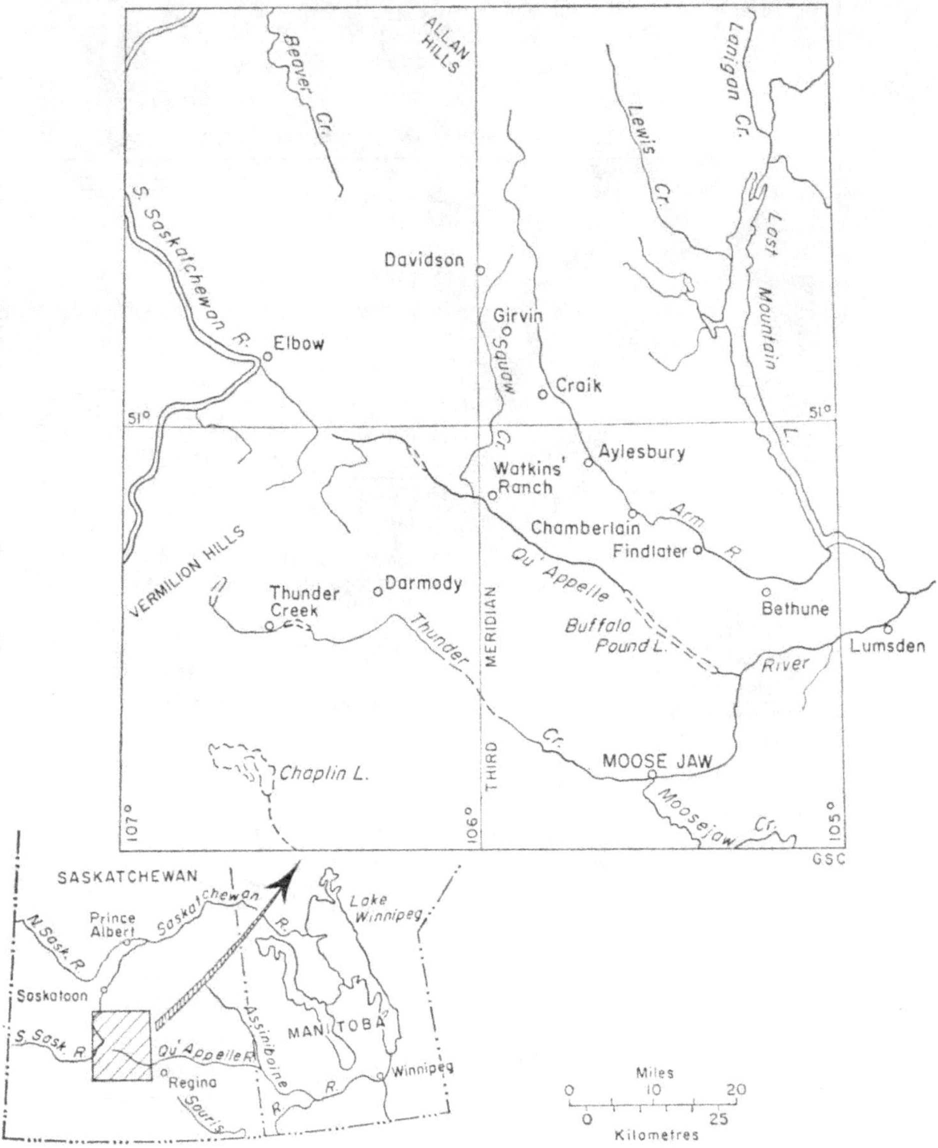

FIGURE 1. Location of the Arm River drainage basin.

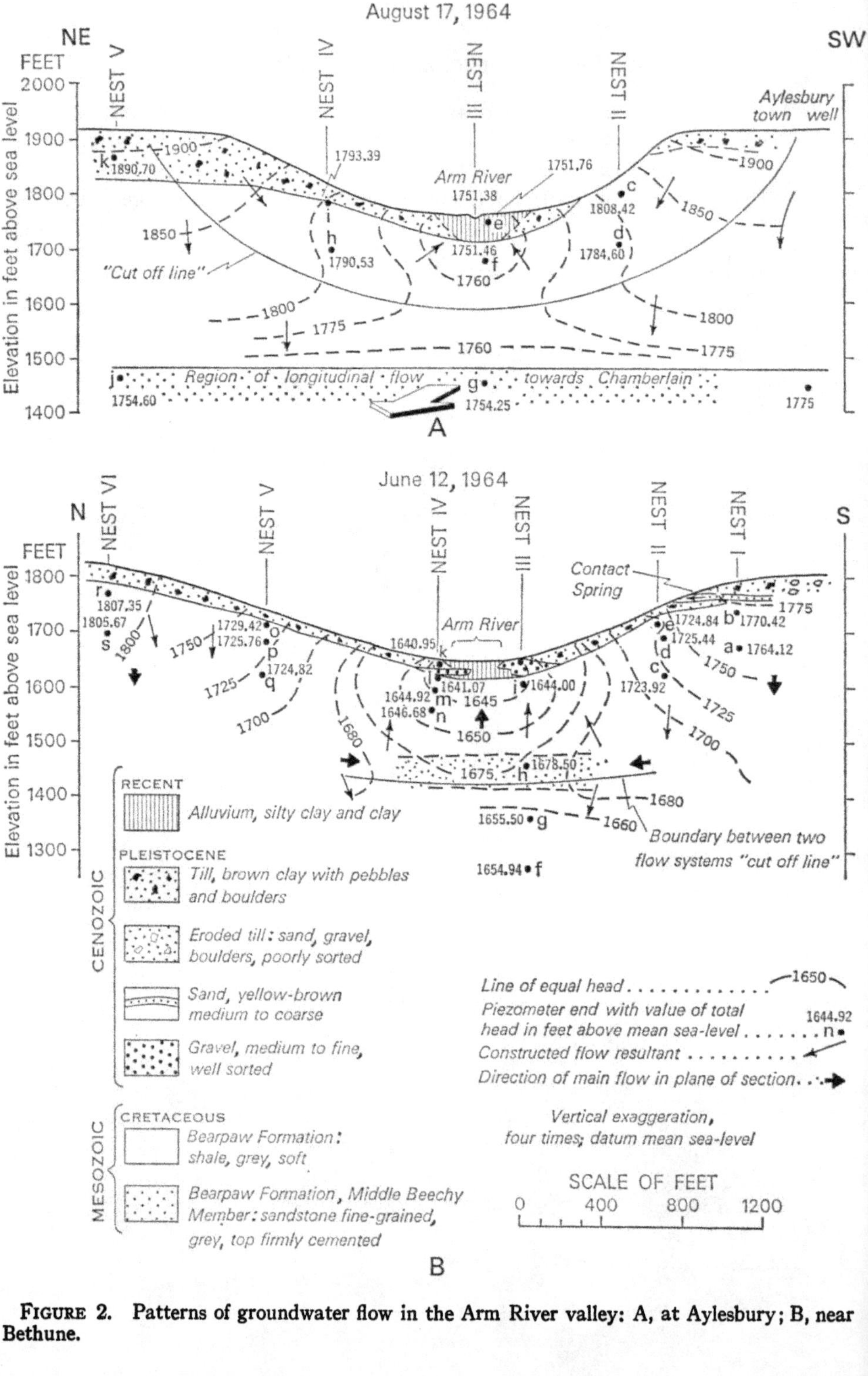

Figure 2. Patterns of groundwater flow in the Arm River valley: A, at Aylesbury; B, near Bethune.

show that the Arm River in its upstream reaches has little influence on the regional groundwater movement (Fig. 2A). The river is associated with a narrow zone of radial flow, superimposed on downward flow to the middle Beechy sandstone. The piezometric map of the Beechy sandstone shows that the main direction of groundwater flow in this area is toward the southeast, in a strip parallel to and underneath the Arm River. Downstream, the drainage influence of the Arm River increases significantly, and from Chamberlain on, it does reach into the Beechy sandstone. Figure 2B shows the flow pattern near Bethune, approximately 20 miles downstream from Chamberlain.

The piezometer measurements reveal also that the groundwater divide coincides with the surface divide to at least the middle Beechy sandstone. Thus, the flow system that exists within the upper 400 feet of the drainage basin is not part of a large regional system as was proposed previously (Meyboom 1962), but constitutes a small regional system whose boundaries coincide with those of the Arm River watershed.

This flow system is characterized by vertical flow in the poorly permeable till and shale, lateral flow in the permeable sandstone, and radial flow in the vicinity of the drainage channel. It follows from the previous paragraphs that the lateral flow in the permeable layer is not everywhere perpendicular to the drainage channel, but that it may be parallel to the stream as well. Downstream from Chamberlain, however, the drainage influence of the stream is such that the bulk of the groundwater flow can be depicted in a two-dimensional cross-section perpendicular to the river. This has been done in Figure 3, which is a schematized elaboration of the flow pattern shown in Figure 2B.

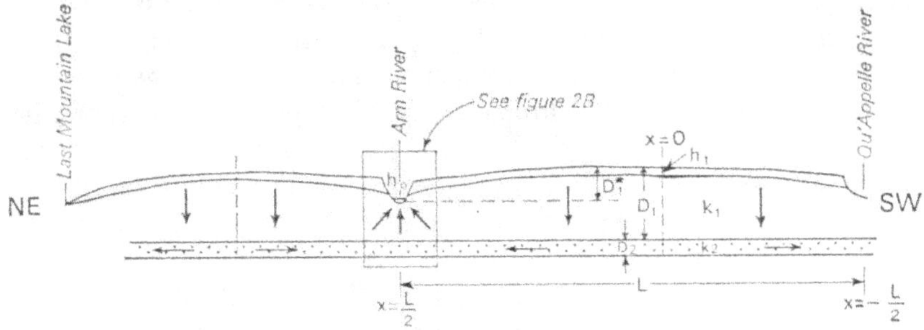

FIGURE 3. Schematized representation of groundwater flow in the Arm River drainage basin near Bethune. h = hydraulic head, k = hydraulic conductivity, D = thickness of strata, L = distance between parallel drainage channels.

Calculation of Groundwater Discharge, Using Steady-State Drainage Equations

Referring to Figure 3, the following parameters have to be considered before quantitative analysis of the flow system is possible:

L = distance between the parallel drainage channels = 9 miles.

h_1 = total hydraulic head of the water table at the divide (in feet above sea level) = 1,850 feet.

h_0 = water level in the drainage channel (in feet above sea level) = 1,643 feet (high-water).

D_1 = thickness of the poorly permeable layer = 370 feet.

D_2 = thickness of the permeable layer = 50 feet.

K_1 = hydraulic conductivity of the poorly permeable layer. At the Bethune cross-section, the mean hydraulic conductivity of the till and shale in the interval from 0 to 120 feet is 0.008 in. per hour. There is one measured value at 7×10^{-4} in. per hour at 300 feet, but the information is insufficient to determine precisely the decrease in permeability with depth. The average value for the entire poorly permeable layer has been taken as 0.005 in. per hour, or 0.01 ft per day.

K_2 = hydraulic conductivity of the permeable layer = 0.6 ft per day.

The configuration shown in Figure 3 is one of symmetrical drainage by an imperfect drain terminating in a poorly permeable layer overlying a permeable layer. The drainage equation for this situation is

$$h_1 - h_0 = Nc_1 + \frac{NL^2}{8(K_1 D_1 + K_2 D_2)} + NLw$$

(Ernst 1963, eq. 15), which states that the total groundwater discharge, N, is the sum of three flow components: a vertical component through the poorly permeable layer, a lateral component in the permeable layer, and a radial component near the drainage channel. Use of the steady-state drainage equation presupposes that the following conditions are satisfied: (i) the strata are of constant thickness, (ii) $\sum D/L < 0.25$, (iii) the water table is nearly horizontal, (iv) drainage takes place by parallel streams, and (v) drainage is restricted to the river. Although the theoretical requirement for a stratified flow medium ($K_1 D_1 \leqslant 0.1 K_2 D_2$) is not fully satisfied, the piezometer measurements underneath the divides to indicate that the schematization employed is permissible. This is substantiated by Ernst's comment that there will always be vertical flow in the poorly permeable layer if $K_1 \ll K_2$ (Ernst 1962, p. 35). These measurements may indicate also strong anisotropy in the permeable layer.

If the configuration shown in Figure 3 were to be solved by means of a modelling method, one would employ the numerical method (Freeze 1966). The result would be a flow net from which the flow could be calculated by counting flow channels and applying Darcy's law. However, the true-scale diagram of the Arm River basin would be difficult to deal with because of the awkward relation between horizontal and vertical dimensions.

Before the drainage equation can be solved, the resistance to flow has to be calculated for each of the three flow components:

1. The *vertical resistance* (also called the c value or seepage coefficient) is given by $c = D/K$. Ernst (1963, p. 61) points out that for the type of configuration in question, it is sufficient to calculate c_1, which is the coefficient D_1^*/K_1, where D_1^* is the thickness of the poorly permeable layer midway between the drainage channels, to a depth equal to the bottom of the channel (see Fig. 3). $c_1 = 21.6 \times 10^3$ days.

2. The *lateral resistance* is given by $1/KD$, in which can be substituted 3.70 sq. ft per day for $K_1 D_1$ and 30 sq. ft per day for $K_2 D_2$.

3. The *radial resistance*, w, of an imperfect drainage channel in a stratified medium has to be calculated according to the equation

$$K_1 w = K_1 w' + \frac{1}{\pi} \ln \frac{D_1}{4r_0}$$

(Ernst 1962, eq. 53), which requires that $r_0/D_1 \leqslant 0.25$, r_0 being the radius of the wetted perimeter (20 feet). Ernst's nomogram (Ernst 1962, Fig. 14) gives the value of $K_1 w'$ as a function of K_2/K_1 and D_1/D_2. In the calculation of w, D_1 is the thickness of the poorly permeable layer at the stream (150 feet). If $K_2/K_1 = \infty$ (which for practical purposes it becomes if $K_2/K_1 \geqslant 20$), Ernst (1962, eq. 54) gives the following direct solution for w:

$$w = \frac{1}{\pi K_1} \ln \frac{4D_1}{r_0}.$$

The direct solution gives $w = 72$ days per ft.

Solving the drainage equation for N, we obtain $N =$ *approx.* 0.10 *in./year*, which is equivalent to a groundwater discharge of approximately 2.75 gallons per minute per square mile (gpm/sq. mile), assuming that N is uniform over the drainage basin. Whether or not this amount of discharge can be measured directly in the river valley remains questionable.

Measurement of Groundwater Discharge

Baseflow

Field measurements in the Arm River valley indicate that near Bethune groundwater discharge is restricted to the river. Consider a strip 1 mile wide, extending across the basin at Chamberlain from divide to divide, parallel to the slope of the land. This strip comprises 11 square miles, and recharge over this strip at a rate of 0.10 in. per year would amount to 58 acre-feet of groundwater discharge per year in the river. If the longitudinal flow component were indeed negligible downstream from Chamberlain,[2] and if the groundwater discharge from the entire profile were indeed restricted to the river itself, hydrometric records of the Arm River should show an annual groundwater flow of 58 acre-feet per mile of stream channel. For the reach Chamberlain–Bethune, this would amount to a year-round baseflow of 1.60 cfs at the gauging station near Bethune. In reality, however, the mean baseflow at Bethune, calculated as an annual average for the period 1958–63, amounts to 0.3 cfs. This means that the river carries about 18 per cent of the calculated discharge. The obvious conclusion is that upstream from Bethune not all discharge is restricted to the river itself.

Disregarding for the moment the longitudinal flow, we shall examine two other discharge processes in the valley: transpiration of groundwater by the valley-bottom vegetation and evaporation from the shallow water table. These two processes are together referred to as evapo-transpiration.

Evapo-transpiration

The valleys of many prairie streams are characterized by a lush growth of trees and shrubs that are absent on the prairie itself. Water table measurements in these densely vegetated areas reveal regular daily fluctuations which indicate that the plants draw water from the zone of saturation (Fig. 4). For these plants Meinzer (1923) coined the term *phreatophytes*.

Phreatophytes live by virtue of the mechanism that ensures nightly recovery of the water table. If it were not for this replenishment, the water table would soon be out of reach of the roots and the vegetation

[2]This assumption is not completely valid (Meyboom *et al.*, 1966). There is a longitudinal component of flow, as can be seen from a comparison of the upward and downward gradients in the Bethune cross-section (Fig. 2B). However, the amount of flow is too small to be included in a first approximation of the groundwater balance.

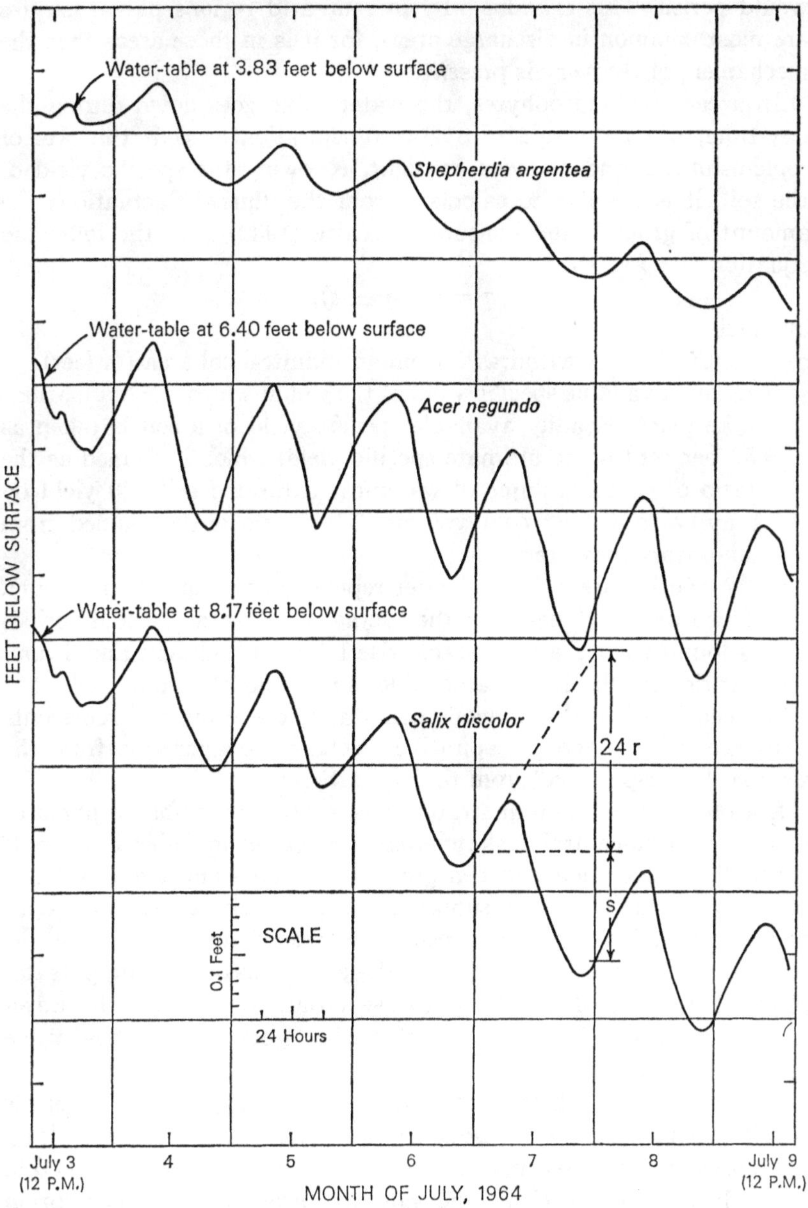

FIGURE 4. Diurnal water-table fluctuations due to transpiration by phreatophytes. From top to bottom the illustration shows weekly graphs of buffaloberry (*Shepherdia argentea*), Manitoba maple (*Acer negundo* L. var. *interius*), and willow (*Salix discolor*). The willow graph shows the White method of calculating consumptive use.

would perish. This explains why in semi-arid regions phreatophytes are most common in discharge areas, for it is in those areas that the mechanism of recovery is present.

In areas of phreatophytes, the water table goes down during the day-time, when the rate of evapo-transpiration exceeds the rate of replenishment, and recovers at night. Knowing the specific yield of the soil, it is possible to calculate from the diurnal fluctuations the amount of groundwater consumed. White (1932) gave the following equation (see Fig. 4):

$$q = y(24r \pm s),$$

in which

q = depth of water withdrawn from an infinitesimal area (in feet).

y = readily available specific yield of the soil in which the fluctuations take place. Readily available specific yield of a soil is taken as 50 per cent of its ultimate specific yield, which is defined as the ratio of (i) the volume of water the saturated soil will yield by gravity to (ii) its own volume. This ratio is determined from laboratory measurements.

r = the hourly rate of groundwater replenishment (in feet per hour). This rate, which has to be the average rate for the 24-hour period, is found from the water-table rise between midnight and 4 a.m.

s = net rise or fall of the water table during the 24 hours.

As mentioned in the previous paragraph, the value of q represents both evaporative and transpirative discharge: evaporation from the soil and "transpiration" from the vegetation.

Seasonal values of groundwater consumption by common phreatophytes in south-central Saskatchewan are set out in Table I. There is a negative correlation between groundwater consumption and depth to water. Groundwater consumption increases with decreasing depth to the water table, partly as a result of increased evaporation from the soil surface. It was found that in south-central Saskatchewan, phreatophytic herbs and shrubs cease to use groundwater when the water table is more than 7 feet below surface. For trees this threshold value appears to lie around 14 feet.

In the unincised parts of the Arm River valley, the phreatophyte belt is about 500 feet wide. Along 1 mile of stream channel this adds up to an area of about 60 acres. In this strip the water table lies from 0 to 7 feet below surface. Using the values of groundwater consumption from Table I and paying due attention to the variable depth to water, it can be calculated that during the growing season of 1964, groundwater consumption by the growth of Manitoba maple downstream

TABLE I

SUMMARY OF DATA ON GROUNDWATER CONSUMPTION BY PHREATOPHYTIC VEGETATION IN SOUTH-CENTRAL SASKATCHEWAN (Meyboom, 1967)

Plant community	Year	Groundwater consumption, C (in.)					K[1] for the period	C/E[2] for the period	Mean depth to the water table (ft)	Readily available spec. yield (%)
		June	July	Aug.	Sept.	Period				
Wolf willow and baltic rush	1963	3.60	8.76	9.84	7.32	29.52	1.16	0.93	1.75	9
	1964	6.00	12.84	11.16	0.72	30.72	1.35	0.91	1.50	9
Baltic rush	1964	5.88	8.40	7.08	1.44	22.80	1.00	0.68	3.00	8.25
Pussy willow	1963	1.55	6.02	5.90	—	13.47	0.65	0.52	1.50	9
	1964	3.24	5.52	1.80	—	10.56	0.52	0.37	4.75	8.25
Manitoba maple	1964	5.88	8.28	5.64	1.32	21.12	0.93	0.63	6.00	8.25
	1964	3.96	7.80	4.80	—	16.56	0.81	0.58	5.00	9
Western cotton wood	1964	10.92	17.52	9.84	3.96	42.24	1.72	1.26	2.00	8.25
Buffaloberry	1964	0.96	1.20	0.48	—	2.64	0.13	0.09	7.25	8.25
	1964	3.96	2.76	1.17	—	7.89	0.38	0.28	4.00	9.75
Hawthorn	1963	0.48	1.80	0.96	—	3.24	0.16	0.13	3.00	6.25

[1]Blaney's consumptive-use coefficient.
[2]Ratio of groundwater consumption (C) and total net water loss (E) from class "A" evaporation pan at Regina airport.

from Chamberlain amounted to 94 acre-feet per mile of stream channel. For a valley vegetation consisting of willow and baltic rush, such as occurs near Findlater, it amounted to about 70 acre-feet per mile during the same period. Considering the extent of the vegetation, these volumes make up for the discharge that could not be accounted for by the baseflow analysis, and it may be concluded that the bulk of natural discharge from this flow system is by evapo-transpiration during the summer.

Conclusions Regarding the Water Balance

If the groundwater balance, expressed in inches per year over the drainage basin, is given in the form of recharge = discharge, in which discharge is the sum of baseflow and evapo-transpiration, we obtain the following approximation for the Arm River drainage basin:

$$0.10 = 0.02 + 0.08$$

or, in terms of precipitation, the average groundwater replenishment in the Arm River basin amounts to less than 1 per cent of the average total annual precipitation.

If the groundwater balance is expressed in gallons per minute per square mile, it reads

$$2.75 = 0.50 + 2.25.$$

Recalling the concept of safe yield expressed by Thomas and Leopold (1964), the ultimate stage of groundwater development in this basin would be reached if the aggregate pumping were to amount to 2.75 gpm/sq. mile. The significance of this value becomes apparent if one considers that the present groundwater use by cities, towns, and villages in southern Saskatchewan amounts to 3.5 gpm/sq. mile (Mollard 1965).

A GROUNDWATER BALANCE INFERRED FROM CALCULATIONS ON RECHARGE

Groundwater Recharge in Hummocky Moraine

The recharge areas shown in Figure 3 are covered by till, which is developed either as ground moraine or as hummocky moraine. The topography of the ground moraine is undulating to gently rolling, and has an average relief of less than 10 feet. The landscape is characterized by numerous small undrained depressions, which are called sloughs.

These sloughs and the intervening low till ridges are commonly orientated in a lobate pattern (Christiansen 1956).

Hummocky moraine has a typical knob-and-kettle topography with a local relief of 20 to 40 feet. Sloughs in hummocky moraine are scattered throughout the area without apparent orientation. An aerial view of the hummocky moraine of the Allan Hills, which constitute the recharge area in the northern part of the Arm River drainage basin, shows till knobs of various dimensions separating irregular, somewhat rounded or perfectly circular sloughs, each one surrounded by a ring of willows.

None of the sloughs in the Allan Hills are permanent. Following winters of average precipitation, the depressions are filled with meltwater during the spring and early summer, but dry up towards the beginning of July. After winters with below-average snowfall the sloughs contain no water in the spring, whereas during years with higher than average precipitation, the depressions may contain water throughout the summer.

Piezometer measurements of a small flow system associated with one of the temporary sloughs in the Allan Hills revealed that during the course of one year the following sequence of flow conditions existed: (1) a winter condition of "normal downward" flow, (2) a spring condition characterized by a groundwater mound underneath the slough, and an associated flow pattern of vertical and lateral dissipation, and finally (3) a condition of inverted water-table relief due to the cone of depression created by the phreatophytic willows and the phreatophytes in the dried-up slough bed. The latter condition existed during summer and fall and was characterized by radial flow into the willow ring, brought about by reversed-shallow and diverted-deep groundwater flow. The sequence is shown schematically in Figure 5.

Much of the recharge efficiency of the slough depends on the duration of the flow conditions 1 and 2. In the experiment described above, which lasted from May 31, 1964 to June 1, 1965, infiltration lasted a total of 187 days, whereas the condition of reversed flow lasted 178 days. During the first period of infiltration (May 31 to July 21, 1964) 1,577 cubic feet of water was added to the groundwater resources. However, from July 21 to January 16, 3,096 cu. ft flowed back towards the willow ring, leaving a negative balance of 1,519 cu. ft at January 16, 1965. From January 16 to June 1, 1965, the total flow away from the willow ring amounted to 4,433 cu. ft. By June 1st, there had thus been a net addition to the regional groundwater resources of 2,914 cu. ft (Meyboom 1966).

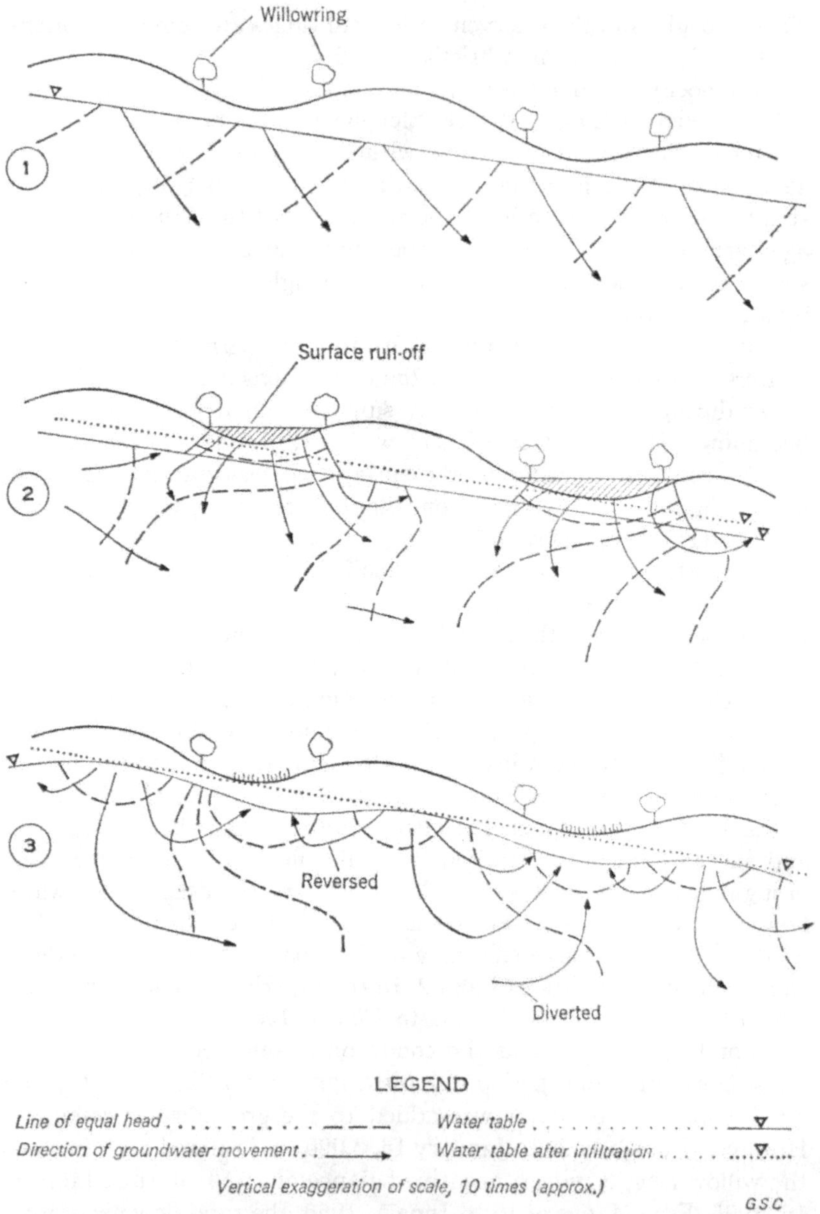

FIGURE 5. Generalized sequence of flow conditions near willow ring and temporary slough: (1) a condition of "normal downward" flow, (2) a condition of dissipating groundwater mounds produced by infiltrating meltwater, and (3) a condition of inverted watertable relief resulting from the cone of depression around the phreatophytes.

It should be stressed that these temporary sloughs can only be recharge areas if the water level in the slough is above the level of the surrounding water table. If the local relief is such that the surrounding water table is at all times higher than the slough level, the slough will be a permanent discharge area. Current research aims specifically at the hydrogeological significance of sloughs, for the small reversible flow systems associated with temporary sloughs may be an important recharge mechanism in the morainic terrain of the plains.

Conclusions Regarding the Water Balance

The water balance of the willow ring showed that from May 31, 1964 to June 1st, 1965, the overall effect of flow conditions 1 and 2 was a net contribution to the regional groundwater resources of 2,914 cu. ft. This volume represents 0.42 inch on the 2-acre watershed around the depression, or 3 per cent of the total precipitation in Davidson during that period. However, if recharge from temporary sloughs is effective only after winters with average or above-average precipitation, the long-term recharge from an area like the Allan Hills will be somewhat less than 3 per cent of the annual precipitation.

To increase the recharge efficiency of this type of hummocky moraine, the third flow condition would have to be eliminated. In other words, evapo-transpiration by the phreatophytes in the depressions would have to be reduced. Destroying the willows would be a solution, but only a partial solution, for if it were not for the willows less snow would be trapped in the low areas, and consequently less meltwater would accumulate in the ponds. Thus if the willows were to be destroyed, they would have to be replaced by snow fences in order to capture sufficient amounts of snow to fill up the pond. Improvement of conditions on the till knobs does not have to be considered, for they are already bare before run-off starts (see also Wolbeer and Husband 1964, p. 141).

A more promising approach towards increasing the efficiency of this type of recharge area may lie in suppressing evapo-transpiration chemically. Waggoner and Hewlett (1965), as well as Waggoner and Zelitch (1965), reported that transpiration can be suppressed effectively by applying the glycerol half-ester of decenylsuccinic acid (GLOSA). GLOSA closes tree stomata when sprayed directly upon the undersides of the leaves. Although there are still many practical difficulties in the spraying of vegetation for water conservation, it may be a more hopeful course of action than destruction of the plants. On the Prairies, the recharge area for the city of Regina, for instance, may be one of the first areas where experiments leading to increased efficiency of the recharge mechanism may become necessary.

A GROUNDWATER BALANCE INFERRED FROM SOIL-MOISTURE BUDGETS

The two previous examples dealt with results obtained from detailed measurements in small areas. With regard to estimates of groundwater recharge over much larger areas, another approach has to be followed, for there is no groundwater instrumentation for most of the tens of thousands of square miles of prairie. The only hydrologic data that are available for the Prairies as a whole are meteorological records and hydrometric records. In the following estimate of recharge, use has been made of meteorological records (Canada Department of Transport 1944–60).

As mentioned in the introduction of this paper, Staple *et al.* (1960) concluded that percolation of soil moisture to the water table is unusual under semi-arid conditions. On the other hand, since there is no evidence for a widespread decline of the water table on the Prairies, recharge must be effective on the few occasions that moisture does pass below the root zone. We shall now discuss what soil-moisture conditions must be satisfied before recharge can take place, and to what extent the frequency and magnitude of recharge can be deduced from soil-moisture budgets, which in turn are derived from meteorological data.

A soil is saturated with respect to water if all its interstices are filled. When the soil is permitted to drain freely, some water will be removed. This amount, expressed as a volume ratio, is called the specific yield of the soil. After gravitational water has drained out, the soil is said to be at *field capacity*. The moisture tension at field capacity is normally between 0.1 and 0.3 atmosphere (atm). Field capacity is the upper limit of moisture available to plant life; the lower limit is reached at the *wilting point*, which corresponds to a moisture tension of about 15 atm. The actual amount of moisture stored in the root zone between moisture tensions of 0.1 and 15 atm depends on the soil texture, and varies from 4.2 inches in sandy loam to 8.8 inches in heavy clay. This amount is called the normal *storage capacity*.

Two concepts that are related to certain moisture conditions are relevant to the following discussion: *soil-moisture deficit* and *soil-moisture surplus*. By soil-moisture deficit is meant the amount of moisture that has to be added to the 4-foot root zone to bring it up to field capacity; whereas a moisture surplus exists when more moisture has been added to the root zone than the amount required to satisfy the transpiration demands of the vegetation and to bring the soil to field capacity. Thus, rain infiltrating into the ground first meets the vegetation demands, and any excess thereafter can only pass to the water table if the soil in the root zone is at field capacity. It is therefore possible to determine whether percolation will take place (or whether it has taken place) by knowing the relation between precipitation, actual and potential evapo-transpiration, and antecedent soil-moisture conditions. This relation, which is generally presented in the form of a soil-moisture budget, can be calculated from meteorological records.

There are several techniques for calculating soil-moisture budgets. The technique used for this paper is the Thornthwaite method of calculating potential evapo-transpiration (Thornthwaite 1948), plus the modulated moisture budget technique devised by Holmes and Robertson (1959). This method, which gives average monthly statements of the moisture budget, takes into account the soil texture, expansion of the roots during the growing season, and the fact that evapo-transpiration withdraws moisture from the root zone at decreasing rates with increasing moisture stress.

Table II presents average monthly moisture *deficits* for 14 stations in the Assiniboine River drainage basin, together with the frequencies at which deficits occurred during the six-monthly periods, April to October, of each year between 1944 and 1960. Of course, even if a certain month is characterized by a moisture deficit during 15 out of 17 years (88 per cent of the time), it does not follow that there was a moisture surplus during the other two years. This becomes apparent when the figures in Table II are compared with those in Table III, which shows the magnitude and frequency of monthly moisture surpluses throughout the Assiniboine basin. Table III indicates that in the Assiniboine basin as a whole, a monthly moisture surplus occurs less than 50 per cent of the time in April, 12 per cent of the time in May, 17 per cent of the time in June, and never or only sporadically during any other month. (In many instances a surplus may occur already in March, but such surpluses have been disregarded as they are more likely to contribute to surface run-off than to groundwater replenishment.) Table III does substantiate Staple's opinion that groundwater recharge on the Prairies is small, but one may not conclude that it is unusual.

Column 3 of this table shows the total average surplus from April to October, all of which was *potential* groundwater replenishment. Column 4 shows the same amount as a percentage of the average total

TABLE II

AVERAGE MONTHLY SOIL-MOISTURE DEFICIT (IN.) FOR THE PERIOD 1944–60, CALCULATED FROM YEAR TO YEAR ACCORDING TO THE MODULATED SOIL-MOISTURE BUDGET TECHNIQUE OF HOLMES AND ROBERTSON (1959), FOR 14 STATIONS IN THE ASSINIBOINE RIVER DRAINAGE BASIN

	April*		May		June		July		August		September		October	
	1	2	1	2	1	2	1	2	1	2	1	2	1	2
Saskatchewan:														
Carlyle	0.10	50	0.73	75	0.85	65	1.24	83	1.41	88	1.20	83	0.36	59
Davidson	0.19	44	0.45	88	0.72	81	1.92	100	2.39	94	0.97	81	0.48	75
Estevan	0.05	50	0.45	88	0.59	59	1.75	100	2.09	100	1.30	82	0.41	50
Indian Head	0.03	35	0.33	88	0.40	76	1.58	94	1.72	94	1.04	82	0.39	59
Kamsack	0.06	41	0.26	94	0.88	71	1.63	94	1.54	94	0.90	82	0.33	64
Moose Jaw	0.18	41	0.60	76	0.82	76	1.73	100	2.07	88	1.11	76	0.53	76
Moosomin	0.03	35	0.35	82	0.52	59	1.02	76	1.32	88	1.01	88	0.40	64
Regina (A)	0.15	35	0.42	59	0.55	52	1.34	82	1.81	94	1.02	82	0.48	52
Yorkton	0.02	28	0.19	88	0.86	71	1.35	82	1.59	100	0.85	76	0.31	59
Manitoba:														
Boissevain	0.02	35	0.24	71	0.36	64	1.09	94	1.25	82	1.16	88	0.44	64
Brandon	0.04	28	0.29	71	0.54	52	1.48	88	1.45	88	1.09	88	0.26	64
Melita	0.01	31	0.32	69	0.40	62	1.34	94	1.36	82	0.95	88	0.27	50
Portage la Prairie	0.15	40	0.36	76	0.54	76	1.24	88	1.30	82	0.69	71	0.22	52
Rivers (A)	0.09	28	0.29	88	0.65	64	1.40	94	1.86	94	0.88	71	0.27	59

**Explanation of columns:*

1. Average monthly moisture deficit (in.) for the period 1944–60.
2. Percentage of years during the period 1944–60 in which moisture deficit occurred during the month indicated.

TABLE III

AVERAGE MONTHLY SOIL-MOISTURE SURPLUS (IN.) FOR THE PERIOD 1944–60, CALCULATED FROM YEAR TO YEAR ACCORDING TO THE MODULATED SOIL-MOISTURE BUDGET TECHNIQUE OF HOLMES AND ROBERTSON (1959), FOR 14 SELECTED STATIONS IN THE ASSINIBOINE RIVER DRAINAGE BASIN

	April*		May		June		July		August		September		October		Period	
	1	2	1	2	1	2	1	2	1	2	1	2	1	2	3	4
Saskatchewan:																
Carlyle	0.23	41	0.10	12	0.42	29	0.08	6	—	—	—	—	—	—	0.83	5
Davidson	0.24	24	0.03	6	—	—	—	—	0.04	6	0.02	6	—	—	0.33	2
Estevan	0.25	36	0.20	12	0.14	18	—	—	—	—	—	—	—	—	0.89	5
Indian Head	0.32	53	0.05	12	0.26	18	—	—	—	—	0.04	6	—	—	0.67	4
Kamsack	0.24	29	—	—	0.11	12	—	—	—	—	—	—	—	—	0.35	2
Moose Jaw	0.09	12	—	—	—	—	—	—	—	—	—	—	—	—	0.09	0.5
Moosomin	0.45	48	0.16	18	0.79	24	0.09	6	—	—	—	—	—	—	1.49	7.5
Regina (A)	0.28	36	0.09	18	—	—	—	—	—	—	—	—	—	—	0.37	2
Yorkton	0.47	60	0.07	6	0.19	12	0.09	6	—	—	—	—	—	—	0.82	5
Manitoba:																
Boissevain	0.24	48	0.28	29	0.71	36	—	—	0.11	6	—	—	0.12	6	1.46	7
Brandon	0.54	50	0.17	18	0.46	24	—	—	—	—	—	—	0.26	6	1.43	7
Melita	0.52	65	0.05	12	0.78	24	—	—	0.04	6	—	—	0.11	6	1.50	7
Portage la Prairie	0.19	18	0.14	6	0.18	6	—	—	—	—	—	—	—	—	0.51	3
Rivers (A)	0.44	54	0.10	12	0.35	29	0.06	6	—	—	0.04	6	—	—	0.99	5

**Explanation of columns:*

1. Average monthly moisture surplus (in.) for the period 1944–60.
2. Percentage of years during the period 1944–60 in which moisture surplus occurred during the month indicated.
3. Total average moisture surplus from April to October (in.).
4. Total average moisture surplus from April to October expressed as percentage of average total annual precipitation 1944–60.

annual precipitation from 1944 to 1960. The average moisture surplus for Davidson (Arm River basin) is strikingly close to the estimates of annual recharge in the Arm River basin, reported elsewhere in this paper.

If the 17 years of records are at all representative for the average conditions in the Assiniboine River drainage basin, it may be said that moisture budgets indicate that the average potential annual groundwater replenishment in this basin varies from 0.09 inch in southwestern Saskatchewan to 1.50 inches in southern Manitoba. Or, in other terms, the potential annual recharge in this area lies between 0.5 and 7.5 per cent of the average total annual precipitation.

GROUNDWATER RECHARGE INFERRED FROM ANNUAL WATER-TABLE FLUCTUATIONS

Recharge or Schneider's Frost Effect?

It can be seen from the soil-moisture budgets that groundwater recharge is most likely to occur in April and May. We may therefore expect a rise of the water table during that period. Typical water-table hydrographs from the Prairies indeed show an abrupt rise in the spring, reaching a maximum during late April or early May and followed by a steady decline throughout the ensuing summer, fall, and winter (Figs. 6 and 7). In areas with a water table at less than 10 feet below surface, the amplitude of the annual fluctuation varies from 2 to 8 feet.

However, not all of the typical spring rise can be attributed to recharge in the sense that it represents the addition of "new" moisture to the groundwater reserves. All or some of it may be caused by moisture that returns to the saturated zone after having been part of the frost wedge in the unsaturated zone.

Schneider (1961) correlated mean daily air temperatures with water-table fluctuations, and concluded that the winter decline of the water table is partly caused by upward-moving moisture resulting in accretion of the frost layer from below. When the air temperature rises above freezing, the water table begins to rise as a result of downward percolation of meltwater from the bottom of the frost wedge. Willis *et al.* (1964) showed that the decline of the water table in prairie soils is accompanied by increases in soil-moisture content above the water table. They substantiated Schneider's opinion that moisture movement from the water table—either as vapour or as liquid flow—

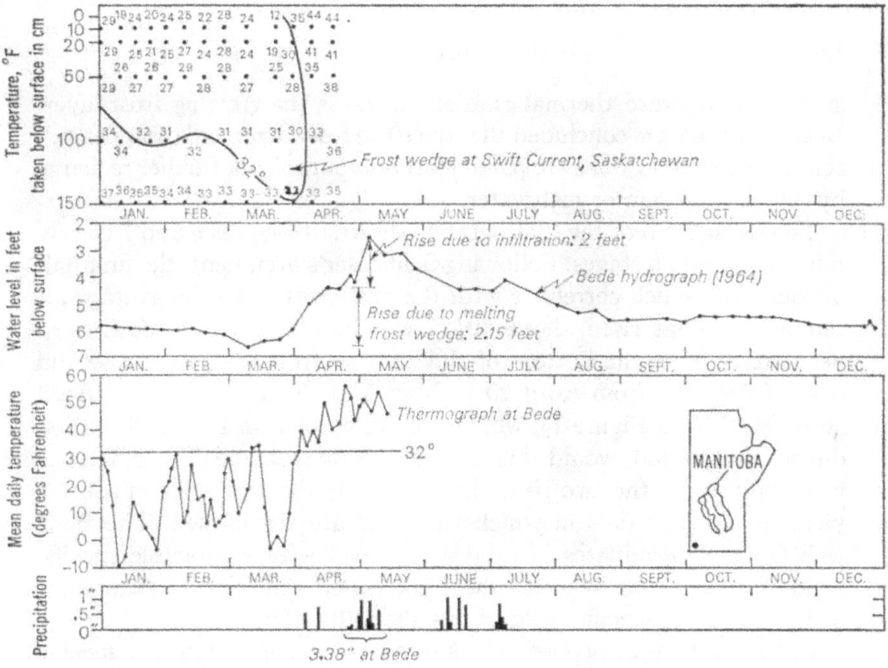

Figure 6. Annual water-table hydrograph at Bede, Manitoba (Bede #1, NW ¼ Sec. 18–5–26, W 1st Mer.) together with measurements of temperature and precipitation at Bede. The soil temperatures from Swift Current, Saskatchewan, illustrate the growth and disappearance of a frost wedge in prairie soil. (Hydrograph courtesy Manitoba Department of Agriculture and Conservation, Water Control and Conservation Branch.)

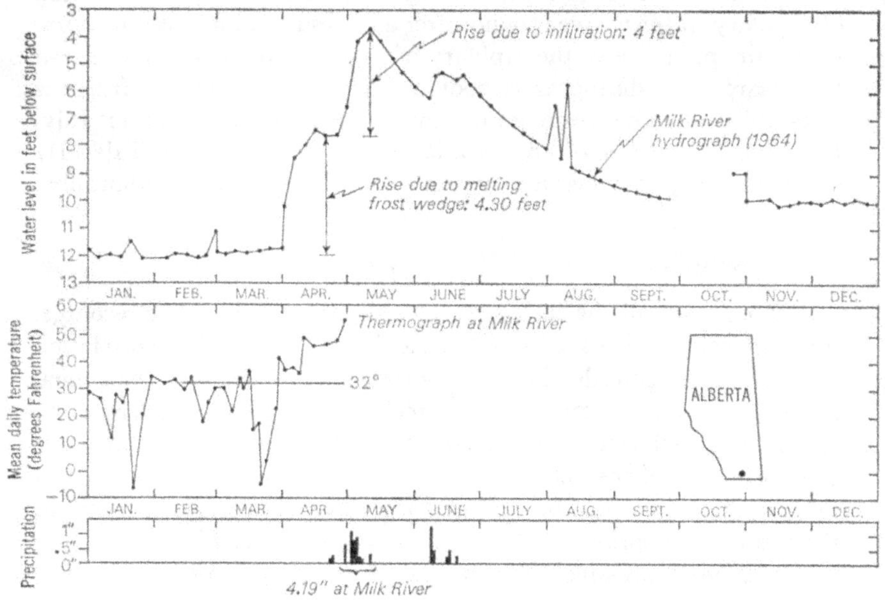

Figure 7. Annual water-table hydrograph at Milk River, Alberta (Sec. 24–2–15, W 4th Mer.), together with measurements of temperature and precipitation at Milk River. (Hydrograph courtesy of Research Council of Alberta, Groundwater Division.)

is along an upward thermal gradient towards the growing frost layer. Both investigators concluded that once the frost layer had disappeared, soil-moisture conditions are particularly favourable for further recharge by percolating rain or meltwater.

The rising limb of the hydrographs shown in Figures 6 and 7 clearly reflects these two stages. Following Schneider's argument, the first half of each rise, which correlates with the first days when the average air temperature has risen above 32° F, can be attributed to downward percolation from the bottom of the melting frost wedge. The second part of the rise (from April 20 to May 5 in Figure 6 and from April 20 to May 10 in Figure 7), which is correlative with the precipitation during that period, would thus represent true recharge. The difference in magnitude of the two rising limbs reflects the difference in specific yield of the materials in which the wells are terminated. The Bede well (Fig. 6) terminates in sand and gravel with a probable specific yield of 20 per cent, whereas the Milk River well (Fig. 7) terminates in till, having a specific yield of less than 10 per cent.

In the absence of precise values of evapo-transpiration and specific yield, it is impossible to calculate the exact amounts of recharge from the graphs shown in Figures 6 and 7. The graphs demonstrate, however, that recharge did take place. The Milk River graph shows some further recharge in June and possibly in October. The sharp peaks in August are probably Lisse effects which are produced by a sudden transition of capillary water to free groundwater as a result of increased pressure in the air spaces above the capillary fringe. Such peaks are not related to recharge and disappear as soon as the original capillary fringe is re-established. The Bede graph shows a secondary peak in July, following 1.73 inches of precipitation early in that month. Table III shows that a July moisture surplus is rare in this part of Manitoba.

Konoplyantsev's Rule

Although not all the spring rise can be attributed to true recharge, some investigators have found a significant geographic correlation between the magnitude of the spring rise, the magnitude of the annual fluctuation, and the total annual precipitation. Konoplyantsev *et al.* (1963) analysed records of 9,000 observation wells throughout the European part of the U.S.S.R., and concluded that the annual water-table fluctuations could be classified according to one simple criterion: the ratio of the spring rise to the annual amplitude. They found that in the "zone of excessive precipitation" the ratio is always about unity.

In the zone of moderate precipitation the ratio was found to lie between 0.85 and 0.70, whereas in the zone of poor precipitation it was found to vary from 0.5 to 0.1. With regard to the magnitude of the annual amplitude, they found for the three precipitation zones the following ranges: 3 to 6 feet, 5.4 to 7.5 feet, and 2.1 to 2.7 feet, respectively.

There is insufficient information to determine the applicability of Konoplyantsev's rule to the Canadian prairies, and the following data are simply presented against the background of his findings. The ratio of spring rise to annual fluctuation for the 1964 records from Alberta and Manitoba[3] lies between 0.75 and 1.00. For the two hydrographs shown in Figures 6 and 7, the ratios are respectively 1.00 and 0.97. On the 1964 records, the average spring rise amounted to 4.00 feet in Manitoba and 5.25 feet in Alberta. The annual amplitude in Manitoba varied from 2.70 to 5.25 feet during 1964, and in Alberta it ranged from 1.61 feet to 8.40 feet.

The magnitude of the annual fluctuation is not only a function of the thickness of the frost wedge and the amount of actual recharge, but also of the place of the observation well in the flow system. This was first noticed by Rasmussen and Andreasen (1959), who commented that the greater water-level fluctuations occur in the upper reaches of a drainage basin, and the smallest fluctuations near the basin outlet.

More information regarding annual water-table fluctuations is available for the prairie regions just south of the international boundary: in North Dakota, South Dakota, and Montana (Hacket 1960, 1964). A summary of the water-table fluctuations in those states is given in Table IV.

TABLE IV

STATISTICS PERTAINING TO THE ANNUAL WATER-TABLE FLUCTUATIONS IN THE AMERICAN STATES OF NORTH DAKOTA, SOUTH DAKOTA, AND MONTANA (FROM DATA BY HACKET 1960, 1964)

State	Period of record	Av. spring rise (ft)	Av. annual ampl. (ft)	Mean ratio spring/year	Max. rise during period	Min. rise during period
North Dakota	1957–61	2.75	3.58	0.78	6.40	0.33
South Dakota	1957–61	2.69	3.16	0.85	10.62	0.00
Montana	1956–60	2.53	3.19	0.74	5.65	0.14

[3]Four Alberta water-table hydrographs were kindly supplied by the Groundwater Division of the Research Council of Alberta. Ten Manitoba records were obtained through courtesy of the Manitoba Department of Agriculture and Conservation, Water Control and Conservation Branch, at Winnipeg.

CONCLUSION

The foregoing discussion presents multiple evidence that groundwater on the Prairies is indeed a renewable resource. The estimates of groundwater recharge, expressed as a percentage of the total annual precipitation, vary from less than 1 per cent to 7.5 per cent, depending on the method used and the location of the area. In absolute values the estimates range from 0.09 to 1.50 inches per year.

REFERENCES

CANADA DEPARTMENT OF TRANSPORT, METEOROLOGICAL BRANCH, Monthly Record of Meteorological Observations in Canada, 1944–60.

CHRISTIANSEN, E. A. (1956), *Glacial Geology of the Moose Mountain Area of Saskatchewan*, Sask. Dept. Mineral Resources, Rept. 21.

——— (1961), *Geology and Groundwater Resources of the Regina Area of Saskatchewan*, Sask. Research Council, Geol. Div. Rept. No. 2.

ERNST, L. F. (1962), *Groundwater Flow in the Saturated Zone and Its Calculation When Horizontal Parallel Open Conduits Are Present* (Wageningen, Holland: Centrum voor Landbouwpublicaties and Landbouwdocumentatie).

——— (1963), "De berekening van grondwaterstromingen tussen evenwijdige open leidingen," *Committee for Hydrological Research T.N.O., Proceedings of the 17th Technical Meeting* (The Hague: State Printing Office), pp. 48–69.

FREEZE, R. A. (1966), "Theoretical Analysis of Regional Groundwater Flow," Ph.D. thesis, University of California, Berkeley.

HACKET, O. M. (1960), *Groundwater Levels in the United States 1956–60, Northwestern States*, U.S. Geol. Survey, Water Supply Paper 1760.

——— (1964), *Groundwater Levels in the United States*, U.S. Geol. Survey, Water Supply Paper 1781.

HOLMES, R. M. and ROBERTSON, G. W. (1959), "A Modulated Soil-Moisture Budget," *Monthly Weather Rev. 87*: 1–7.

KONOPLYANTSEV, A. A., KOVALEVSKY, V. S., and SEMENOV, S. M. (1963), *Regional Regularities of the Natural Regime of Unconfined Groundwaters in the Territory of the European Part of the U.S.S.R.*, International Assoc. Sci. Hydrology, Berkeley Assembly, Publ. No. 64, pp. 384–390.

MEINZER, O. E. (1923), *Outline of Groundwater Hydrology*, U.S. Geol. Survey, Water Supply Paper 494.

MEYBOOM, P. (1962), "Patterns of Groundwater Flow in the Prairie Profile," *Proc. Third Canadian Hydrology Symposium* (Natl. Res. Council of Canada), pp. 5–33.

——— (1966), "Unsteady Groundwater Flow near a Willow Ring in Hummocky Moraine," *J. Hydrol. 4*: 38–62.

——— (1967), *Groundwater Studies in the Assiniboine River Drainage Basin, Part II: Hydrologic Characteristics of Phreatophytic Vegetation in South-Central Saskatchewan*, Geol. Survey Canada, Bull. 139, Part II.

MEYBOOM, P., VAN EVERDINGEN, R. O., and FREEZE, R. A. (1966), *Patterns of Groundwater Flow in Seven Discharge Areas in Saskatchewan and Manitoba*, Geol. Survey Canada, Bull. 147.

MOLLARD, J. D. (1965), "A Reconnaissance Appraisal of Groundwater Potential and Development in Saskatchewan, Canada," *Groundwater*, *3*: 5–11.

RASMUSSEN, W. C. and ANDREASEN, G. E. (1959), *Hydrologic Budget of the Beaverdam Creek Basin, Maryland*, U.S. Geol. Survey, Water Supply Paper 1472.

SCHNEIDER, R. (1961), *Correlation of Groundwater Levels and Air Temperatures in the Winter and Spring in Minnesota*, U.S. Geol. Survey, Water Supply Paper 1539–D.

STAPLE, W. J., LEHANE, J. J., and WENHARDT, A. (1960), "Conservation of Soil Moisture from Fall and Winter Precipitation," *Can. J. Soil Sci. 40*: 80–88.

THOMAS, H. E. and LEOPOLD, L. B. (1964), "Groundwater in North America," *Science*, *143*, No. 3610: 1001–6.

THORNTHWAITE, C. W. (1948), "An Approach toward a Rational Classification of Climate," *Geograph. Rev.* Jan. 1948: 55–95.

TODD, D. K. (1959), *Groundwater Hydrology*. (New York: John Wiley & Sons Inc.).

TÓTH, J. (1962), "A Theoretical Analysis of Groundwater Flow in Small Drainage Basins," *Proc. Third Canadian Hydrology Symposium* (Natl. Res. Council of Canada), pp. 75–106.

VAN EVERDINGEN, R. O. (1963), *Groundwater Flow-Diagrams in Sections with Exaggerated Vertical Scale*, Geol. Survey Canada, Paper 63–27.

WAGGONER, P. E. and HEWLETT, J. D. (1965), "Test of a Transpiration Inhibitor on a Forested Watershed," *Water Resources Res. 1*: 391–7.

WAGGONER, P. E. and ZELITCH, J. (1965), "Transpiration and Stomata of Leaves," *Science*, *150*, No. 3702: 1413–20.

WHITE, W. N. (1932), *Method of Estimating Groundwater Supplies Based on Discharge by Plants and Evaporation from Soil. Results of Investigations in Escalante Valley*, U.S. Geol. Survey, Water Supply Paper 659–A.

WILLIS, W. O., PARKINSON, H. L., CARLSON, C. W., and HAAS, H. J. (1964), "Water Table Changes and Soil Moisture Loss under Frozen Conditions," *Soil Sci. 98*: 244–8.

WOLBEER, J. J. and HUSBAND, W. H. W. (1964), "Saskatchewan Studies of Small Watersheds," *Proc. Fourth Canadian Hydrology Symposium* (Natl. Res. Council of Canada), pp. 133–46.

THE REVERSE OSMOSIS MEMBRANE SEPARATION PROCESS AND ITS APPLICATION FOR WATER PURIFICATION*

S. Sourirajan

THE "REVERSE OSMOSIS PROCESS" is a simple technique for the separation of substances in fluid solutions. It consists in letting the fluid mixture flow under pressure through an appropriate porous membrane. The membrane-permeated fluid is enriched in one or more constituents of the mixture. No heating of the membrane and no phase-change in product recovery are involved in this separation process.

This process is an exciting new development in the field of solute–solvent separation in general, and water purification in particular. It is at a very early stage of development, the basic principles involved are still controversial, and no currently available theory on the mechanism of the process is beyond question. However, whatever is known about the process is useful, and what is yet to be known appears full of promise. The object of this paper is to review briefly some of the fundamental aspects of this separation process and to illustrate its possible application for water purification and water pollution control.

THE PREFERENTIAL SORPTION–CAPILLARY FLOW MECHANISM

The Gibbs adsorption theorem expressed in the form

(1)†
$$\Gamma = -\frac{1}{RT}\left[\frac{\partial\sigma}{\partial(\ln a)}\right]$$

predicts the existence of a monomolecular layer of fresh water at the

*National Research Council of Canada Contribution No. 9731.

†For nomenclature used in this and subsequent equations, see the section at the end of the paper.

air–solution interface for aqueous sodium chloride solutions [3, 5, 8, 16].* Yuster [31] first suggested the possibility of developing a practical desalination process based on the concept of skimming this surface layer of fresh water. Obviously, the problems involved in trying to skim a monomolecular layer of fresh water are formidable. But it is clear from the Gibbs equation that the thickness of the freshwater layer is a function of the nature of the interface. If the latter is such that there exists at the interface a multimolecular layer of fresh water, then, from an engineering standpoint, the situation would seem different.

The above considerations led to the conceptual model given in Figure 1 for recovering fresh water from aqueous salt solution [21, 32].

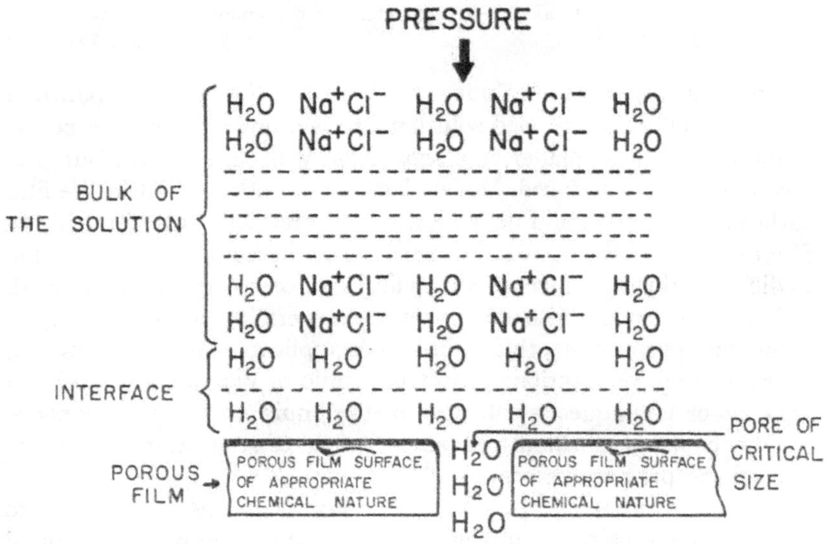

FIGURE 1. Schematic representation of the preferential sorption capillary flow mechanism.

Here, the solution is not in contact with air, but with a solid material in the form of a porous membrane. If only the surface of the porous membrane in contact with the solution is of such chemical nature that it has a preferential sorption for water or preferential repulsion for the solute, then a multimolecular layer of preferentially sorbed fresh water could exist at the membrane–solution interface. A continuous removal of this interfacial water can then be effected by letting it flow under pressure through the membrane capillaries.

*Numbers in brackets refer to the list of references.

The above model also gives rise to the concept of a critical pore diameter for maximum separation and permeability, which is twice the thickness of the interfacial pure water layer (Fig. 2). If the pore

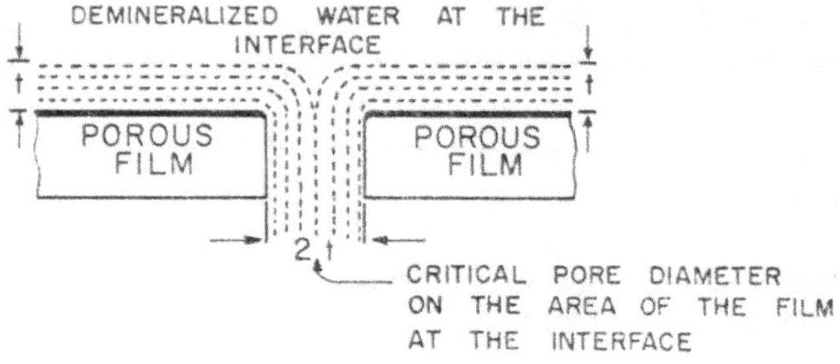

FIGURE 2. Critical pore diameter for maximum separation and permeability.

diameter is larger, permeability will be higher but solute separation will be lower, since the feed solution also will flow through the pores; if the diameter is smaller, the separation will be maximal, but permeability will be reduced. When there are no pores at all in the film surface, then there could be no flow of the interfacial fluid through the film material by the above mechanism, and the fluid permeability due to diffusion through the non-porous film surface can only be very small.

The above model also illustrates the generality of this separation technique. In principle, this technique is applicable for the separation, concentration, or fractionation of inorganic or organic substances in aqueous or non-aqueous solutions in the liquid or the gaseous state, and hence it opens a new and versatile field of separation technology in chemical process engineering [24].

The preferential sorption–capillary flow mechanism gives rise to two basic characteristics of this separation process in its most general application: (i) with respect to a given solution containing components A and B, the membrane-permeated product can be enriched either in A or in B, depending upon the chemical nature of the membrane surface in contact with the solution; and (ii) with respect to a given membrane–solution system, wherein the membrane surface has a preferential sorption for the solvent, practically any degree of solute separation is possible depending on the porous structure of the membrane and other operating conditions. These two characteristics are borne out experimentally [21–29]. For example, using *n*-heptane–ethyl alcohol mixture as the feed solution, the membrane-permeated product shows alcohol enrichment for cellulose acetate films, and *n*-heptane enrichment for polyethylene films. Also, using cellulose acetate films of different porosities, a wide range of solute separations has been obtained for a given feed solution system [24]. The former result is particularly interesting, since it shows that this process is not simple ultrafiltration.

From an industrial standpoint, the application of the reverse osmosis technique to a given separation problem essentially entails choosing the appropriate chemical nature of the film surface, and developing methods for making films containing the largest number of pores of the required size on the area of the film at the interface. This approach formed the basis of the successful development of a porous film of industrial significance for saline water conversion.

The first step in the practical development of the reverse osmosis process for saline water conversion was the discovery, made independently by Breton [1] and Sourirajan [32], that cellulose acetate had a preferential sorption for water from aqueous salt solutions. The second step was the joint development by Loeb and Sourirajan [12–14, 30] of a method for making porous cellulose acetate membranes capable of giving both high flow rates and high degrees of demineralization of aqueous sodium chloride solutions. The latter accomplishment has led to the current world-wide interest in this separation process.

Porous Cellulose Acetate Membrane Technology

The Loeb–Sourirajan technique for making cellulose acetate desalination membranes is essentially as follows [12–14, 30].

The film-casting solution contains cellulose acetate dissolved in acetone, to which is added a water-soluble additive that does not adversely affect the solubility of cellulose acetate in acetone. While all the necessary and sufficient requirements for the choice of a successful additive are not yet known, several electrolyte and non-electrolyte substances have been effectively employed as additives [11, 15]. In their original development, Loeb and Sourirajan used an aqueous solution of magnesium perchlorate as the additive.

Using the above casting solution, the membrane is cast on a glass plate having 0.01-inch side runners. In the original development this casting operation was done at $-5°$ to $-10°$ C. The solvent is then allowed to evaporate in air from the surface of the membrane at the casting temperature for a definite time—3 to 4 minutes for films cast at $-10°$ C. The membrane–plate assembly is then immersed in ice-cold water for at least an hour while gelation occurs, and the additive is leached out, yielding a tough, solid porous film on the plate.

The membrane is then peeled off from the glass plate and stored under water at all times. The surface of the film, which was away from that of the glass plate and exposed to air during casting, is always held in contact with the feed solution during desalination experiments. Each film is subjected to a temperature and pressure treatment before testing it for its desalination characteristics. The temperature treatment consists in heating the film gradually in water from the laboratory temperature to the required temperature, where it is kept for about 10 minutes and subsequently cooled rapidly. The pressure treatment consists in pumping distilled water for at least an hour over the surface of the film mounted in the desalination cell, at a pressure about 15 per cent higher than the maximum intended operating pressure.

The above casting technique yields porous cellulose acetate films of total thickness about 0.003 to 0.004 inch. They have a relatively very dense microporous structure on an extremely thin layer of the film surface which was exposed to air during casting; the remainder of the film material, underneath this thin surface layer, is a spongy porous mass containing comparatively large pores. The electron micrograph studies of Riley, Gardner, and Merten [19] show that the thickness of the dense surface layer is only about 0.25 micron. It is the microporous structure of the dense surface layer that is significant for desalination and causes the major resistance to fluid flow through the membrane.

The temperature and pressure treatments of the film change its porous structure. The temperature treatment shrinks the film and reduces the size of the micropores, while the surface layer also becomes denser. The pressure treatment stabilizes the porous structure of the film, including that of the dense surface. The combined result of the temperature and pressure treatments is a dense and stable microporous surface structure, which maintains the separation characteristics of the film for several months under the normal laboratory operations. If the film is allowed to get dry at any time, its porous structure changes, affecting its desalination characteristics adversely.

CA-NRC-18 Type Films

Depending upon the exact composition of the film-casting solution and other casting conditions, several types of porous cellulose acetate desalination membranes can be made, differing in their porous structure and hence in their relative separation and permeability characteristics. Unless otherwise stated, the experimental results presented in this paper were obtained using a particular type of membranes designated earlier [28] as CA-NRC-18 type films. These films were made in the laboratory by the general Loeb–Sourirajan technique, using the following composition (weight per cent) for the film-casting solution: acetone, 68.0; cellulose acetate (acetyl content = 39.8%), 17.0; water, 13.5; and magnesium perchlorate, 1.5. The film-casting conditions were: casting temperature, −10° C; time interval between casting and immersion in ice-cold water, 4 minutes; duration for film setting in cold water, about 1 to 2 hours; and total film thickness, about 0.004 inch.

Apparatus and Experimental Details

The apparatus and the experimental procedure employed in the laboratory investigations of this separation process have been reported [23]. The desalting cell, shown in Figure 3, is simple in design and

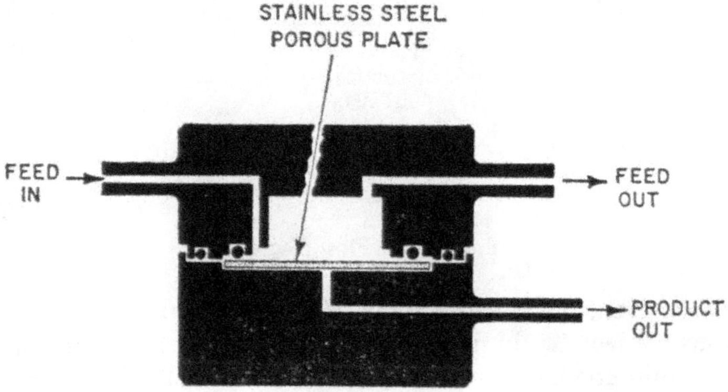

FIGURE 3. Cell.

construction. It is made of Type 310 stainless steel and consists of two detachable parts. The upper part is a high-pressure chamber through which flows the feed solution under pressure. The lower part is the membrane stand through which the desalted water leaves. The wet preshrunk membrane is mounted on a stainless steel porous plate embedded in the lower part of the cell. Between the membrane and the porous plate is placed a wet Whatman filter paper which protects the membrane from abrasion and also aids the flow of the desalted water through the porous plate. The porous plate and the Whatman filter paper offer practically no resistance to liquid flow under operating conditions. The upper and lower parts of the cell are set in proper alignment with rubber O-ring contacts between the high-pressure chamber and the wet membrane. A pressure-tight joint is obtained by clamping the cell tightly between two thick plates. The effective area of the membrane in the cell is 7.6 sq. cm. All the data presented in this paper relate to this area and to 25° C unless otherwise specified.

A flow diagram of the experimental set-up is shown in Figure 4.

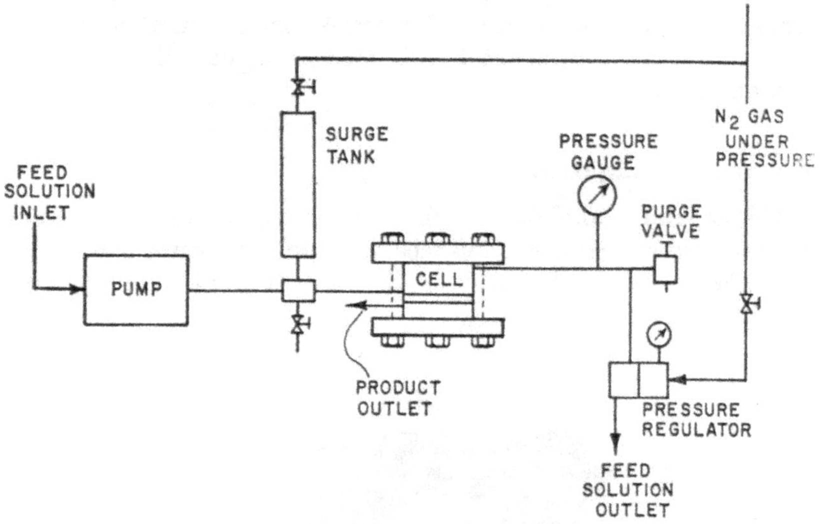

FIGURE 4. Flow diagram.

A motor-driven, controlled-volume, Milton Roy duplex pump is used to pump the feed liquid under pressure through the system. All parts of the pump coming into contact with the feed liquid are made of either Hastalloy or stainless steel. The surge tank is a stainless steel high-pressure cylinder used to minimize the pressure fluctuations in the cell. Under the operating conditions, the fluid pressure in the cell is indicated by a liquid-sealed Ashcroft pressure gauge. The purge valve is used to drain the system when necessary. A stainless steel Grove pressure regulator is used to maintain a constant operating pressure in the cell. Nitrogen gas under pressure from commercial gas cylinders is used to load the dome of the Grove regulator. Monel metal high-pressure tubings and HIP high-pressure fittings made of Type 316 stainless steel are used throughout the system.

The experiments are usually carried out at laboratory temperature under conditions of single-pass flow. Several solutions of different substances may be studied in conjunction with several membranes of different pore structures. In each experiment, the pure water permeability, [PWP], the mole per cent salt removed, and the product rate, [PR], are determined at the pre-set operating conditions. The relative concentrations of the solute in the feed and product solutions are determined either gravimetrically or by refractive index measurements using a Bausch and Lomb precision refractometer, or by specific resistance measurements using a conductivity bridge. Here the terms "product" and "product rate" refer to the membrane-permeated solution.

Effect of Shrinkage Temperature on Membrane Performance

At present no definite statements can be made on the size, number, and distribution of pores on the surface of any particular film having desalination properties, nor can they be predicted for a given separation and permeability level. A film is hence best described in terms of its separation, product rate, and pure water permeability data for a given feed solution (reference system) at a specified set of operating conditions. Without prior temperature treatment, the CA-NRC-18 type films have high pure water permeabilities ($>$250 gallons per day per sq. ft of membrane surface at 1,500 psig), but very little desalination characteristics for $0.5M$ [NaCl–H_2O] feed solution. The preshrunk films give higher desalting and, of course, lower product rates. By varying the temperature and time of hot-water treatment, different levels of solute separation are obtainable depending on the initial porous structure of the film surface. Figure 5 illustrates the variation of the separation and permeability characteristics of a number of laboratory-made films as a function of shrinkage temperature.

Basic Questions

From a practical standpoint the above experimental results are interesting enough. However, there are three basic questions in relation to the full scientific and industrial development of this separation process: (i) What are the precise physico-chemical criteria of preferential sorption or preferential repulsion? (ii) What is the mechanism of pore formation in the process of casting high-flow porous membranes? (iii) What are the factors governing flow of fluids through porous membranes having separation characteristics?

No unequivocal answer to any of these questions can be given at this time. As more experimental data become available the answers

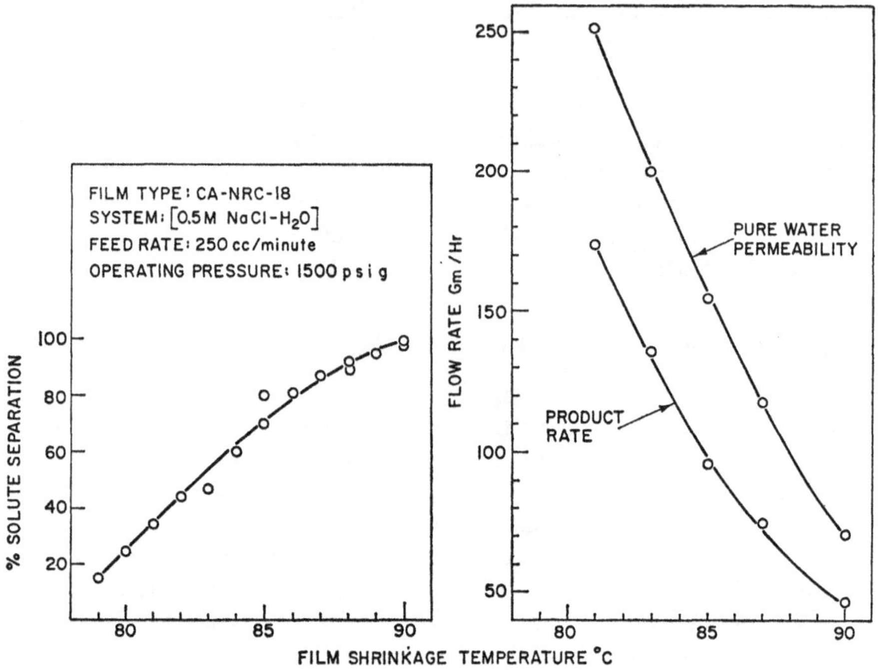

FIGURE 5. Effect of shrinkage temperature on the separation and permeability characteristics of porous cellulose acetate membranes; data of Sourirajan and Govindan [28].

may be expected to unfold. However, it is obvious that interfacial forces, such as London dispersion forces, dipole–dipole interactions, and hydrogen bonding, are of importance in connection with the first question. The details of the film-casting conditions are obviously of critical importance for producing films capable of giving both high separation and high permeability. Further developments in porous membrane technology can lead to the production of films capable of giving at least a 10-fold increase in product rates at any given level of solute separation and set of operating conditions, compared to those obtained with the best present-day films.

The third question is of fundamental importance in engineering. It is concerned ultimately with the problem of predicting the separation and permeability characteristics of a given membrane for various solution systems and operating conditions from a minimum number of experimental results. The following is a summary of some of the useful relations and concepts developed in this laboratory in relation to this question [4, 7, 28].

CAPILLARY FLOW, EFFECTIVE PRESSURE, OSMOTIC PRESSURE, AND MAXIMUM SEPARATION

The effective driving pressure (ΔP) for the capillary flow of the preferentially sorbed fluid and that of the feed solution through the pores of the membrane surface may be given by the relation

$$\Delta P = P - \Delta\pi \tag{2}$$

where

$$\Delta\pi = \pi_F - \pi_P; \tag{3}$$

π_F is the osmotic pressure of the concentrated membrane boundary layer solution and π_P is that of the product solution. As the feed rate on the membrane surface approaches infinity, π_F approaches the osmotic pressure of the feed solution. In the following discussions and calculations, unless otherwise stated, π_F is approximated to the osmotic pressure of the feed solution.

Equation (2) is general in its application and accounts for the name "reverse osmosis" for this separation process. It is valid for all levels of solute separation. When there is no solute separation,

$$\Delta\pi = 0 \quad \text{and} \quad \Delta P = P \tag{4}$$

and when there is 100 per cent solute separation,

$$\Delta\pi = \pi_F \quad \text{and} \quad \Delta P = P - \pi_F. \tag{5}$$

For a given membrane–solution system, the actual level of solute separation is determined by the relative amounts of the preferentially sorbed fluid and the feed solution permeating through the membrane under the driving pressure ΔP. Further, some degree of solute separation is possible under any operating pressure which establishes flow of the fluid through the membrane, provided of course that the membrane surface has a preferential sorption for the solvent material.

While equation (2) is true whatever be the value of the osmotic pressure of the feed solution, it says nothing about the separation characteristics of any membrane. In other words, whether actual solute separation is possible does not depend on the osmotic pressure of the feed solution, but on the nature of the membrane.

When $P < \pi_F$, equation (2) gives also the maximum possible solute separation, whatever the membrane used, under which condition

$$\Delta\pi = P \quad \text{and} \quad \Delta P = 0. \tag{6}$$

Based on equation (6), Table I gives the maximum solute separation possible for the system [NaCl–H_2O] at different operating pressures and feed solution concentrations. The data illustrate the thermodynamic significance of osmotic pressure as applied to this separation process.

Flow of Fluids through Porous Membranes Having Separation Characteristics

At least two factors govern fluid flow through porous membranes having separation characteristics: (i) the size of the pores on the membrane surface is only a few times larger than the size of the permeating molecules, and (ii) the interfacial forces are important enough to cause solute separation. Under such conditions, the simple Poiseuille equation for fluid flow cannot apply, and it is hence insufficient to predict solute separation and product rate. One can, however, study the experimental separation and product rate data from the point of view of the deviation from Poiseuille flow. Such a study may lead to an understanding of the separation effect on flow. Another approach is to consider that, under the conditions of the experiment, water (or solvent) transport through the membrane is proportional to the effective pressure, and solute transport is due to pore diffusion through membrane capillaries; the proportionality constant used in the water transport equation is obtained from the pure water permeability data. The latter approach leads to results of practical interest in predicting membrane performance. Whatever method of analysis is used, in order for it to be valid, it must be applicable to the entire 0 to 100 per cent range of solute separation. Further, it is the intermediate range of separation which offers the real testing ground for any hypothesis concerning the transport of materials through porous membranes having separation characteristics. The transport equations given below have been tested and found valid for a wide range of solute separations.

Predictability of Product Rates for Related Solution Systems

At high feed-flow rates, the product rates obtained through a particular membrane for any two feed-solution systems may be given by the relations

$$[PR]_1 = \bar{K}(f_c)_1(f_P)_1\,\Delta P_1\,\rho_1/\mu_1, \tag{7}$$

$$[PR]_2 = \bar{K}(f_c)_2(f_P)_2\,\Delta P_2\,\rho_2/\mu_2, \tag{8}$$

TABLE I

MAXIMUM SOLUTE SEPARATION POSSIBLE FOR THE SYSTEM [NaCl–H_2O] AT DIFFERENT OPERATING PRESSURES AND FEED SOLUTION CONCENTRATIONS; DATA OF SOURIRAJAN AND GOVINDAN [28]

Feed solution concentration		Osmotic pressure	Maximum solute separation possible at the operating pressure (psig)				
Molality	Wt. %	(psi at 25° C)	125	250	500	1,000	1,500
0.0625	0.36	42	100	100	100	100	100
0.125	0.73	84	100	100	100	100	100
0.25	1.44	165	75.8	100	100	100	100
0.50	2.84	331	37.8	75.5	100	100	100
0.75	4.20	495	25.3	50.5	100	100	100
1.0	5.52	673	18.6	37.2	74.3	100	100
2.0	10.47	1417	8.0	16.0	33.0	69.0	100
3.0	14.92	2264	4.7	9.3	19.3	40.0	62.3
4.0	18.95	3232	3.0	6.2	12.5	26.0	40.5
5.0	22.62	4324	2.8	5.8	8.8	18.4	28.0

where [PR] = product rate (g/hr) for a given area of film surface, $\bar{K}$ = a constant characteristic of the porous structure of the film, f_c is a numerical factor which is a function of the feed-solution concentration, and f_P is a numerical factor which is a function of the operating pressure. ΔP is given by equation (2); ρ and μ refer to the density and viscosity, respectively, of the product solution; and subscripts 1 and 2 designate the respective feed solutions. The factors f_c and f_P give a measure of the deviation from Poiseuille flow under the given experimental conditions.

If, in the case of two particular feed solutions, $(f_c)_1 = (f_c)_2$ at constant feed molality, and $(f_P)_1 = (f_P)_2$ at constant operating pressure, then for such systems under experimental conditions of constant feed molality and operating pressure, equations (7) and (8) may be combined to give

$$\text{(9)} \qquad [\mathrm{PR}]_2 = [\mathrm{PR}]_1 \, (\mu_1/\Delta P_1 \, \rho_1) \, (\Delta P_2 \, \rho_2/\mu_2).$$

The above conditions seem to be valid for feed solutions containing cations and anions of the same respective valency; for such solutions, it has also been found that the relative separation and product rate data are uniquely fixed for each type of film. They have hence been termed "related solution systems" [23]. Provided the relative separation data are known, equation (9) enables the prediction of relative product rates for such systems under experimental conditions of constant feed molality and operating pressure. This is illustrated in Figures 6 and 7 for the systems [$NaCl$–H_2O] and [$NaNO_3$–H_2O], taking the former as the reference system and using the experimental relative separation data.

Some Empirical Correlations for Predicting Membrane Performance

The effect of operating pressure (P), in the range 250 to 1,500 psig, on solute separation and product rate for the systems 0.5M [$NaCl$–H_2O], [Na_2SO_4–H_2O], and [$MgSO_4$–H_2O], and the effect of feed concentration (m) on product rate for the systems 0.25 to 3.0M [$NaCl$–H_2O] and 0.25 to 1.5M [Na_2SO_4–H_2O], [$MgCl_2$–H_2O], and [$MgSO_4$–H_2O] at 1,500 psig operating pressure, have been well correlated by Govindan and Sourirajan by means of the following empirical equations [4].

Effect of pressure:

$$\text{(10)} \qquad x = \bar{a}P/(\bar{b}P + 1),$$

$$\text{(11)} \qquad [\mathrm{PR}] = [\bar{A} \exp(-P/P_{\max}) + \bar{B}]\Delta P \, \rho/\mu.$$

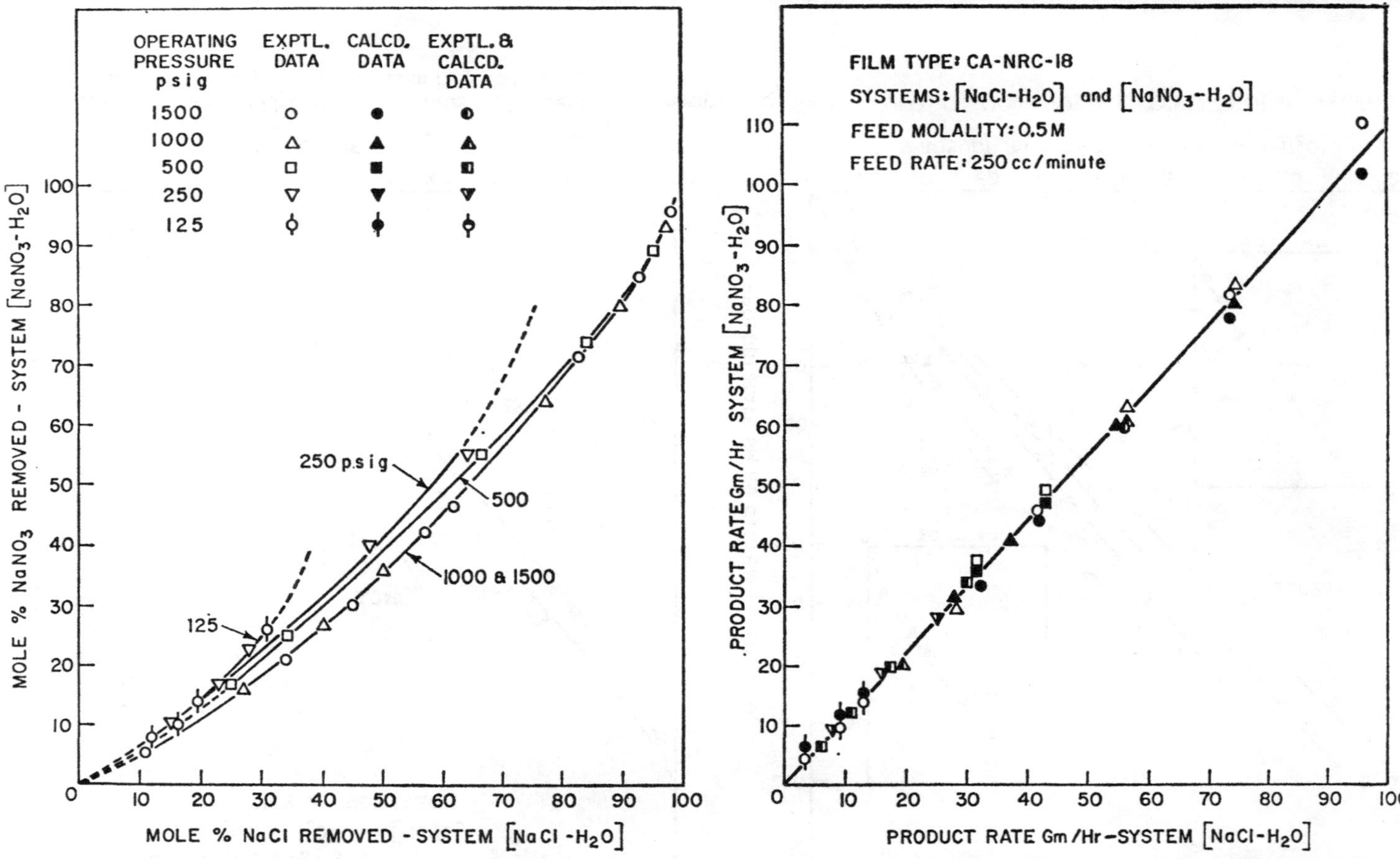

FIGURE 6. Predictability of product rates at different operating pressures for the system [$NaNO_3$–H_2O] using [NaCl–H_2O] as the reference system; data of Sourirajan and Govindan [28].

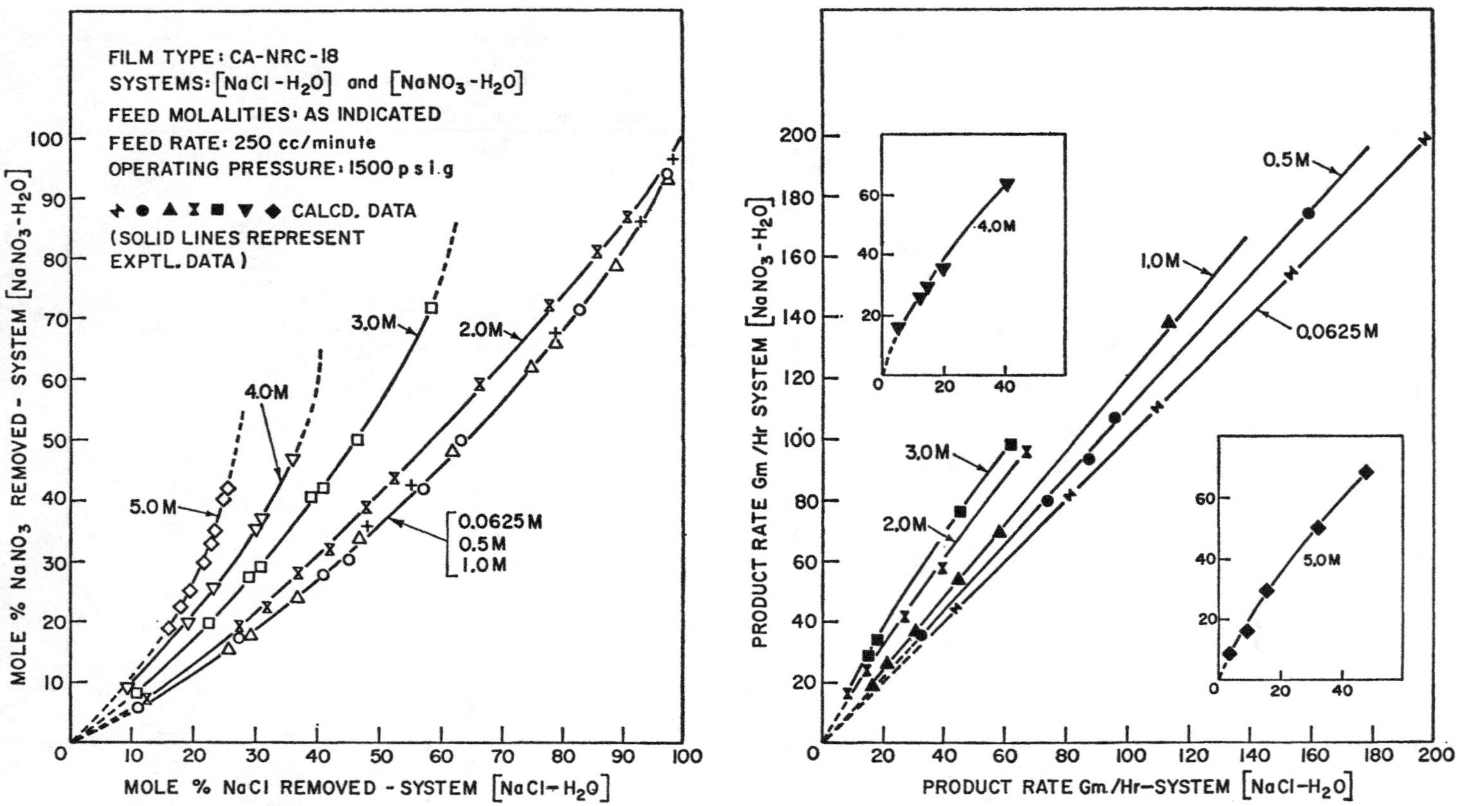

FIGURE 7. Predictability of product rates at different feed concentrations for the system [$NaNO_3$–H_2O] using [NaCl–H_2O] as the reference system; data of Sourirajan and Govindan [28].

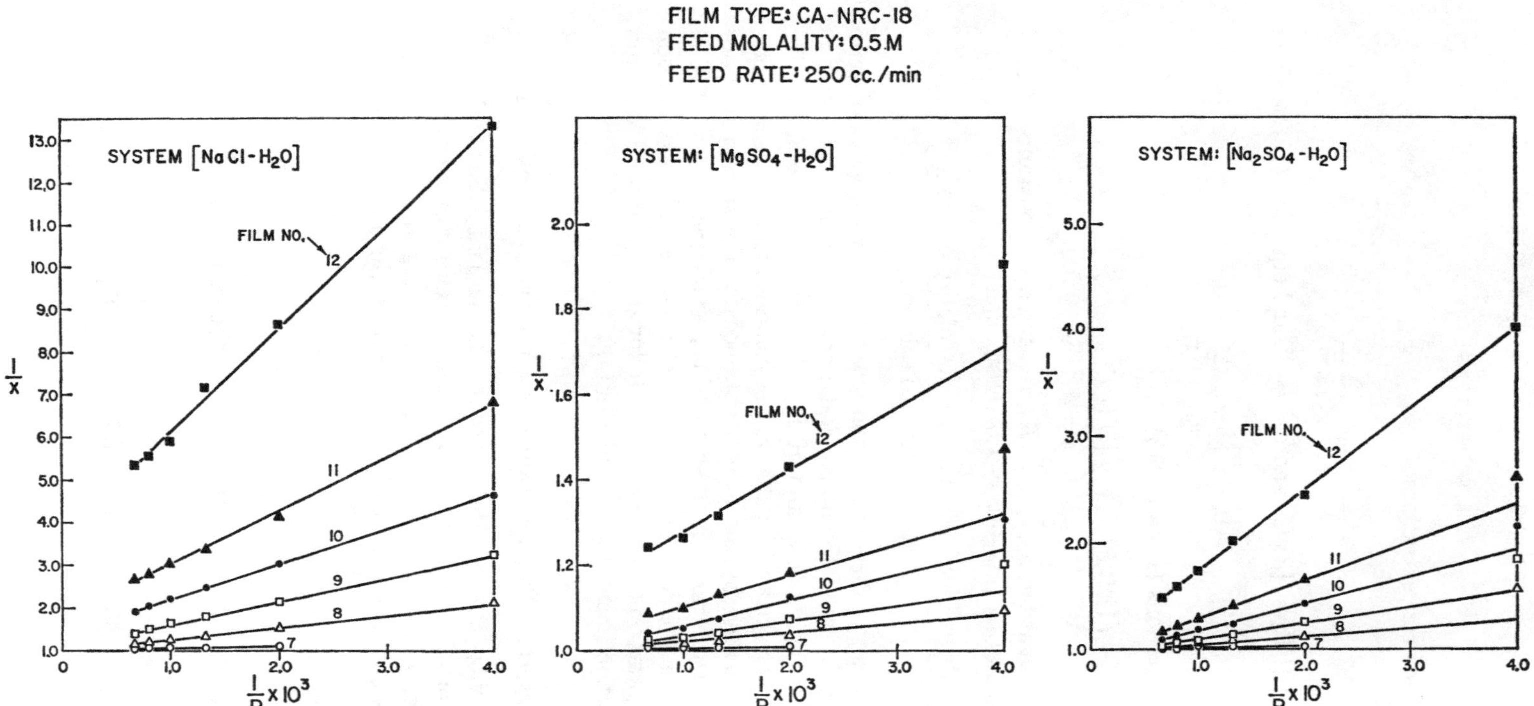

Figure 8. Effect of pressure on solute separation for the systems [NaCl–H_2O], [Na_2SO_4–H_2O], and [$MgSO_4$–H_2O]; data of Govindan and Sourirajan [4].

Effect of feed concentration:

$$\frac{[PR]}{\Delta P}\frac{\mu}{\rho}=\frac{K_1}{K_2+m^n}. \tag{12}$$

When $m = 0$, [PR] = [PWP] and $\Delta P = P$, and equation (12) becomes

$$\frac{[PWP]}{P}\frac{\mu_w}{\rho_w}=\frac{K_1}{K_2}. \tag{13}$$

Combining equations (12) and (13),

$$\left(\frac{[PWP]}{P}\frac{\mu_w}{\rho_w}\right)\Big/\left[\left(\frac{[PR]}{\Delta P}\frac{\mu}{\rho}\right)-1\right]=\frac{1}{K_2}m^n. \tag{14}$$

In the above equations $\bar{a}$, $\bar{A}$, $\bar{b}$, $\bar{B}$, K_1, K_2, and n are constants, P_{max} = maximum operating pressure = 1,500 psig, and

$$x=\frac{\text{molality of feed solution }(m)-\text{molality of product}}{\text{molality of feed solution}};$$

ρ_w and μ_w refer to the density and viscosity, respectively, of pure water. The validity of the above equations for the systems tested is illustrated in Figures 8, 9, and 10 [4]. The probable general validity of the above correlations for the reverse osmosis membrane separation process is indicated by the results obtained for the system sucrose-water [27]. In the range of their validity, equations (10), (11), and (12) enable the prediction of the effect of pressure and concentration on solute separation and/or product rate for any film from [PWP] and two sets of experimental [PR] and x data.

Solute Transport by Pore Diffusion through Membrane Capillaries

The following analysis developed by Kimura and Sourirajan [7] enables the prediction of the effect of feed concentration on membrane performance. Referring to Figure 11, and using the nomenclature given at the end of this text, the main steps in the analysis are given below.

Pure water permeability constant:

$$A = N_{BP}/P. \tag{15}$$

N_{BP} is obtained in appropriate units from the pure water permeability data.

Water transport:

$$N_B = A[P - \{\pi(X_{A2}) - \pi(X_{A3})\}]. \tag{16}$$

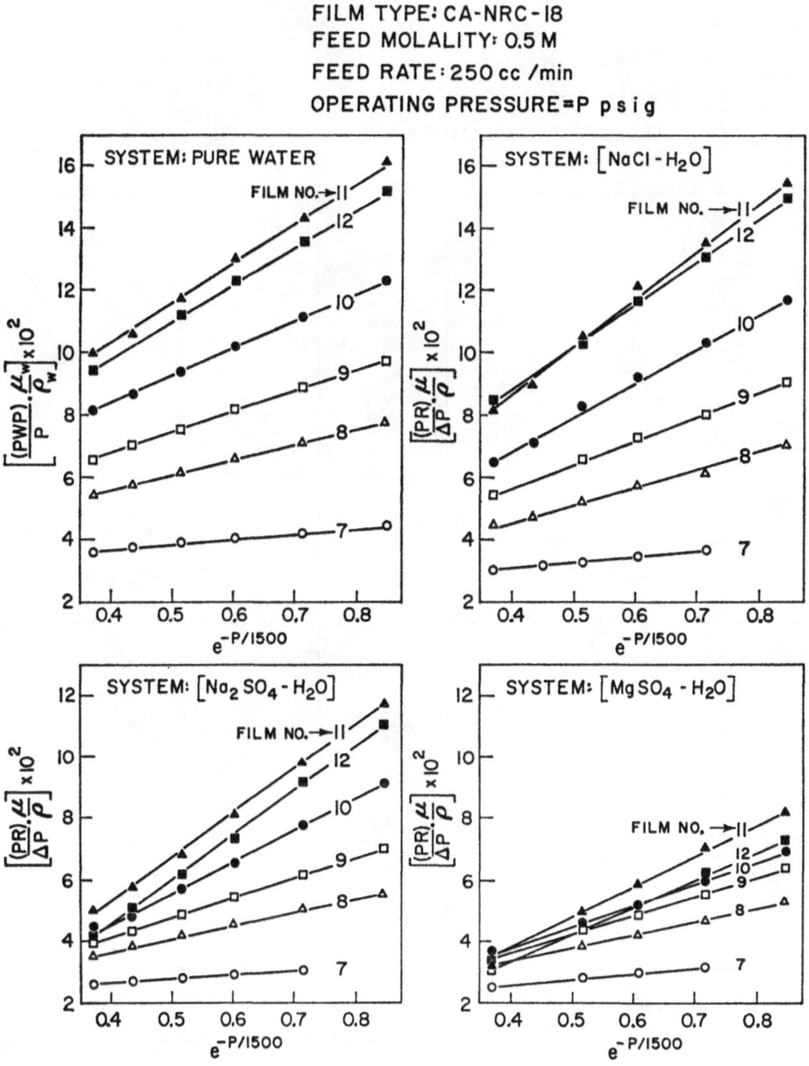

FIGURE 9. Effect of pressure on product rates for the systems [NaCl–H_2O], [Na_2SO–H_2O] and [$MgSO_4$–H_2O]; data of Govindan and Sourirajan [4].

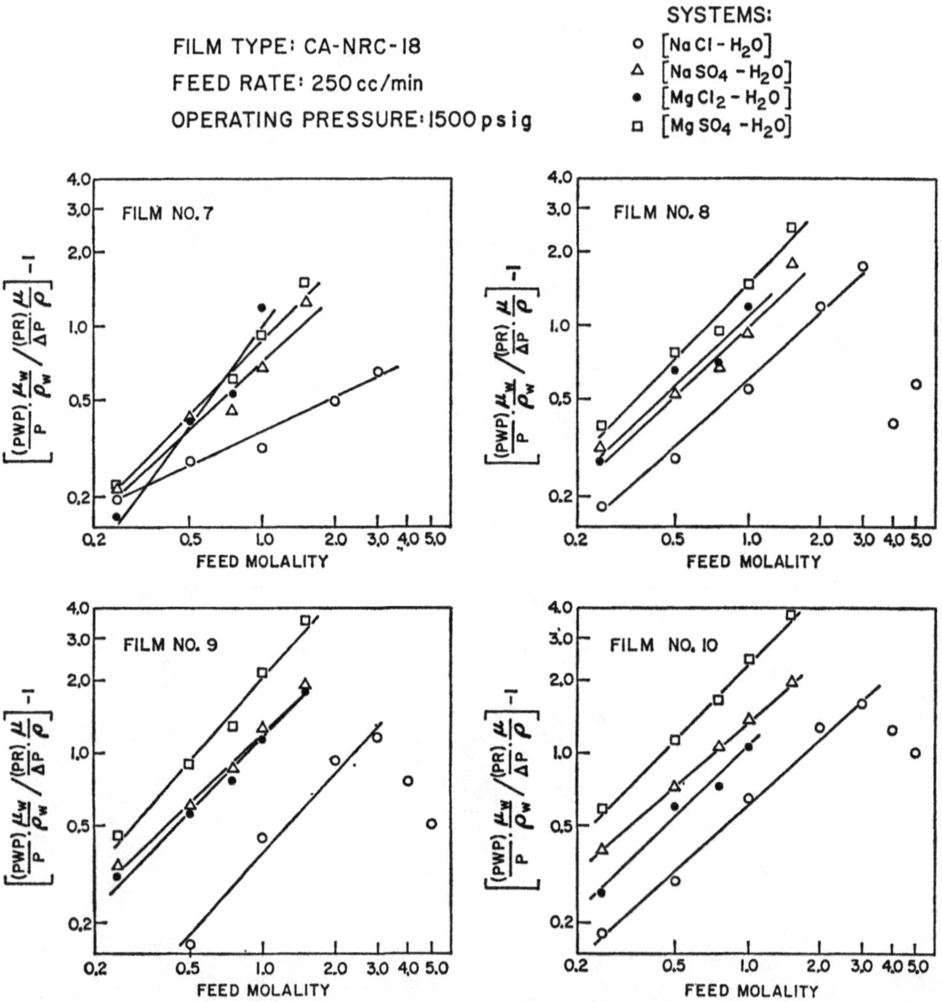

FIGURE 10. Effect of feed concentration on product rates for the systems [$NaCl-H_2O$], [$Na_2SO_4-H_2O$], [$MgCl_2-H_2O$], and [$MgSO_4-H_2O$]; data of Govindan and Sourirajan [4].

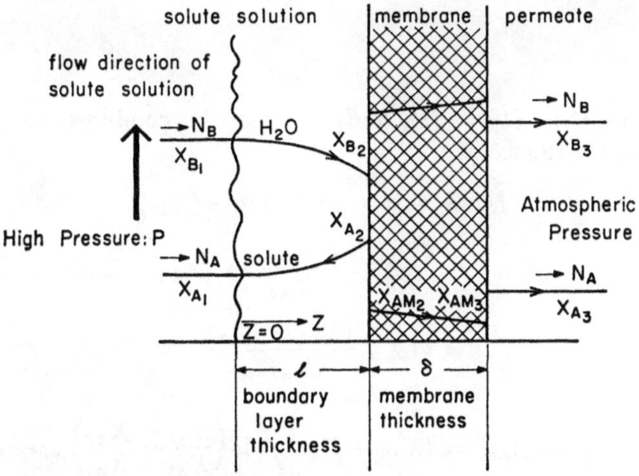

FIGURE 11. Transport of solute and water through membrane; model of Kimura and Sourirajan [7].

Solute transport:

$$N_A = C(D_{AM}/\delta)\,(X_{AM2} - X_{AM3}). \tag{17}$$

Relative distribution of solute between aqueous solution and membrane: assume that

$$CX_A = KC_M X_{AM}; \tag{18}$$

then equation (17) becomes

$$N_A = C(D_{AM}/K\delta)\,(X_{A2} - X_{A3}). \tag{19}$$

Mass transfer in the boundary layer:

$$N_A = X_A(N_A + N_B) - D_{AB}\, C dX_A/dZ. \tag{20}$$

Using the stoichiometric equation,

$$X_{A3} = N_A/(N_A + N_B) \tag{21}$$

and the boundary conditions

$$Z = 0, \qquad X_A = X_{A1},$$

$$Z = l, \qquad X_A = X_{A2},$$

equation (20) can be integrated to give

$$\ln\left(\frac{X_{A2} - X_{A3}}{X_{A1} - X_{A3}}\right) = \frac{1}{Ck}\,(N_A + N_B) \tag{22}$$

where

$$k = D_{AB}/l. \tag{23}$$

Equations (16), (19), (21), and (22) may be combined to give the following relations:

$$N_B = A[P - \pi(X_{A2}) + \pi(X_{A3})] \tag{16}$$

$$= \frac{CD_{AM}}{K\delta} \cdot \frac{1 - X_{A3}}{X_{A3}} \cdot (X_{A2} - X_{A3}) \tag{24}$$

$$= kCX_{B3} \frac{(X_{B1} - X_{B2})}{(X_A)_{\text{l.m.}}}, \tag{25}$$

where

$$(X_A)_{\text{l.m.}} = (X_{A2} - X_{A1}) \Big/ \ln\left(\frac{X_{A2} - X_{A3}}{X_{A1} - X_{A3}}\right). \tag{26}$$

Using the same notations, the solute separation (x) and product rate in grams per hour can be expressed as

$$x = \frac{m_1 - m_3}{m_1} = 1 - \frac{1 - X_{A1}}{X_{A1}} \cdot \frac{X_{A3}}{1 - X_{A3}} \tag{27}$$

and

$$[\text{PR}] = N_B \cdot S \cdot \bar{M}_B \cdot 3{,}600 \Big/ \left[1 - \frac{1}{1 + 1{,}000/[m_1 M_A(1 - x)]}\right]. \tag{28}$$

The above analysis gives rise to the concept of an effective solute transport parameter $D_{AM}/K\delta$ for the particular membrane–solution system. The use of the above relations for predicting membrane performance needs a knowledge of the variation of $D_{AM}/K\delta$ with feed concentration, and the mass transfer coefficient k for different experimental conditions. Analysing the experimental [PWP], [PR], and x data for different film–solution systems, Kimura and Sourirajan made two important observations: (i) for the CA-NRC-18 type films, the parameter $D_{AM}/K\delta$ remains constant, at least in the feed concentration range 0.0625 to $4.0M$; and (ii) the mass transfer coefficients between the membrane and the bulk of the feed solution obtained by the analysis of the reverse osmosis data are in agreement with those determined experimentally by the diffusion current method [9, 18] as illustrated in Figure 12, which is applicable for the particular desalting cell described earlier.

On the basis of the above observations, the effect of feed concentration on solute separation and product rate at a given operating pressure can be predicted for the CA-NRC-18 type films from a single set of experimental [PWP], [PR], and x (and hence X_{A1} and

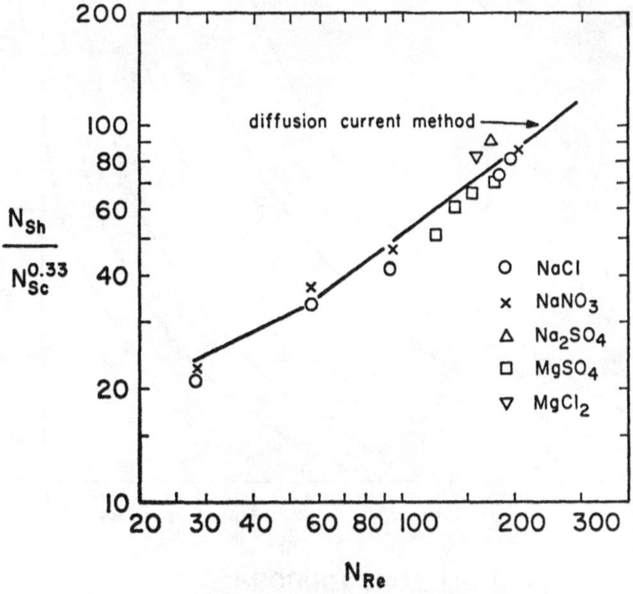

FIGURE 12. Mass transfer coefficient between the membrane and the bulk of the feed solution in the cell; data of Kimura and Sourirajan [7].

X_{A3}) data as follows. The values of A, X_{A2}, $D_{AM}/K\delta$ are first calculated using equations (15), (16), and (24) respectively. For any other feed concentration and feed rate, k is obtained from Figure 12 using the diffusivity data available in the literature [2, 17, 20], the values of A and $D_{AM}/K\delta$ are assumed constant, and those of X_{A2}, X_{A3}, and N_B are calculated by a trial and error procedure using equations (16), (24), (25), and (26). Finally, x and [PR] are obtained from equations (27) and (28) respectively. Figure 13 illustrates the results of such calculations carried out for the system [NaCl–H_2O]. The solid lines express the calculated results, which agree remarkably well with the experimental results.

APPLICATION OF REVERSE OSMOSIS TECHNIQUE FOR WATER PURIFICATION

Evidently one of the most important applications of the reverse osmosis technique is in the general field of water purification (including saline water conversion), water renovation, and water pollution control. Almost the entire current research effort in reverse osmosis seems related to this one field of application, more particularly to

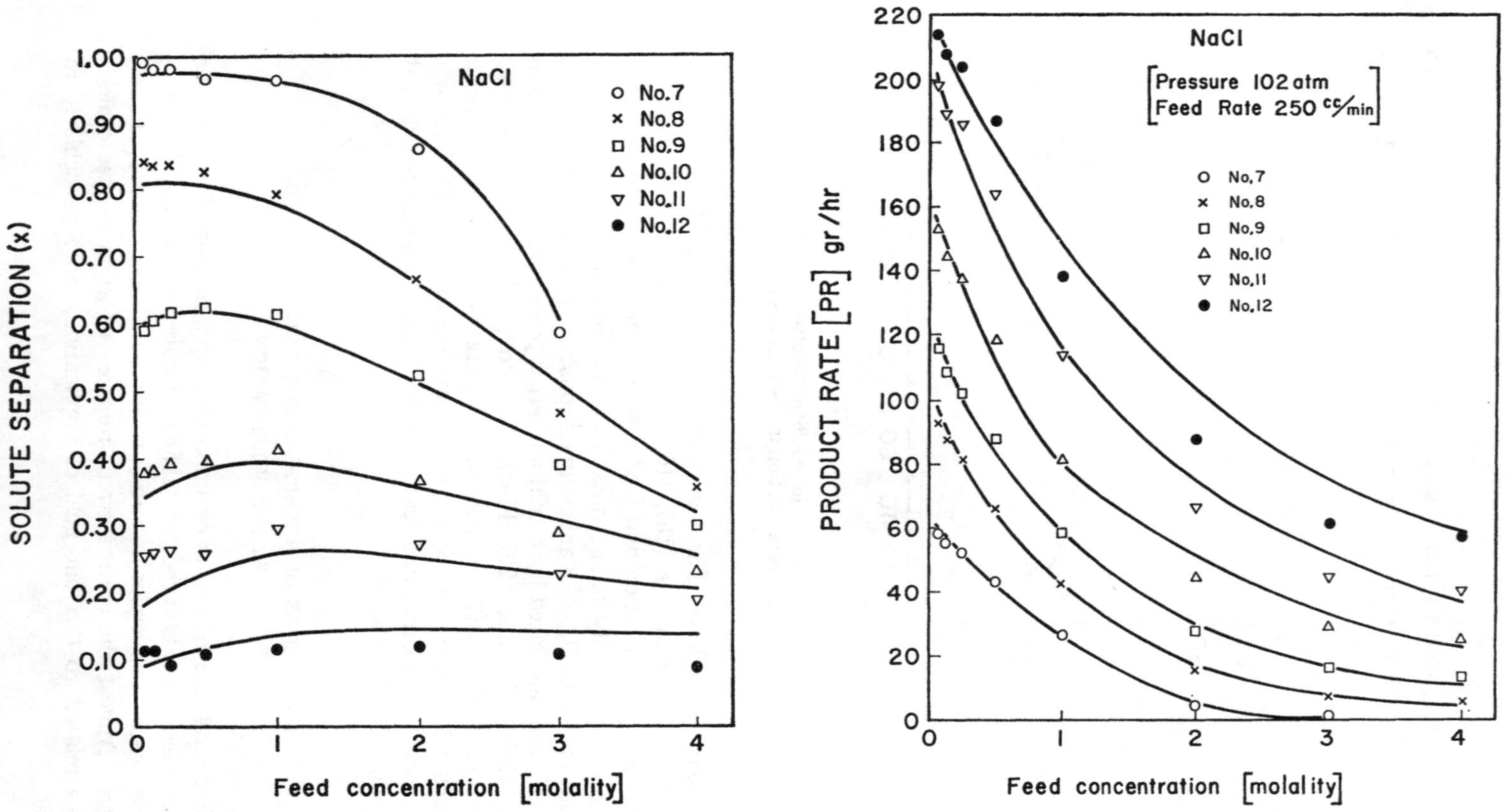

FIGURE 13. Predictability of solute separation and product rate as a function of feed concentration for the system [NaCl–H_2O]; data of Kimura and Sourirajan [7].

saline water conversion. This is due to the timely importance of this subject and also to the extensive government support available for such work, especially in the United States.

The successful application of this technique for the separation of a wide variety of inorganic, organic, and surface-active substances in aqueous solution has been demonstrated [21, 23, 25–29]. The Loeb–Sourirajan type of porous cellulose acetate membrane is particularly useful for water conversion applications involving solution systems which do not physically or chemically affect the membrane during operation. The extent of separation and product rate obtainable depends on the porous structure of the membrane and the chemical nature of the solution. The ability of a given cellulose acetate membrane to separate various inorganic ions in aqueous solution increases with increase in the valency of the ion. With respect to anions, the level of separation is in the order citrate > tartrate = sulphate > acetate > chloride > bromide > nitrate > iodide > thiocyanate, which is the same as the lyotropic series. When organic solutes of various molecular sizes are involved, more than one mechanism could control the separation process. The solute molecule might be retained on the film surface purely by ultrafiltration, i.e. by virtue of the fact that its molecular size is bigger than that of the pore on the film surface, or by the negative absorption of the solute at the membrane–solution interface. In the latter case, the size of the pores on the membrane surface need not be smaller, and could be bigger, than the size of the molecules involved. In many cases, both mechanisms may combine to give advantageous results.

A set of illustrative data is given in Table III and Figure 14 on the performance of CA-NRC-18 type films for saline water and actual sea water conversion [28]. Table II illustrates the possible use of the

TABLE II

REMOVAL OF TRITONS FROM AQUEOUS SOLUTIONS; DATA OF SOURIRAJAN AND SIRIANNI [29]
(Film type, CA–NRC–18; feed concentration, 2 g Triton/100 g water; feed rate, 120 cc/min; Operating pressure, 1,500 psi)

Film shrinkage temp. (°C)	Solute triton type	Wt. % solute separation	Product rate (gal/day/sq. ft)
86	N-128	98.6	32.5
89	X-165	99.1	29.4
90	X-205	99.1	29.5
89	X-305	~100	26.2

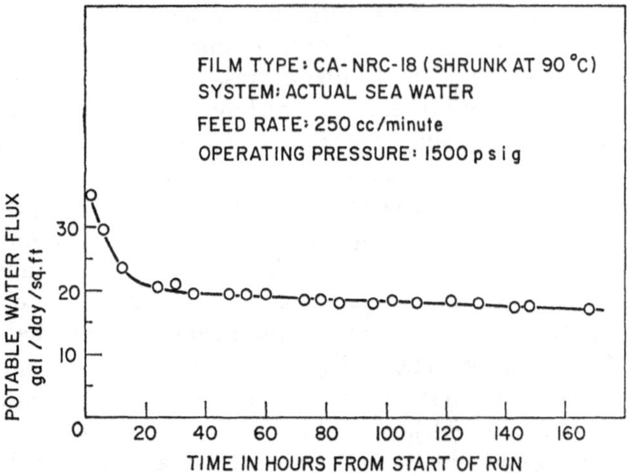

FIGURE 14. Variation of potable water flux with time in a continuous run with sea water; data of Sourirajan and Govindan [28].

above membranes for the separation of the surface-active substances in aqueous solution. Ironside and Sourirajan [6] have demonstrated that the above membranes are effective for the purification of sewage waters, and waters contaminated by ABS type detergents or paper-mill lignin solutions. The above results indicate the possible industrial application of the technique for saline water conversion, water renovation, and water pollution control.

Under contract with the Office of Saline Water (U.S. Department of the Interior), several organizations are currently building or operating reverse osmosis pilot plants for water conversion applications. These plants use porous cellulose acetate membranes made by the general Loeb–Sourirajan technique described earlier. Scientists at the University of California, Los Angeles, have built and operated successfully for more than a year a reverse osmosis pilot plant at Coalinga, California. This plant is of particular interest since it utilizes porous cellulose acetate membranes cast in the form of tubes at the laboratory temperature [10, 15].

CONCLUSION

The concept of preferential sorption and capillary flow has already led to the discovery of a new separation process of tremendous significance in chemical process engineering. Further researches on a wide

TABLE III

APPLICABILITY OF CA-NRC-18 TYPE FILMS FOR SALINE WATER CONVERSION; DATA OF SOURIRAJAN AND GOVINDAN [28]

Film treatment							
Shrinkage temp. (°C)	Pressure (psig)	Solute	Feed rate (cc/min)	Operating pressure (psig)	Solute concn. in feed (wt. %)	Solute concn. in product (ppm)	Product rate (gal/day/sq. ft)
88	250	NaCl	300	100	0.25	363	4.7
87	700	NaCl	300	600	0.25	400	52.4
88	700	NaCl	300	600	0.50	300	34.0
87	700	Na_2SO_4	300	600	0.25	150	53.3
87	700	Na_2SO_4	300	600	0.50	300	50.7
90	1,700	NaCl	250	1,500	1.44	<100	38.5
90	1,700	NaCl	250	1,500	2.84	280	31.3
90	1,700	NaCl	250	1,500	4.20	420	24.1
90	1,700	NaCl	250	1,500	5.53	550	18.2
90	1,700	Actual sea water	250	1,500	3.33 (equivalent NaCl)	<300	27.0

variety of membranes and solution systems with particular reference to the precise physico-chemical criteria of preferential sorption, mechanism of pore formation during film casting, and factors governing flow of fluids through porous membranes having separation characteristics could contribute much to the practical development of this membrane separation process in all its applications, including water purification.

NOMENCLATURE

a = activity of solute
$\bar{a}$ = constant
A = pure water permeability constant, g-mole H_2O/cm^2 sec atm
$\bar{A}$ = constant
$\bar{b}$ = constant
$\bar{B}$ = constant
C = molar density of solution, g-mole/cm^3
d = diameter of circular membrane, cm
D = diffusivity, cm^2/sec
D_{AB} = diffusivity of solute in water, cm^2/sec
f_c = numerical factor
f_P = numerical factor
h = depth of cell, cm
k = mass transfer coefficient, cm/sec
K = distribution ratio of solute between solution and membrane
$\bar{K}$ = constant
K_1 = constant
K_2 = constant
l = effective boundary layer thickness, cm
m = molality
M = concentration in molality units
$\bar{M}$ = molecular weight, g/mole
n = constant
N = flux through membrane, g-mole/cm^2sec
N_{Re} = ud/ν
N_{Sc} = ν/D_{AB}
N_{Sh} = kd/D_{AB}
P = operating gauge pressure
P_{max} = maximum gauge pressure in the operating range
[PR] = product rate, g/hr
[PWP] = pure water permeability, g/hr

R = gas constant
S = effective membrane area, cm^2
T = absolute temperature
u = velocity of solution parallel to membrane, cm/sec
x = solute separation
X = mole fraction
Z = distance, cm
Γ = adsorption of solute, mole/cm^2 of surface
δ = effective membrane thickness, cm
μ = viscosity of product
μ_w = viscosity of water
ν = kinematic viscosity
π = osmotic pressure
$\pi(X_A)$ = osmotic pressure corresponding to mole fraction X_A
ρ = density of product
ρ_w = density of pure water
σ = surface tension of solution

Subscripts

A = solute
B = water (solvent)
BP = pure water permeation
M = membrane phase

In equations (7)–(9): 1 and 2 designate the respective feed solutions
in equations (16)–(28): 1 = feed solution, 2 = concentrated boundary layer, 3 = product

REFERENCES

1. Breton, E. J., Jr. (1957), *Water and Ion Flow through Imperfect Osmotic Membranes*, U.S. Dept. Interior, Office of Saline Water Research and Development, Progress Rept. 16.
2. Davies, R. J. (1933), *Phil. Mag.* **15**: 489–511.
3. Goard, A. K. (1925), *J. Chem. Soc.* **127**: 2451–8.
4. Govindan, T. S. and Sourirajan, S. (1966), *Ind. Eng. Chem. Process Design Develop.* **5**: 422–9.
5. Harkins, W. D. and McLaughlin, H. M. (1925), *J. Am. Chem. Soc.* **47**: 2083–9.
6. Ironside, R. and Sourirajan, S. (1967), *Water Res.* **1**: 179–80.
7. Kimura, S. and Sourirajan, S. (1967), *A.I.Ch.E.J.* **13**: 497–503.
8. Langmuir, I. (1917), *J. Am. Chem. Soc.* **39**: 1848–1906.
9. Lin, C. S., Denton, E. B., Gaskill, H. S., and Putnam, G. L. (1951), *Ind. Eng. Chem.* **43**: 2136–43.

10. LOEB, S. (1966), *Desalination*, **1**: 35–49.
11. LOEB, S. and MCCUTCHAN, J. W. (1965), *Ind. Eng. Chem. Prod. Res. Develop.* **4**: 114–21.
12. LOEB, S. and SOURIRAJAN, S. (1961), *Sea Water Demineralization by Means of a Semipermeable Membrane*, Dept. of Engineering, University of California, Los Angeles, Rept. 60–60.
13. ——— (1963), *Advan. Chem. Ser. No.* **38**: 117–32.
14. ——— U.S. Patent 3,133,132, May 12, 1964.
15. MANJIKIAN, S., LOEB, S., and MCCUTCHAN, J. W., First International Symposium on Water Desalination, Washington, D.C., Paper SWD/12, October 1965.
16. MCBAIN, J. W. and DUBOIS, R. (1929), *J. Am. Chem. Soc.* **51**: 3534–49.
17. ÖHOLM, L. W. (1936, 1938), *Finska Kemistsamfundets Medd.* **45**: 71–76; **47**: 115–23.
18. REISS, L. P. and HANRATTY, T. J. (1962), *A.I.Ch.E.J.* **8**: 245–7.
19. RILEY, R., GARDNER, J. O., and MERTEN, U. (1964), *Science*, **143**: 801–3.
20. ROBINSON, R. A. and STOKES, R. H. (1959), *Electrolyte Solutions*, 2nd ed. (Butterworths, London), pp. 513–15.
21. SOURIRAJAN, S. (1963), *Ind. Eng. Chem. Fundamentals*, **2**: 51–55.
22. ——— (1963), *Nature*, **199**: 590–1.
23. ——— (1964), *Ind. Eng. Chem. Fundamentals*, **3**: 206–10.
24. ——— (1964), *Nature*, **203**: 1348–9.
25. ——— (1964), *J. Appl. Chem.* **14**: 506–13.
26. ——— (1965), *Ind. Eng. Chem. Prod. Res. Develop.* **4**: 201–6.
27. ——— (1967), *Ind. Eng. Chem. Process Design Develop.* **6**: 154–60.
28. SOURIRAJAN, S. and GOVINDAN, T. S., First International Symposium on Water Desalination, Washington, D.C., Paper SWD/41, October 1965.
29. SOURIRAJAN, S. and SIRIANNI, A. F. (1966), *Ind. Eng. Chem. Prod. Res. Develop.* **5**: 30–34.
30. UNIVERSITY OF CALIFORNIA, OFFICE OF PUBLIC INFORMATION, Press Release "New Water Desalting Process Developed at UCLA," August 23, 1960.
31. YUSTER, S. T., Personal communication, September 1956.
32. YUSTER, S. T., SOURIRAJAN, S., and BERNSTEIN, K. (1958), *Sea Water Demineralization by the Surface Skimming Process*, Department of Engineering, University of California, Los Angeles, Rept. No. 58–26.

PART VI

THE BIOLOGICAL NECESSITIES AND HAZARDS OF WATER

BIOLOGICAL ASPECTS OF THE WATER PROBLEM

F. R. Hayes, F.R.S.C.

BIOLOGICAL EFFECTS of water are brought about by substances dissolved in it. While there is a great deal of natural variability in waters, we are here concerned with materials added by man, usually without thought of the consequences. A very few things may be put into public waters with the idea of improving them; one thinks for example of fluoride to prevent tooth decay. There are also additions such as chlorine to counteract man-made damage. But the great majority of additives are unwanted, and their effects are grouped under the general name of pollution.

The historic idea of pollution concerns the potential of public water supplies to spread epidemics. Even in the early years of this century, typhoid fever and other diseases were major causes of death. Since about 1920, however, these enteric diseases have contributed so little to our total sickness and death that an outbreak today is usually the result of an accident and becomes front-page news. The good and continually improving record is a tribute to the stringent control measures developed by the sanitary engineering profession. The techniques of sanitary engineering were totally appropriate for the health problems they have solved. But the biological effects of today's additives do not pose any immediate danger to health, and their abatement calls for a quite different research approach.

Industrial complexes are often established in thinly populated areas where there is abundant water power or a mineral deposit. For example, Newfoundland waters receive millions of tons of so-called "tailings," made up of finely divided low-grade iron ore. These are distinctly toxic to fish and also destroy spawning grounds and smother plant growth. Other mines produce zinc and copper, which are toxic to fish even in very low concentrations. Attempts have been made to use certain lakes as settling basins, isolated from the surrounding waters. Research is required both on toxicities and control methods.

Wastes from pulp and paper manufacture are also troublesome in Newfoundland. The most serious effluent is sulphite waste liquor, which has some toxic effects on fish, and—what is worse—a high affinity for oxygen, which depletes the waters and so kills off life there. Control includes attempts by biologists to induce owners to modify plant design. Research is required into the species composition and tolerance of healthy aquatic communities.

Reference has been made to the effects of additives on health via epidemics, and on aquatic life. However, the current concern about water is related to the production in it of excess fertility. Our streams and lakes, especially in heavily populated areas, are receiving large quantities of phosphate and nitrate, originating in sewage and in wastes from the manufacture and use of synthetic chemicals, such as detergents. These waters have become foul-smelling, filled with objectionable plant growths, unpleasant for bathing and boating, and depleted of game fish. We know little about the course of chemical degradation of the new synthetics in nature, or of their toxic effects. Research is also necessary to develop substitutes more readily attacked by aquatic bacteria.

The drains of a city carry away two types of liquids: storm water and used or spent water from houses and industries. Ideally there should be two separate systems, but in practice they are usually combined. During fine weather the sanitary drainage can be managed and treated, but during storms the rain water overflows the system and carries raw waste into the river or lake. Treatment consists of inducing bacterial decomposition of the solids, which are settled out, allowing the supernatant fluid to be discharged. The solids may be recovered and sold as garden fertilizers such as Milorganite or Torganic. Unfortunately the supernatant fluid still contains high concentrations of phosphate and nitrate, which promote excess fertility in the lake. The engineering problem has been solved but the biological problem has not. Research today is directed towards means of removing the nutrient salts and towards forecasting the biological effects following abatement.

In some watersheds, farm animals contribute considerably more wastes than humans, and the drainage from certain land areas supporting large animal populations has led to downstream fish kills and groundwater contamination. Farm animals in the United States are said to produce ten times as much waste as the human population. There is as yet no single method generally satisfactory for the treatment of animal manure.

Many observers are of the opinion that chemical fertilizers added to farm land contribute to the enrichment of waters, but there is as yet little definite information. Most of the phosphate applied to soils is tightly bound, but nitrates leach through the soil and can more easily reach drainage waters.

Pesticides sprayed over agricultural land also find their way into open waters. Forest sprays often go directly into rivers and kill both the fish and their food organisms. In the world's largest aerial forest-spraying programme, over half the forests of New Brunswick have been repeatedly treated with DDT, which has killed young salmon and insects in the rivers there. Although human illness traceable to pesticides in public waters has not been reported, there is an accumulating residue of DDT in the bodies of people; the average has now reached about a tenth of a gram per person. Pesticides have also been reported in tuna fish far out to sea, as well as in antarctic penguins and arctic snowy owls. The sublethal and subclinical long-term effects of these substances deserve fundamental investigation in order to clarify the potential medical problem.

Before we turn to a general question—What happens to the biological system as a lake receives fertilizer?—a few words are called for on semantics. In his book *Nineteen Eighty Four*, George Orwell defines the Newspeak language of the future. In Newspeak the expression of unorthodox opinions, above a very low level, is well-nigh impossible. The word "pollution" is a good example of Newspeak. It carries an unpleasant and offensive emotional appeal: something to View with Alarm. We dislike the idea of building up the fertility of a lake with an extract from city sewers. Yet many centuries ago monks were adding horse manure to their carp ponds to improve their Friday dinners. And when we sprinkle our lawns with treated human faeces we call it enrichment or fertilization: reassuring words, enabling us to Point with Pride.

The effect on fishing of emptying nutrients into open water is usually to destroy the game fish which are prized by anglers, and to substitute for them a larger crop of coarse fish, which may yield a better income to commercial fishermen. The biologist cannot classify the whole process as either good or bad, and he needs a neutral word. Despite misgivings it seems necessary to attempt to popularize the word *eutrophication*, which means the enrichment of water by nutrients, whether intentional or unintentional, and without reference to the desirability or otherwise of the effects.

It is instructive to follow case histories where the growth of cities has steadily enriched neighbouring waters. Records are available for a large series of lakes, principally European, where the sequence of biological events has been observed for a century or more.

A noteworthy example is Lake Zürich, Switzerland, a lake composed of two basins separated by a narrow passage. Less than a hundred years ago both basins were clear, clean, and supported a commercial crop of trout and whitefish. Since shortly before the turn of the century, however, one basin has received urban drainage from small communities numbering altogether over 100,000 people. The city of Zürich lies at one end of the lake but contributes no sewage to it. Hand in hand with the increased urban fertilization, there developed about 75 years ago algal scums, malodorous and displeasing to the eye. The lake ceased to be an attractive site for general vacationing, boating, and bathing. Moreover, since the cities and their industries got their water from the lake, expensive filtering and purifying systems had to be installed to remove the greatly increased masses of organisms and their accompanying obnoxious odours and flavours.

Decomposition of the added organic matter produced a deficiency of oxygen in the deeper water, with the result that trout and whitefish disappeared altogether and were replaced by coarse fish. There were also increased deposits of silt in the lake which would hasten its extinction by filling it up. The shallower of the two lakes, which received no urban drainage, changed little during the century and still retains its "virgin" lake characteristics.

Returning to Canada, in the years following the war there was considerable interest in the intentional addition of fertilizers to lakes with the object of improving angling. Actually CIL marketed a "correct" mixture of nitrogen, phosphorus, and potassium for the purpose. In natural trout waters and open lakes the amounts added were usually insufficient to produce any detectable change in the fishing. On the other hand, in small, artificial farm fish-ponds, especially in the southern United States, it has been possible to grow good crops of coarse fish for the table.

When ordinary fertilizer is added to a pond most of it disappears in a few days. (Of the nutrients going into Lake Erie today only about one tenth ever reach the outlet.) The disappearance of nutrients was formerly attributed to plant growth, but this hypothesis was found to be untenable when tested with radioactive tracer techniques. The correct explanation reached me from a popular book by a biologist attached to the post-war atom bomb test at Bikini. The book, by David Bradley, was called *No Place to Hide*—not a bad title for the pollution problem either. Here are some extracts from Bradley's diary:

Seventh day after the explosion

Most of the radioactivity dispersed in the water seems to have settled out. The water-counting lab has nearly gone out of business in favour of ship monitoring jobs. An area of radioactive infection aboard the ship is the green and brown algae which grow along the waterlines. For some reason or other the algae do not release their radioactivity and so the water lines remain so hot that one may pick up a respectable radiation coming through the steel walls of the hull.

Day 15

Today we went dredging. Our first netful of sand dumped upon the fantail of our boat proved to be so radioactive that in a panic I had the whole catch thrown overboard. None of us expected the bottom to show such intensities at this late date.

These observations give a central clue to the understanding of eutrophication. It appears that there is a single pool of nutrient material, divided between the water and solids in a lake, with most of it in the solids. For comparison one might think of the distribution of money between a bank and the street outside, most of the money being in the bank. Bradley was observing something like the distribution of marked bank-notes to people in the street. They soon found their way into the bank, not because the bank was actively absorbing them or growing on them, but simply through normal exchange. Similarly, the disappearance of nutrients from water is a consequence of an experimental arrangement in which material is added to the water phase of the system. Were the opposite technique followed, of removing, say, phorphorus from lake water, a continuous replacement from the solids would be expected.

The oxygen relations of red blood cells in their plasma provide another analogy to the lake nutrient system. Oxygen is distributed between the cells and plasma in dynamic equilibrium. Under ordinary conditions nearly all the oxygen is in the cells. Any disturbance of either phase will cause an appropriate rearrangement of the system. For example, the addition of oxygen to the plasma would be followed by a "loss" to the cells and vice versa. To the physiologist the plasma, or fluid phase, is merely an innocuous transporter between the active parts of the system.

Unfortunately we do not yet know the time relations for lake equilibration. Thus if the phosphate and nitrate supply to, for example, Lake Erie were stopped tomorrow, the first decline in its level of fertility might not be observed for many years. There is a layer of sediment at the bottom of the lake about 5 cm thick, which, like a current account in the bank, can at once make up any nutrient deficiencies in the water. The nuisance growths of algae form another source. To elucidate the exchange mechanism and provide a time scale for it, the combined talents of biochemists, physical chemists, and bacteriologists will be required.

Mention should be made of physical obstructions in rivers which prevent salmon from reaching their spawning grounds. An example from early in the century was the dumping of rock at Hell's Gate on the Fraser River during railroad construction. A great deal of work has since been required at the site to restore and retain the salmon runs. In more recent times there are many so-called fish-versus-power problems which arise when rivers are dammed to produce electricity. Again, the removal of trees in forestry operations causes rivers to dry up in summer.

Research should be directed towards the understanding of multiple uses of water resource, so that even in treated rivers fish might be kept alive. They require a safe passage upstream, through reservoirs and to their spawning grounds, as well as arrangements for the young to pass downstream over a series of dams without delay or injury. Many of the biological effects of dams have only recently been discovered, and the modifications they cause in fish behaviour are more diverse than had been expected.

BIBLIOGRAPHY

BRADLEY, D. (1948), *No Place to Hide* (Boston). (Biologist's diary on Bikini atom bomb tests.)

ELSON, P. F. and KERSWILL, C. J. (1964), "Forest Spraying and Salmon Angling," *Atlantic Salmon Journal for 1964*, No. 3: 20–29 (New Brunswick forests).

HASLER, A. D. (1947), "Eutrophication of Lakes by Domestic Drainage," *Ecology*, *28*: 383–95 (long-term effects on European lakes).

HAYES, F. R. (1964), "The Mud-Water Interface," *Oceanog. and Marine Biol., Ann. Rev. 2*: 121–45 (reactions between water and sediment).

HAYES, F. R. and PHILLIPS, J. E. (1958), "Radiophosphorus Equilibrium with Mud, Plants and Bacteria under Oxidized and Reduced Conditions," *Limnol. Oceanog. 3*: 459–75 (exchange mechanism with lake solids).

ORWELL, G. (1949), *Nineteen Eighty Four* (New York), Appendix on the principles of Newspeak.

TAYLOR, V. R. (1965), "Water Pollution and Fish Populations in the Province of Newfoundland and Labrador in 1964," *Canadian Fish Culturist*, Issue 35: 3–15 (mines and pulp mills).

VARIOUS AUTHORS (1965), *Restoring the Quality of Our Environment* (Washington, D.C.: Supt. of Documents). (Report and recommendations of a Presidential Panel on Environmental Pollution.)

AQUATIC COMMUNITIES AND THEIR ADAPTATIONS TO THEIR ENVIRONMENT

Gordon A. Riley

THE AQUATIC ENVIRONMENT is, in general, benign. Its inhabitants have ready access to some of the main requirements of living beings, such as water itself and the major chemical elements that are required by living tissues. It has a moderate temperature, with a total seasonal variation that seldom exceeds 30° C and may be considerably less. In the extreme case of the deep ocean, an animal conceivably can spend its whole life in an environment that does not vary by as much as 1° C in temperature.

Surface waters permit light penetration in sufficient abundance for plant growth to a depth of some metres, but these waters are about 20 times as opaque to potentially harmful ultra-violet radiation as they are to visible and photosynthetically usable light. Water gives support to many delicate and soft-bodied creatures that could not exist on land. Speaking in broadly phyletic terms, the aquatic environment harbours a greater biological diversity than any other part of the biosphere, although speciation is less extreme than in some terrestrial groups. This lack of extreme speciation is perhaps evidence of an environment lacking in pronounced stresses.

To be sure, there are aquatic environments that we think of as anything but benign, and at least a limited number of plants and animals have become adapted to such places. A few algae and bacteria can grow in thermal springs with a temperature of 70° C and, in some cases, a chemical composition quite different from that of most natural waters. There are cold-adapted and dark-adapted algae that live embedded in the under-side of polar ice. Mussel beds along the arctic shore have been observed to lie buried in ice for as much as eight months out of the year, during which time more than half of the water content is transferred out of the cells and lies frozen in intercellular spaces [1].* Great

*Numbers in brackets refer to the list of references.

Salt Lake, with a salinity of about 204 g/kg, supports a limited fauna and flora, as do temporary ponds in arid, alkaline regions.

These cases of extreme environmental stress are very limited geographically, compared with vast areas of marine and fresh waters which support a productive community living under the milder sort of conditions mentioned earlier. In general, such communities grow actively on a year-round basis. There may be seasonal variations in growth rate, but only in the most extreme polar conditions is there a dormant period comparable to that of land plants.

AQUATIC POPULATIONS

The richest part of the aquatic environment is commonly the shore zone. Here, if the substrate is suitable for rooted aquatic vegetation or attached algae, one is likely to find a community that is more productive than either the adjacent land or the deeper waters off-shore. At some point in deeper water this kind of growth is limited by the availability of light. The maximum depth may be as little as a metre or two in turbid lakes, or it may be more than 100 metres for red algae growing in blue tropical waters. In greater depths attached forms cannot exist, and there begins the realm of the small floating algae known as phytoplankton.

These algae are microscopic, single-celled or colonial forms belonging to a number of different orders. They are adapted in various ways for a life that seems precarious, in that they must somehow maintain themselves in near-surface waters where light is sufficient for growth, despite mixing processes that tend to carry them down into deeper water and despite their own tendencies to sink.

A few members of the phytoplankton, such as the blue-green algae, are lighter than water and tend to float up towards the surface. There are flagellated forms which can maintain a favourable depth range if turbulence is not too extreme. Most non-motile forms are heavier than water, and adaptations to avoid excessive sinking speeds include small size and elaborations of shape which increase the surface area. Such adaptations can also serve a useful function in increasing the rate of absorption of phosphate, nitrate, and other micronutrients. In spring and summer in most lakes, as well as in the ocean, the supply of these micronutrients is likely to be the most important factor limiting the growth of green plants.

However, the most characteristic feature of these plants in enabling them to inhabit the surface waters is their rapid rate of multiplication. Although many are lost to the depths and serve only as food for deep-living animals, a few will be retained in the surface layer or returned to it by random mixing processes, and this is sufficient to keep the population growing. The phytoplankton grows rapidly and is rapidly consumed or dissipated. The general range of total plant production in lakes and in the ocean is about the same as that of terrestrial communities, but the biomass of living organisms present at any one time is very small.

The planktonic animals living in association with the phytoplankton and depending upon it for food belong to a variety of taxonomic groups. They have a common share in a few adaptations which are necessary for successful planktonic existence. They must be capable of more or less continuous activity in order to maintain a favourable position in the water column. Truly planktonic animals must be capable of this kind of suspension in the water through the entire life cycle, and commonly through a considerable range of environmental conditions. Alternatively, some shallow water forms are able to develop resting stages which tide them over unfavourable periods. Some animals which are not truly planktonic acquire this mode of existence during certain periods in the life cycle. Notably these include the larvae of many bottom-living invertebrates and some fish larvae.

All of these creatures, whether temporary or permanent members of the zooplankton, have as a prime requisite the ability to acquire their food by collecting small particles which exist in a rather thin suspension in the water. The mechanisms for doing this are various. Certain protozoa entrap particles in pseudopodial nets, and others feed by ciliary entrainment. Ciliary feeding is common in many other forms as well. The branchial baskets of certain Crustacea have a complex and well-integrated system for creating water currents with some of their appendages and for filtering particles out of the stream with others, with the net result that particles are concentrated and passed to the mouth. This does not exhaust the list of filter-feeding types, but it illustrates the adaptability of living creatures to meet this prime necessity.

Bottom sediments in lakes and the ocean present a more varied environment than that of the overlying water, and in general the animals living there tend to be larger, more abundant, and more diverse. There are filter-feeders living on the slurry of plankton and detritus that exists just above the bottom. There are animals which burrow through the sediments, feeding indiscriminately, as do earthworms on land. There are animals with various kinds of devices for clearing organic matter from mud–water interfaces and the surfaces of sand particles and rocks.

Some of the bottom animals are of course carnivores. There are varying degrees of ability to tolerate the anoxic conditions that often develop in soft sediments and, to a lesser degree, in water overlying the bottom.

Although the bottom fauna as a whole is diverse, the adaptations are so narrowly specialized that a particular kind of bottom is likely to have a fairly limited array of species. Commonly half a dozen species are overwhelming dominant on a particular bottom type, constituting 70 to 90 per cent of the total biomass [2], and in cases where the bottom is patchy, an almost totally different fauna may occupy another area only a few metres away.

The maintenance of a fauna that is well adapted to a particular bottom type is apparently no problem. When free-swimming planktonic larvae have reached a size suitable for metamorphosis, and are carried helplessly over the bottom by water movements, they are able to delay the change to adulthood awhile, pending arrival over a bottom suitable for adults. This observation has been well documented, but present knowledge is insufficient to specify what sensory mechanisms enable them to do this.

TROPHIC RELATIONS

The utilization of the products of green plant growth is partitioned between animals and bacteria. The latter grow throughout the water column and on the bottom, although generally they are most abundant and perform their functions most effectively on the bottom. These functions are both general and specific, involving the decomposition of any organic matter not otherwise utilized. This puts them in competition with animals for some organic remains, but they are also capable of degrading refractory materials that animals cannot digest.

Despite the presence of bacteria, most aquatic environments contain considerable quantities of non-living organic matter, particulate, colloidal, and dissolved, which has not yet been decomposed. The non-living fraction often exceeds the total organic content of the living community, especially in the deep ocean, where it is several orders of magnitude larger than the living fraction [3]. Since all of this material is originally derived from living organisms, either by death and decomposition or by direct excretory and secretory processes, the rate of turnover must be very slow.

The reasons for this slow turnover cannot be evaluated with any degree of clarity, although a number of factors can be mentioned. For example, the total quantity of dissolved organic matter in deep ocean waters is about 1 mg per litre [4], and in some freshwater environments it may be one or even two orders of magnitude higher. The waters of our earth contain between 1 and 2×10^{12} metric tons of this material—an impressive figure, which nevertheless represents a thin bacterial medium. This fact at least partly accounts for the slow rate of turnover.

We do not know nearly as much as we would like to know about the reservoir of non-living organic matter that exists in the aquatic environment. Modern biochemical techniques are only now becoming equal to the task of dealing with the complex array of chemical substances that exists in very dilute solution in natural waters. Study of these substances is a matter of increasing interest, because we are beginning to see that their relations with living organisms are more complicated than was formerly realized. This is not just a simple, one-way path of decomposition of dead organisms to inorganic materials. There are some reversible steps in the process. Dissolved organic materials can be converted into particles by adsorption on near-surface bubbles [5, 6] and probably on other particles, and it has been experimentally demonstrated that the particles so formed will support the growth of filter-feeding animals [7] and will provide a suitable substrate for bacterial growth.

These particles with their attached bacteria have achieved a rather remarkable "steady state" in some experiments, in which the rate of utilization of organic matter by bacteria is approximately balanced by additions from the dissolved fraction. Moreover, bacteria are able literally to create particles of organic matter as a substrate for themselves. The known facts are simply that filtered sea water inoculated with bacteria will develop aggregated masses of particulate organic matter in the course of a few days. The mechanism of formation is obscure; the most likely explanation is that bacterial attack on colloids alters the electrical charges that normally keep the colloids dispersed. In short, there is an array of relationships between the living and non-living components of the aquatic environment, some of which can turn the dissolved and colloidal portions back into the food chain without going all the way through the cycle to inorganic elements.

Bacteria grow most effectively on surfaces. In natural waters they are commonly found on plankton and on non-living particulate organic matter. The quantity of such surfaces is limited, and experimentally it has been shown that an increase in surface area accelerates bacterial growth [8] and is likely to result in utilization of most of the organic matter present. This kind of result negates a statement commonly seen in the literature, that these dissolved materials probably are largely humates and other substances which are relatively poor bacterial nutrients.

The basic production of any aquatic environment depends upon the rate of cycling of essential nutrients. Phytoplankton growth is limited in most bodies of water during much of the year by the quantity of phosphate, inorganic sources of nitrogen, and other trace elements. This in turn depends upon the rate of production of these micronutrients by animal excretion and bacterial decomposition. The existence of a large pool of dissolved and colloidal organic matter, which must be degraded to inorganic materials before it can be used by the green plants, has led aquatic biologists to feel that this is where the real bottle-neck in the system lies. And because the bottom is a more effective site for decomposition and regeneration of nutrients than the water column, some of our most productive freshwater environments are shallow bodies of water which have a large ratio of mud surface to water volume and sufficient vertical mixing to return regenerated nutrients to the surface layer quickly. For the same reasons, shallow coastal areas and off-shore banks in the oceans tend to be productive. In deeper parts of the ocean there is a fairly rich store of inorganic nutrients, which are the products of decomposition over a period of some hundreds of years. There the problem is not so much rates of regeneration as it is rate of return of the nutrients to the surface layer, so that productivity tends to be controlled by physical processes of mixing and upwelling. These are relatively slow processes because of the thermal stability of ocean waters, and with minor exceptions deep oceanic areas are less productive than coastal waters.

STABILIZING FACTORS IN THE AQUATIC ENVIRONMENT

The multiplicity of species and of trophic pathways is the keynote of success in the development of long-term stability in the aquatic environment. A reasonable balance is required between producers and consumers in order to achieve a smooth energy-flow through the system. Temporary overproduction of either producers or consumers can disrupt the system, with results ranging from mild reduction in overall productivity to cataclysmic destruction.

A multi-species balance is most readily achieved in a relatively constant environment, and hence tropical associations have been regarded with good reason as being mature from an evolutionary standpoint [9]. In higher latitudes many plankton species are ephemeral and sharply limited as to season. Long-term stability requires a succession of species that are well suited to the environment of the moment. This succession ordinarily is achieved without serious disruption, although some seasonal imbalance is likely to exist. For example, growth of green plants is reduced in winter, when the light intensity is minimal for photosynthesis, and during that period a considerable stock of unutilized nutrients accumulates in the water column. The imbalance swings in the opposite direction in spring, when increasing vernal radiation triggers a short, sharp burst of phytoplankton growth that uses up most of the nutrients that are immediately available. The production is in excess of immediate consumer needs and probably is not used as effectively as it would be if production were distributed over a longer period.

These are minor imbalances. More drastic examples have been noted in connection with summer blooms of blue-green algae in lakes and ponds, and the so-called red tides [10, 11] in marine coastal waters. These blooms commonly are associated with warm, calm weather and an excessive nutrient supply which generally, although not always, is a result of pollution. The organisms involved are able to maintain themselves in a thin surface stratum, and to carry on photosynthesis at a level near the maximum quantum yield, as long as the nutrient supply continues to be adequate. The animal population is not geared to utilize this plant material as rapidly as it is produced, and the situation is worsened by the fact that some of these algae produce noxious external metabolites. In the later stages of these blooms, their death and decomposition can, in extreme cases, cause mass mortality of fishes and bottom invertebrates.

These are pathological conditions arising largely from unnatural causes. Only a few types of environments have achieved long-term stability at a similarly high level of production approaching the theoretical maximum. These include the littoral zone of some ponds and lakes, fresh and salt water marshes, turtle grass communities, and coral reefs. The requirements for such a community appear to be a substrate rich in potential nutrient supply and a sufficiency of water, so that none of the ordinary chemical factors will be limiting, and in addition the community must be confined to a thin stratum, so that the plants have a full opportunity to make the most of the solar energy available.

In contrast, the more typically terrestrial community tends to be limited by lack of sufficient water or carbon dioxide, and the more typically aquatic one by a suboptimal rate of supply of inorganic nutrients. The net result is that most plant communities operate at a level between 10 and 50 per cent of maximum efficiency [12]. However, in general, the community gains stability by sacrificing efficiency. The simple facts of the case become apparent enough if crash blooms are compared with a more normal aquatic association.

Let us suppose that instead of a bloom concentrated in the immediate surface layer, we have a phytoplankton population that is distributed through the upper 20–30 metres of water. Some of the solar radiation that impinges on the surface of the water will be absorbed by the water itself, before it has an opportunity to reach the plants at the lower levels. Inevitably this reduces the overall efficiency of production in relation to incident radiation. However, the plants will be able to scavenge such nutrients as are available from a larger volume of water, thus postponing ultimate nutrient deficiency. The animals can feed more efficiently in a moderate concentration of phytoplankton and are less liable to the toxic effects associated with extreme bloom conditions. A large fraction of the food they assimilate will be used for immediate metabolic needs, and the excretory products will be returned to the water to a large degree as ammonia, phosphate, and other substances that can be used immediately for further phytoplankton growth. Thus the system acquires built-in potentialities for further growth, although it is by no means the closed system that exists in a balanced aquarium.

As nutrients become more deficient, the phytoplankton growth rate is reduced. There is a tendency for the plants to store products of photosynthesis as carbohydrate or lipid until such time as the nutrient intake permits further production of protoplasm. This concomitant of nutrient deficiency has been observed in nature and also in culture experiments. Two major ecological consequences arise therefrom. First, an increase in energy sources for animal metabolism is supplied at minimum cost in terms of nutrient input. Secondly, the accumulation of storage products increases the sinking rate of the phytoplankton, which tends to reduce the concentration of phytoplankton in the surface layer and to increase its total depth range [13, 14]. Theoretically there is a further reduction in the potential efficiency of production; but the increase in the volume of water containing growing phytoplankton provides an additional source of nutrients to help alleviate the deficiency, so that in actual fact production is increased.

The basic environmental factors that control productivity are highly variable. However, the internal adjustments to changing conditions, which have just been described, provide built-in stability in phytoplankton populations and associated consumers. There are large variations, both seasonal and regional, in radiation, nutrient supply, and other important environmental factors, but biological populations are considerably less variable.

Admittedly the extent of these compensations has not been fully realized until recently. For example, the older literature speaks of the blue waters of the Sargasso Sea as a biological desert in comparison with the richer temperate and boreal waters. This is true enough in terms of numbers of phytoplankton cells per litre of surface water, where the ratios of cell concentrations are of the order of 10:1 or even 30:1. But the low concentration of phytoplankton in the Sargasso Sea is partly compensated by its more extensive vertical distribution. It can grow actively in the upper 100 metres, more or less, in contrast with 30–40 metres in some of the more northern waters. As a result, the total population underlying a unit area of sea surface will vary by a factor of only three or four to one.

This is also true of rates of production of plant material. For example, measurements of phytoplankton productivity have been made on the Fladen Ground [15, 16], a productive area in the North Sea that is commercially important for its fisheries, and in the Sargasso Sea off Bermuda [17, 18]. The two sets of data were comparable, consisting of assessments of rates of carbon fixation by means of experimental determinations of C^{14} uptake. Ratios of total productivity in the two areas were of the order of 3:1.

The stabilizing factors that have been discussed qualitatively above have been examined more critically by means of mathematical models [19]. These models formulate the interrelationships of phytoplankton, zooplankton, and a limiting nutrient such as phosphate, in a way that incorporates the checks and balances that have been described. The model obviously is simpler than nature in many ways, both in the biological interrelations and in the choice of key environmental factors that control levels of productivity. However, in areas such as the Fladen Ground and the Sargasso Sea, where detailed information is available for testing purposes, the model yields realistic results. The kinds of basic environmental factors that need to be considered in this sort of model are radiation, temperature, the rate of mixing between the surface waters and subsurface layers, and the concentration of nutrients existing in a more or less steady state underneath the productive zone, which will refertilize the surface layer when they are delivered to it by mixing processes. This problem has been examined particularly with respect to summer populations, which are not highly variable and hence conform more or less to the requirements of the model. In summer, radiation is nearly constant over wide ranges of latitude and does not need to be regarded as a variable. The other environmental factors in the model are extremely variable geographically, so that if their effects were cumulative, the plankton would vary by a ratio of more than 30:1. Instead, the internal adjustments postulated in the model result in a reduction in plankton variability quite similar to that observed in nature. In a comparison of model results based on environmental data from the Fladen Ground and the Sargasso Sea, the calculated ratio of surface chlorophyll concentrations in the two areas is 15:1, but the carbon content of the total phytoplankton population per unit area of sea surface is only about 4:1.

CONCLUSIONS

In this brief survey, some aspects of the aquatic community are clear enough. The aquatic environment is an equable one which ordinarily does not impose extreme stress on its inhabitants, although there are some rather specialized adaptations that are necessary in order to make full use of the available potentialities. The most obvious adaptations have to do with general life habit—with modes of feeding that are consistent with the various kinds of food available. Beyond this, there are built-in physiological adaptations that tend to stabilize the biological system, the immediate effect being to minimize effects of environmental fluctuations in any one area; but there are overtones, in that these same adaptations make it possible to establish viable ecosystems in all sorts of geographical regions, some of which seem forbidding at first glance.

There is fragmentary evidence of a third level of adaptation. Certain physiological reactions and behavioural responses of aquatic organisms are difficult to explain in terms of adaptive advantage to the individual, e.g. the diurnal migration of zooplankton. There has been wide speculation as to possible advantages of this mode of life, and also there have been a few solid attempts to evaluate the advantages and disadvantages in ecological and physiological terms [20, 21]—with somewhat equivocal conclusions. In a community in which about half the species perform this migration and the other half do not, one would hardly expect to find an overwhelming advantage in one mode of life or the other. However, one can make a fairly good case for the hypothesis that diurnal migration of at least some of the population can contribute to the long-term stability of the community as a whole [22]. An equally good case can be made for the proposition that certain other modes of behaviour would be more advantageous from the standpoint of short-term gains, but that these would be deleterious to the community over the long term.

Thus there are indications of community evolution, which might seem to oppose the doctrine of survival of the fittest, but do not actually do so. Rather there is a suggestion that the community is a sort of loosely organized symbiosis. Individual species compete with others that have similar needs, but these basic needs are supplied only by continued community interaction. Hence a species which disrupts the community will reduce its own chances for survival.

On the other hand, drastic alteration of the environment may provide an opportunity for disruptive, weed-like growths of certain species which hitherto were harmless members of a stable community. This happens under certain experimental conditions, and also in cases of marked pollution of natural waters. Given sufficient time, such communities might become restabilized by processes of natural evolution. But we need not and should not accept that long-delayed solution to our problems of water resources.

REFERENCES

1. KANWISHER, J. W. (1955), "Freezing in Intertidal Animals," *Biol. Bull. 109*: 56–63.
2. SANDERS, H. L. (1956), "Oceanography of Long Island Sound, 1952–1954. X. The Biology of Marine Bottom Communities," *Bull. Bingham Oceanogr. Coll. 15*: 345–414.
3. RILEY, G. A., VAN HEMERT, D., and WANGERSKY, P. J. (1965), "Organic Aggregates in Surface and Deep Waters of the Sargasso Sea," *Limnol. Oceanogr. 10*: 354–63.
4. DUURSMA, E. K. (1960), "Dissolved Organic Carbon, Nitrogen, and Phosphorus in the Sea," *Netherlands J. Sea Res. 1*: 1–147.
5. SUTCLIFFE, W. H., BAYLOR, E. R., and MENZEL, D. W. (1963), "Sea Surface Chemistry and Langmuir Circulation," *Deep-Sea Res. 10*: 233–43.
6. RILEY, G. A. (1963), "Organic Aggregates in Seawater and the Dynamics of Their Formation and Utilization," *Limnol. Oceanogr. 8*: 372–81.
7. BAYLOR, E. R. and SUTCLIFFE, W. H. (1963), "Dissolved Organic Matter in Seawater as a Source of Particulate Food," *Limnol. Oceanogr. 8*: 369–71.
8. ZOBELL, C. E. and ANDERSON, D. Q. (1936), "Observations on the Multiplication of Bacteria in Different Volumes of Stored Sea Water and the Influence of Oxygen Tension and Solid Surfaces," *Biol. Bull. 71*: 324–42.
9. DUNBAR, M. J. (1960), "The Evolution of Stability in Marine Environments. Natural Selection at the Level of the Ecosystem," *Am. Naturalist, 94*: 129–36.
10. CONOVER, S. M. (1954), "Observations on the Structure of Red Tides in New Haven Harbor, Connecticut," *J. Mar. Res. 13*: 145–55.
11. SLOBODKIN, L. B. (1953), "A Possible Initial Condition for Red Tides on the Coast of Florida," *J. Mar. Res. 12*: 148–55.
12. RYTHER, J. H. (1960), "Organic Production by Plankton Algae, and Its Environmental Control," *The Ecology of Algae* (Spec. Pub. No. 2), Symposium Pymatuning Lab., Univ. Pittsburgh, pp. 72–83.
13. STEELE, J. H. and VENTSCH, C. S. (1960), "The Vertical Distribution of Chlorophyll," *J. Mar. Biol. Assoc. 39*: 217–26.
14. SMAYDA, T. J. and BOLEYN, B. J. (1966), "Experimental Observations on the Flotation of Marine Diatoms. II. *Skeletonema costatum* and *Rhizosolenia setigera*," *Limnol. Oceanogr. 11*: 18–34.

15. STEELE, J. H. (1958), "Plant Production in the Northern North Sea," *Mar. Res., Scot. Home Dept. 7*: 1–36.
16. STEELE, J. H. and BAIRD, I. E. (1961), "Relations between Primary Production, Chlorophyll, and Particulate Carbon," *Limnol. Oceanogr. 6*: 68–78.
17. MENZEL, D. W. and RYTHER, J. H. (1960), "The Annual Cycle of Primary Production in the Sargasso Sea off Bermuda," *Deep-Sea Res. 6*: 351–67.
18. MENZEL, D. W. and RYTHER, J. H. (1961), "Zooplankton in the Sargasso Sea off Bermuda and Its Relation to Primary Production," *J. Conseil, 26*: 250–8.
19. RILEY, G. A. (1965), "A Mathematical Model of Regional Variations in Plankton," *Limnol. Oceanogr., 10,* Suppl.: R202–R215.
20. MCLAREN, I. A. (1963), "Effects of Temperature on Growth of Zoo-plankton and the Adaptive Value of Vertical Migration," *J. Fish. Res. Bd. Can. 20*: 685–727.
21. NAPORA, T. A. (1964), "The Effect of Hydrostatic Pressure on the Prawn, *Systellaspis debilis.*" *Narragansett Mar. Lab., Occas. Pub. No. 2*: 92–94.
22. HARRIS, E. (1959), "The Nitrogen Cycle in Long Island Sound," *Bull. Bingham Oceanogr. Coll. 17*: 31–65.

PRÉSENCE DE BACTÉRIES RÉDUCTRICES DU SOUFRE DANS LES RIVIÈRES POLLUÉES PAR LES EAUX RÉSIDUAIRES DES USINES DE PRÉPARATION DES PÂTES À PAPIER

Raymond Desrochers

LES EFFETS des eaux résiduaires, déversées, sans traitement préalable, dans les cours d'eau, se manifestent principalement de deux façons : premièrement, en affectant directement les êtres aquatiques, et deuxièmement, en modifiant le milieu dans lequel vivent ces organismes.

Des tests biologiques ou bio-essais permettent de déterminer si les substances polluantes sont toxiques pour les organismes aquatiques, si elles ont des effets répulsifs ou si elles sont inoffensives. Les effets toxiques des eaux sulfiteuses furent étudiés, entre autres, par Williams *et al.* (1953), Hoglund (1961), et Grande (1964), et leurs effets répulsifs, par Hoglund (1961), Jones *et al.* (1956), et Grande (1964).

Ces deux effets, toxique et répulsif, se font malheureusement sentir à des concentrations différentes : les doses létales diminuant l'acuité des sens olfactifs, exercent leur action sans que l'animal ait l'instinct de fuir, alors que les doses faibles repoussent le poisson, établissant ainsi une barrière chimique aux migrations, mais sans affecter sérieusement la santé de l'animal (Hoglund 1961).

Des tests chimiques et biochimiques ainsi que des échantillonnages biologiques servent à mesurer les changements profonds caractéristiques d'une pollution intense; diminution sensible de l'O_2 dissous due à la grande demande biologique d'oxygène de certaines eaux résiduaires, telles les eaux sulfiteuses dont le B.O.D. est 10 fois plus élevé que celui des égouts domestiques (Eldridge 1959); abaissement du pH de l'eau par suite du caractère acide des eaux sulfiteuses (Williams *et al.* 1953; Grande 1964); augmentation des substances organiques et inorganiques solubles; accumulation sur le fond des solides en suspension, etc.

A la suite de ces modifications profondes, de nouvelles populations animales et végétales mieux adaptées aux conditions nouvelles s'installent, prolifèrent et souvent, occupent tout l'espace disponible au détriment des autres espèces. Par exemple, les *Sphaerotilus*, bactéries filamenteuses, forment un véritable tapis et nuisent au développement normal des autres organismes, tels les œufs de poissons (Smith et Kramer 1963). Mais surtout, les bactéries sont très actives et utilisent l'oxygène pour la décomposition de la matière organique, ce qui rend souvent le milieu anaérobie. Les bactéries de la putréfaction se multiplient alors rapidement et libèrent dans l'eau des produits toxiques qui aggravent le degré de pollution. Les bactéries réductrices du soufre font partie du groupe de microbes qui ne prolifèrent que lorsque le milieu est devenu réducteur.

LES BACTÉRIES RÉDUCTRICES DU SOUFRE

Les bactéries réductrices du soufre ont la propriété, comme leur nom l'indique, de réduire les composés inorganiques du soufre : sulfates, sulfites, thiosulfates, etc. (Postgate 1959), et de libérer de l'hydrogène sulfuré. Pour cette réduction, les sulfato-réducteurs ont besoin d'une source d'hydrogène. Une grande variété de substances organiques peuvent être utilisées à cette fin : tartrate, citrate, pyruvate, acides gras, acides aminés, peptones, alcools simples, monosaccharides, certains dissaccharides, etc. (ZoBell 1957).

Deux genres bactériens possèdent cette propriété de réduire les sulfates : le genre *Clostridium* (Campbell *et al.* 1957), de l'ordre des Eubactériales, qui compte une espèce sulfato-réductrice thermophile, et le genre *Desulfovibrio*, de l'ordre des Pseudomomadales. Ce dernier genre surtout fut étudié; la plupart des travaux traitant de la réduction des sulfates se rapportent à des bactéries de ce genre.

Ces microbes sont ubiquistes et furent isolés des milieux les plus divers : boues marines et lacustres, marais, eaux d'égouts, sols humides, etc. (ZoBell 1957). Ce sont des anaérobies stricts se développant seulement lorsque les conditions d'oxydo-réduction leur sont convenables. Leur présence peut-être décelée par les odeurs d'hydrogène sulfuré qui se dégagent des habitats peuplés de ces germes. Ce gaz est toxique pour les organismes aquatiques et est aussi une source de pollution de l'air.

TOXICITÉ DE L'H_2S POUR LES ORGANISMES AQUATIQUES

Les sulfures en général, et surtout l'hydrogène sulfuré, sont très toxiques pour les poissons d'eau douce. Doudoroff et Katz (1950), à la fin d'une revue des études faites sur le sujet, concluent que l'H_2S peut être toxique à certains poissons d'eau douce à des concentrations plus faibles que 1 ppm. Jones (1964) rapporte que des concentrations de moins de 2.4 ppm d'hydrogène sulfuré sont létales pour l'épinoche. Ce gaz a pour effet de diminuer la consommation d'oxygène par les vertébrés aquatiques. Werner (1963) trouva que le L.C.50 (concentration en parties par million qui tue 50 pour cent des animaux en expérience dans à peu près 4 heures) d'H_2S pour *Daphnia Pulex* est d'environ 2.82 ppm.

L'hydrogène sulfuré, formé dans les zones polluées anaérobies, cause donc une pollution très sérieuse lorsqu'il est entraîné dans des zones où vivent divers organismes aquatiques. Une forte mortalité de poissons attribuable à la libération subite d'hydrogène sulfuré par des opérations de dragage fut signalée sur les côtes de la Colombie-Britannique par Hourston et Herlinveaux en 1957. Des phénomènes semblables furent également rapportés par Copenhagen (1934) et Butlin (1949). En faibles concentrations, l'hydrogène sulfuré produit également un effet répulsif chez certaines espèces de poissons (Jones 1964).

POLLUTION DE L'AIR PAR L'HYDROGÈNE SULFURÉ

L'odorat humain est très sensible à l'hydrogène sulfuré et peut le déceler dans des mélanges d'H_2S et d'air dans des proportions de 1 à 10,000,000 (Moncrieff 1944). L'hydrogène sulfuré de l'air provient surtout des raffineries de pétrole et des cokeries, mais il se dégage aussi des eaux résiduaires des usines de pâte à papier utilisant le procédé Kraft. Ce gaz peut également provenir d'étangs contaminés. Drummond et Postgate (1955) rapportent un cas où l'odeur d'H_2S se dégageant d'un étang contaminé causait tellement d'ennuis aux résidents qu'on a dû le faire combler.

ÉTUDE D'UNE POPULATION DE BACTÉRIES RÉDUCTRICES DU SOUFRE DANS LA RIVIÈRE OTTAWA

Nous avons fait, au cours de l'année 1961, une étude dans la rivière Ottawa, afin de déterminer s'il s'établissait une population de bactéries réductrices du soufre dans une rivière où étaient déversées des eaux ayant servi à la préparation de la cellulose selon le procédé au sulfite.

A première vue, les eaux sulfiteuses semblent contenir les substances favorables au développement des sulfato-réducteurs : soufre sous forme de sulfite et de sulfate, et substances organiques pouvant servir de source d'hydrogène : pentoses, hexoses, alcools, etc. (Eldridge 1959). De plus, en aval du point des déversement des eaux sulfiteuses, se jettent les égouts de la ville de Hawkesbury, source abondante d'azote et de phosphore.

Nous savions également, à la suite de l'étude de Piché en 1954, que certaines zones, en aval de Hawkesbury, devenaient anaérobies au cours de l'été. Les conditions nous semblaient donc favorables au développement des bactéries réductrices du soufre.

Des prélèvements furent faits tous les mois, pendant une période d'un an, à six stations différentes de la rivière Ottawa, entre Baie de l'Orignal et Pointe-Fortune aux endroits indiqués sur la carte (figure 1), soit sur un secteur de seize milles.

Les sites de prélèvement sont, dans l'ordre :

1. Baie de l'Orignal, 3⅔ milles en amont du pont de Hawkesbury.
2. Pont de Hawkesbury, ⅔ de mille en aval des usines de la C.I.P.
3. Ile Lorrain, 1 mille en aval du pont de Hawkesbury et ⅔ de mille en aval du point de déversement des égouts domestiques de la ville de Hawkesbury.
4. Ile Stevens, 3 milles en aval de l'île Lorrain.
5. Chute-à-Blondeau, 4 milles en aval de l'île Stevens.
6. Pointe-Fortune, 5 milles en aval de Chute-à-Blondeau.

Chaque échantillon était soumis aux analyses suivantes : détermination de l'oxygène dissous, du pH, du B.O.D., de l'H_2S, et comptage des bactéries réductrices du soufre.

Les résultats de ces travaux montrèrent que le nombre de bactéries réductrices du soufre augmente en aval des sources de pollution, soit après le déversement des eaux résiduaires de l'usine de cellulose et des eaux des égouts domestiques de la ville de Hawkesbury, mais que ces bactéries ne sont pas actives dans les eaux de la rivière sauf pendant une courte période de l'année et à la station 2 seulement. En effet, à deux reprises nous avons noté la présence d'H_2S à cet endroit alors que la population des bactéries réductrices du soufre atteignait l'ordre de 1.1×10^6 par cm^3 (Desrochers et Fredette 1959).

Cette station était située entre la rive et une petite île, et lorsque le niveau de la rivière était bas, à la fin de l'été, il se formait à cet endroit un étang plus ou moins fermé et séparé du corps de la rivière, ce qui favorisait le développement de conditions anaérobies et la prolifération des bactéries réductrices du soufre.

Nous étions également intéressé à savoir ce qui se passait l'hiver sous la glace. Gaufin et Tarzwell (1955) ont démontré que la zone polluée s'allonge au cours de l'hiver mais que, par contre, l'activité bactérienne

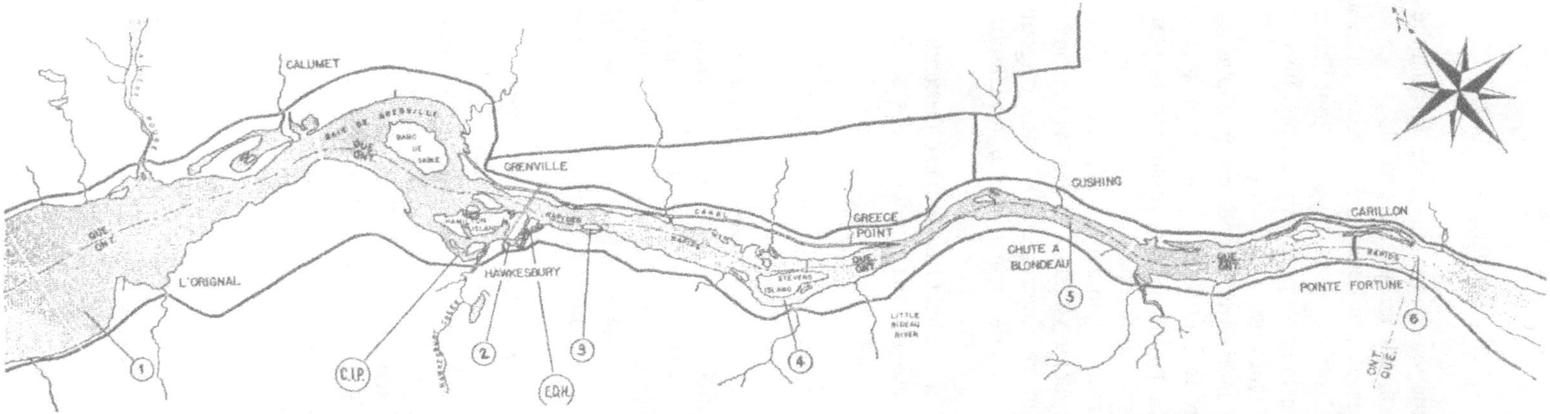

FIGURE 1. Secteur de la rivière Ottawa entre Original et Pointe Fortune. Les endroits de prélèvement sont numérotés de un à six. C.I.P., usine de la Canadian International Paper; E.D.H., égouts domestiques de la ville de Hawkesbury.

étant réduite, les fluctuations journalières de la quantité d'O_2 dissous sont de plus faible amplitude en hiver qu'en été.

Nos analyses montrèrent que l'eau de la rivière Ottawa, en aval des sources de pollution, est suffisamment oxygénée tout l'hiver. La mortalité du poisson, souvent constatée au printemps un peu plus en aval, ne peut donc être attribuée à l'asphyxie.

La zone polluée de la rivière s'étend sur une plus grande distance en hiver qu'en été car le B.O.D. est plus élevé à la station la plus éloignée des sources de pollution, soit la station 6, pendant la saison froide que pendant la saison chaude.

Par contre, au printemps, pendant la période de la crue des eaux, le B.O.D. a presque la même valeur à toutes les stations, ce qui signifie que la dilution des eaux résiduaires et des eaux d'égouts se fait convenablement à cette période de l'année et que la pollution est beaucoup moins sérieuse.

Le pH de l'eau de la rivière Ottawa n'est descendu à moins de 6 pendant la période de nos travaux à aucune des stations.

BACTÉRIES RÉDUCTRICES DU SOUFRE DANS LES SÉDIMENTS

Nous n'avons pas fait de numération des bactéries réductrices du soufre dans les sédiments. Kimata *et al.* (1955) firent une étude des populations de bactéries réductrices du soufre dans les boues du fond d'un cours d'eau et de la mer et constatèrent qu'il y avait une relation entre la quantité d'H_2S des boues et le nombre de bactéries réductrices du soufre présentes dans ces boues. Ils constatèrent également que la production d'H_2S était influencée par la quantité de sulfate et de matière organique de la boue et de l'eau recouvrant cette boue. Il ne fait donc aucun doute que des eaux résiduaires contenant à la fois des sulfates et des substances organiques sont favorables au développement des bactéries réductrices du soufre, si le milieu devient anaérobie comme c'est le cas pour les sédiments. L'H_2S produit dans ces sédiments remonte à la surface de la boue et rend le fond inhospitalier pour la faune benthique. Ce phénomène expliquerait l'absence de faune benthique normale dans des cours d'eau recevant les eaux résiduaires des usines de pâte à papier.

CONCLUSION

Les bactéries réductrices du soufre étant des anaérobies stricts exigeant un potentiel d'oxydo-reduction très bas, ne se développent que dans les milieux fortement pollués et, par conséquent, ne sont actives que dans les cas de pollution très intense comme l'a montré notre étude. Ces conditions extrêmes exigées par les sulfato-réducteurs ne se rencontrent pas souvent dans tout le volume d'un cours d'eau recevant des eaux résiduaires. Mais souvent celles-ci sont déversées le long des berges où elles emplissent des fosses ou des mares à peu près stagnantes, surtout pendant la périodes des eaux basses, créant ainsi des habitats propices aux bactéries de la putréfaction. Ces endroits putrides, en plus d'être une source de pollution de l'eau et de l'air, présentent un aspect désagréable et souvent répugnant.

C'est un fait noté par plusieurs (Beak 1963; Waldichuk 1962) que tout le volume de l'eau disponible pour la dilution des eaux résiduaires n'est pas toujours utilisé efficacement, ce qui cause une forte pollution locale, pourtant évitable à peu de frais. A Hawkesbury, par exemple, on a remédié à la situation par une meilleure distribution des eaux résiduaires. L'endroit s'y prêtait admirablement bien puisque ces eaux se déversaient à la tête de rapides puissants. On avait malheureusement négligé d'utiliser cette situation géographique susceptible de permettre une plus complète dilution des eaux des l'usine et de celles des égouts de la ville. La même négligence peut être constatée à plusieurs endroits, surtout le long des cours d'eau importants.

Les bactéries réductrices du soufre sont également actives dans les boues des lacs et des cours d'eau. L'accumulation de déchets solides sur les fonds, en plus de détruire les habitats de la faune benthique, favorise le développement d'un milieu anaérobie propice à la putréfaction. L'été lorsque la température de l'eau est plus élevée et le métabolisme bactérien plus actif, la fermentation sulfhydrique est très intense, les gaz s'accumulent dans les sédiments; puis, lorsque la pression est assez forte, des masses de déchets se détachent du fond et montent à la surface libérant sur leur passage les gaz toxiques qu'elles contiennent. Nous avons, à maintes reprises, observé ce phénomène à l'embouchure de la rivière du Lièvre près de Masson sur la rivière Ottawa. Le lit de la rivière, à cet endroit, est recouvert de fibres cellulosiques et d'autres débris de bois.

Pour lutter efficacement contre ce type de pollution, le meilleur moyen consiste à éliminer les déchets solides des eaux résiduaires. On éviterait ainsi que des résidus inoffensifs soient transformés, par l'action des bactéries réductrices du soufre et d'autres microbes, en substances toxiques capables d'empoisonner la faune benthique qui habite normalement les eaux propres et saines.

BIBLIOGRAPHIE

BEAK, T. W. (1963), "Water Pollution Problems of the Pulp and Paper Industry," *Tappi, 46*: 160A–166A.

BUTLIN, K. B. (1949), "Some Malodorous Activities of Sulphate-Reducing Bacteria," *Proc. Soc. Appl. Bact. 12*: 39–42.

CAMPBELL, L. L. Jr., FRANK, H. A., et HALL, E. R. (1957), "Studies on the Thermophilic Sulfate Reducing Bacteria. I. Identification of *Sporovibrio desulfuricans* as *Clostridium nigrificans*," *J. Bact. 73*: 516–21.

COPENHAGEN, W. J. (1934), "Occurrence of Sulphides in Certain Areas of the Sea Bottom on the South African Coast," *Fish. Mar. Biol. Surv. Union S. Afr. Rept. No. 11*: 3–18. Cité par ZoBell (1957).

DESROCHERS, R. et FREDETTE, V. (1959), "Etude d'une population de bactéries réductrices du soufre," *Can. J. Microbiol. 6*: 349–54.

DOUDOROFF, P. et KATZ, M. (1950), "Critical Review of Literature on the Toxicity of Industrial Wastes and Their Components to Fish. I. Alkalies, Acids, and Inorganic Gases," *Sew. and Indust. Wastes, 22*: 1432–58.

DRUMMOND, J. P. M. et POSTGATE, J. R. (1955), "A Note on the Enumeration of Sulphate-Reducing Bacteria in Polluted Water and on Their Inhibition by Chromate," *J. Appl. Bact. 18*: 307–11.

ELDRIDGE, E. F. (1959), "Composition of Sulfite Waste Liquor," in *Biological Problems in Water Pollution* (USDHEW Div. of Wat. Supply and Poll. Cont., Taft Sanitary Engineering Center), pp. 255–6.

GAUFIN, A. R. et TARZWELL, C. M. (1955), "Environmental Changes in a Polluted Stream during Winter," *Amer. Midland Naturalist, 54*: 78–88.

GRANDE, M. (1964), "Water Pollution Studies in the River Otra, Norway. Effects of Pulp and Paper Mill Wastes on Fish," *Air Water Pollut. 8*: 77–88 (*Biol. Abst. 46*: 1730).

HOGLUND, L. B. (1961), "The Reactions of Fish in Concentration Gradients. A Comparative Study Based on Fluviarium Experiments with Special Reference to Oxygen, Acidity, Carbon Dioxide, and Sulphite Waste Liquor (SWL)," *Rept. Inst. Freshwater Res. Drottningholm, 43*: 1–17 (*Biol. Abst. 42*: 712–13).

HOURSTON, A. S. et HERLINVEAUX, R. H. (1957), "A 'Mass Mortality' of Fish in Alberni Harbour, B.C.," *Fish. Bd. Progr. Rept. Pacific Coast Sta. No. 109*: 3–6.

JONES, J. R. E. (1964), *Fish and River Pollution* (London: Butterworths).

JONES, B. F., WARREN, C. E., BOND, C. E., et DOUDOROFF, P. (1956), "Avoidance Reactions of Salmonid Fishes to Pulp-Mill Effluents," *Sew Indust. Wastes, 28*: 1403–13.

KIMATA, M., KADOTA, H., HATA, Y. et TAJIMA, T. (1955), "Studies on the Marine Sulphate-Reducing Bacteria. 1. Distribution of Marine Sulphate-Reducing Bacteria in the Coastal Waters Receiving a Considerable Amount of Pulp Mill Drainage," *Bull. Japan. Soc. Sci. Fish. 21*: 102–8.

MONCRIEFF, R. W. (1944), *The Chemical Senses* (Leonard Hill, London).

PICHÉ, L. (1954), *Rapport sur la pollution de la rivière Ottawa et de ses principaux tributaires entre Ottawa-Hull et l'Ile de Montréal en 1954* (Montréal: La ligne anti-pollution de Québec).

POSTGATE, J. R. (1959), "Sulphate Reduction by Bacteria," *Ann. Rev. Microbiol. 13*: 505–20.

SMITH, L. L. Jr. et KRAMER, R. H. (1963), "Survival of Walleye Eggs in Relation to Wood Fibres and *Sphaerotilus natans* in the Rainy River, Minnesota," *Trans. Amer. Fish. Soc. 92*: 220–34.

WALDICHUK, M. (1962), "Some Water Pollution Problems Connected with the Disposal of Pulp Mill Wastes," *Can. Fish. Culturist, 31*: 3–34.

WERNER, A. E., (1963), "Sulphur Compounds in Kraft Pulp Mill Effluents," *Can. Pulp and Paper Ind. 16*: 35–43.

WILLIAMS, R. W., MAINS, E. M., ELDRIDGE, W. E. et LASATER, J. E. (1953), "Toxic Effects of Sulfite Waste Liquor on Young Salmon," *Washington Dept. Fish Res. Bull. No. 1*: 1–111.

ZOBELL, C. (1957), "Ecology of Sulphate Reducing Bacteria," in *Sulphate Reducing Bacteria, Their Relation to the Secondary Recovery of Oil* (Science Symposium, St. Bonaventure University), pp. 1–24.

WATER-BORNE VIRAL INFECTIONS

Donald M. McLean

STEADILY INCREASING DEMANDS upon supplies of fresh water for domestic, industrial, and recreational purposes, especially during the past decade, have provided enhanced opportunities for microbial and chemical pollution of available sources. Although extensive investigations of coliform bacteria, and to a lesser extent of streptococci, have yielded information of great epidemiological importance, relating to their method of spread by water and to the use of halogens to achieve their inactivation, relatively little direct information of this type is available for viruses. In domestic situations, water is used not only for drinking, and for washing of household utensils, clothing, and persons, but also for conveyance of sewage, bathroom, laundry, and kitchen wastes. Contamination of drinking-water by sewage, which frequently contains viruses pathogenic for man, provides a most convenient mechanism for widespread dissemination of these agents. In recreational areas, natural lakes and streams may also become contaminated by sewage, whereas in artificially constructed swimming-pools and wading-pools, pollution is most frequently introduced through the secretions and excretions of bathers.

RECENT STUDIES

Drinking-water has been incriminated as the vehicle of spread of infectious hepatitis virus in more than 200 outbreaks [1],* following the initial recognition of this mode of dissemination during an epidemic amongst students at Sackville, New Brunswick, in 1930 [2]. Although one hepatitis outbreak in upstate New York was attributed to consumption of water which was chlorinated but not otherwise treated [3], many outbreaks have arisen through the drinking of raw water from wells which became contaminated by seepage from cesspools [4] or septic

*Numbers in brackets refer to the list of references.

tanks [5]. Stasis of water in wells subject to constant addition of virus from nearby sources promotes accumulation of hepatitis virus to high titres of infectivity for human subjects; but flowing water in streams provides a means for continuous dilution, so that accumulation at a particular point is unlikely, unless virus is added constantly from an upstream source, e.g. a sewage plant, as happened at Bathurst, N.S.W., Australia [6].

Swimming-pools have been incriminated as sources of infection of bathers who subsequently developed pharyngo-conjunctival fever due to adenovirus types 3 and 7 [7, 8] or exanthemata due to coxsackievirus A16 [9]. Echovirus types 3 and 11 were recovered from water at three of four wading-pools in Albany, New York, during the summer of 1959 [10]. None of the water samples contained detectable residuals of free chlorine. However, no viruses were recovered from water at an adjacent swimming-pool where the average free chlorine residual was maintained at or above 0.2 ppm. Parainfluenza–1 virus was isolated from water obtained from an inadequately halogenated swimming-pool in Toronto during early 1962 [11]; and in the same city, coxsackievirus B1 was recovered from a swab immersed in a wading-pool in August 1964 [12]. Maintenance of adequate residuals of halogen continuously in swimming-pools ensures prompt inactivation of most viruses introduced by bathers.

At beaches along Lake Erie and Lake Huron, where exchange of water between the shore and the deep portion occurred continuously, coliform bacteria have been detected in low concentrations, but in docks and estuaries where the water was stagnant, gross bacterial contamination was found [11, 12]. In small lakes with little or no turnover of water, high microbial populations have been detected. Likewise, although no viruses have been recovered from water obtained along the Ontario shore line of the Great Lakes, enteroviruses and reoviruses were isolated from swabs immersed in the stagnant terminal branches of the upper Illinois River near Chicago [13]. These swabs were located both upstream and downstream from the outfalls of three sewage treatment plants, thus demonstrating that stagnation permitted the build-up of viral concentration. Similarly, clams and oysters raised in calm stretches of sea water receiving raw sewage effluent at Raritan Bay, New Jersey [14], and Pascagoula, Mississippi [15], ingested sufficient amounts of infectious heptatis virus contained in the sewage to induce outbreaks of illness amongst humans who consumed these seafoods uncooked.

At a sewage plant at Santee, California, a substantial reduction of infectivity titres of effluents was noted following activated sludge treatment of sewage containing high concentrations of enteroviruses, but almost 98 per cent of effluents still yielded virus [16]. The prevalence of enterovirus isolations decreased to 22 per cent after holding the activated sludge effluent in an oxidation pond for an average period of 30 days. Only 10 per cent of samples yielded enteroviruses after the pond effluent was treated with 15 ppm chlorine for 30 minutes; and percolation of the chlorinated effluent through natural sand and gravel 10 to 12 ft thick resulted in complete loss of infectivity. This water was then used successfully for recreational purposes. Similarly, at a sewage plant where coxsackievirus A13 was introduced into the headworks, virus was recovered repeatedly from the aeration tank effluent [17]. In a bench-model activated sludge unit, the concentrations of coxsackievirus A9 and poliovirus–1 in the effluent were reduced by 79 to 99 per cent following addition of virus to the unit continuously throughout 48 hours, but the effluent retained some infectivity [18].

EXPERIMENTAL METHODS AND MATERIALS

This paper reports investigations of the dispersal of two species of poliovirus which are completely non-pathogenic for man, following their introduction into swimming-pools, lakes, creeks in the field, and into a laboratory model of an aeration-type sewage treatment plant. The Sabin vaccine strain of poliovirus–2 was selected for this field-work, and Sabin poliovirus–3 was used in the laboratory model.

Swimming-Pools

At an outdoor recirculating pool of 25,000 gallons capacity, an inoculum containing approximately 100,000 50 per cent Tissue Culture Infective Doses (5.0 $\log_{10}TCD_{50}$) per ml. of Sabin poliovirus–2, together with 0.2 per cent sodium fluorescein, was ejected from the rear of a raft at the rate of 10 ml per minute. Before the pool was inoculated, the protein content of the stock virus preparation was reduced by precipitation with protamine sulphate 0.25 mg per ml, followed by deposition of the virus from the supernatant by ultracentrifugation at 100,000*g* for 1 hour. The virus pellet was reconstituted with 0.15*M* sodium chloride to the original volume. This partially purified virus preparation showed a free chlorine demand of less than 0.1 ppm.

Samples of water were collected for assay of virus content, within 3 inches of the raft whilst it was held stationary, or immediately after it had been drawn past a designated point along the pool deck. To each 10 ml water sample, 0.1 ml of 1.5 per cent sodium thiosulphate was added immediately to inactivate halogens. Water samples were centrifuged at 2,000 rpm for 30 minutes to deposit bacteria. To each 3.6 ml of supernatant, 0.4 ml of 10-fold concentrated medium ELY* was added, and the mixture was inoculated in 0.8-ml amounts into each of four drained roller tubes containing monolayers of rhesus or cynomolgus monkey kidney cells. Whenever appropriate, serial decimal dilutions of the water samples in medium ELY were also inoculated into tissue cultures. After 4 days' incubation on roller drums at 37° C, all tubes were examined for cytopathic effects. The virus content of each sample was expressed as the logarithm to the base 10 of the number of 50 per cent tissue culture infective doses of virus per ml (log TCD_{50} per ml).

Free residuals of chlorine were attained by the addition of HTH† to water in the pool before commencement of the test. The residual was determined by Palin's orthotolidine test. Elemental bromine was liberated from dispersed particles of Di-Halo (R) (bromo-chloro-dimethylhydantoin) or dissolved potassium iodide by the addition of stoichiochemical amounts of HTH. The concentrations of these elements were also determined colorimetrically by Palin's method.

Lakes and Streams

Inocula usually contained 5.0 to 6.0 log TCD_{50} of Sabin poliovirus–2 per ml, and the concentration of sodium fluorescein was increased to 1 per cent. No attempt was made to remove extraneous protein from the stock virus before use in tests. Sodium thiosulphate was not added to bottles before the collection of 10-ml water samples. An Ott flowmeter‡ was used to measure the rate of water flow in streams, but surface wave motion at lakeshore sites interfered with attempts to detect the presence of water currents.

Sewage Plant Model

Inocula consisted of 60 to 350 ml of effluent from an aeration tank to which Sabin poliovirus–3 was added, to give final concentrations of 4.5 to 6.0 log TCD_{50} per ml. These inocula also contained sodium

*Medium ELY: Earle's saline with lactalbumin hydrolysate 0.5%, yeast extract 0.1%, penicillin 1,000 U per ml, and streptomycin 0.5 mg per ml.

†HTH: "High test hypochlorite," a commercial preparation containing calcium hypochlorite, yielding about 70% of "available" chlorine.

‡Ott flowmeter: distributed by Overseas Instruments Ltd., Kingston, Ontario.

fluorescein 2 per cent. After addition of these virus pulses to the columns, aeration tank effluent was run in during the subsequent week or longer. In some experiments, Sabin poliovirus–3 was added directly to the aeration tank. All tests were run at room temperature (23° C). The virus content of liquid collected from aeration tanks and sewage disposal columns was assayed after centrifugation at 2,000 rpm for 30 minutes, by inoculation of 1:10 and higher dilutions of supernatant into tissue culture tubes. Owing to the toxicity of sewage effluents it was usually impossible to assay the virus content of undiluted fluids.

The sewage disposal columns were 15 cm wide and contained 14 to 32 cm lengths of sand, garden soil, or silty clay [19, 20]. The sand or the soil layer was placed between 10 to 20 cm lengths of crushed stones. Backfill of 20 cm of soil was placed above the upper stone layer. Aeration tank effluent containing virus and fluorescein was run into the upper stone layer about 5 cm above the stone–sand interface. The effluent was collected at the bottom of the lower layer of stones. In some experiments, cores of sand were removed daily from the column 3 cm below the upper interface and examined for virus content.

RESULTS

Swimming-Pool

1. *Raft stationary.* In the absence of any halogen, no virus was detected 20 or 60 seconds after ejection [12]. In the presence of 1.0 ppm free chlorine, minimal infectivity was detected 20 seconds after ejection, but none was found thereafter (Table I). Virus was detected as long

TABLE I

VIRUS DISPERSAL IN POOL WATER, RAFT STATIONARY

	Free residuals of halogen (ppm)								
		Cl	Br			I			
Time (sec)	None	1.0	2.5	6.0	7.0	0.4	2.0	4.0	5.0
0	2.3*	1.0	3.7	3.7	2.5	2.5	1.5	1.7	2.5
10	—	—	1.3	1.5	0	2.3	1.3	1.0	0.5
20	0	+	2.0	0	0	1.5	0.5	0	0
40	—	0	+	0	0	1.7	0.7	0	0
60	0	0	+	—	0	0.7	—	—	0

*Log_{10} TCD_{50} of poliovirus-2 per ml of water.

as 60 seconds after ejection in the presence of 2.5 ppm bromine, but no virus was isolated from water more than 10 seconds after ejection when the bromine residual was 6.0 ppm or higher. Virus infectivity persisted for at least 60 seconds in the presence of 0.4 ppm iodine and for 40 seconds when 2.0 ppm was detected, but residuals of 4.0 ppm or higher resulted in removal of infectivity between 10 and 20 seconds after ejection.

2. *Raft moving past fixed point.* Virus was detected 20 to 60 seconds after the raft had passed when no halogen was present [12]. Although no virus was detected in water containing 0.8 and 1.0 ppm free chlorine at any interval after the raft had passed, the virus concentration in the water sampled at the time the raft traversed the designated point was unusually low. No virus was detected 10 seconds or more after the raft had passed, when bromine residuals were 6.0 ppm or higher, and when the iodine residuals were 2.0 ppm or greater. However, virus infectivity was detected as long as 40 seconds after the raft had passed when only 0.4 ppm iodine was present (Table II).

TABLE II

VIRUS DISPERSAL IN POOL WATER, RAFT PASSING FIXED POINT

	Free residuals of halogen (ppm)								
	None		Cl		Br		I		
Time (sec)	*a*	*b*	0.8	1.0	6.0	7.0	0.4	2.0	5.0
0	0.7	0.7	0.5	0.7	2.3	1.2	2.0	1.5	1.3
10	1.0	+	0	—	0	0	1.0	0	0
20	0.5	+	0	0	0	0	0.5	0	0
40	1.3	0	0	0	0	0	1.3	0	0
60	1.3	0	0	0	—	—	0	—	0

These results show that the infectivity of virus ejected from a point source such as a nozzle, which is an experimental model of the mouth of a bather, decreases fairly rapidly both as a result of dilution and by dispersal, because of the mild water currents which are always present in a recirculating pool. This decrease of infectivity following ejection is hastened both by the addition of viricidal substances such as halogens, and by movement of the source.

Lakes

For tests 1 to 4, Sabin poliovirus–2 was added to water 1 to 2 ft deep at points 10 to 20 ft off-shore from a stony beach along Lake Huron.

Virus was detected in water obtained 3 to 10 minutes subsequently, within a radius of 5 ft of the point of addition, where the collector remained standing (Table III). In tests 1 and 2, the wind was calm, the waves were 2 to 3 inches high, and virtually no onward movement of the fluorescent zone was observed during the subsequent 15 minutes. During test 3, a strong wind was blowing, waves were about 1 ft high, and virus was detected close to the point of addition as long as 5 minutes subsequently. Onward spread of the fluorescence was observed, and virus was detected up to 10 ft distant at 3.5, 5.5, and 8.5 minutes after addition. In test 4, waves were 2 ft high, and rapid dispersal of virus and fluorescence was noted.

For tests 5 to 10, virus was added to lake water 3 to 6 ft deep from a motor boat moving at 3 to 5 knots. Samples were collected while cruising through the fluorescent zone at successive intervals of 1 minute. In quiet water, virus was recovered 2 to 5 minutes after addition. In choppy water, which rendered steering of the boat difficult, virus was recovered up to 10 minutes after addition. However, the enhanced virus load in test 10 may account for the prolonged persistence of virus (Table III).

TABLE III

VIRUS DISPERSAL IN LAKE WATER

Time after addition (min)	Virus titres in water (log TCD_{50} per ml)									
	Collector stationary				Collector moving in boat					
	Quiet		Choppy		Quiet				Choppy	
	1	2	3	4	5	6	7	8	9	10
Inoculum	5.5	5.0	6.0	6.0	5.5	6.0	5.5	5.5	6.0	7.0
0.1	3.0	3.0	—	—	—	—	4.0	1.5	—	—
0.25	2.0	1.5	3.5	3.5	—	—	—	1.5	2.5	1.5
1	0	0.5	0.5	0	0.5	0.5	1.0	0.5	1.5	1.5
2	1.0	2.0	0.5	—	0.5	0.5	0.5	+	1.0	1.0
3	—	0.5	1.0	—	0	+	—	0	+	1.0
4	—	—	+	—	0	0.5	0	0	+	1.0
5	—	—	+	—	0	+	+	0	+	0
8	—	—	0	—	—	0	0	—	0	+
10	+	—	0	—	0	0	0	—	+	0.5
15	0	—	—	—	—	0	—	—	—	—

These results show that despite extensive wave activity of lake water, this movement is confined to the surface, and relatively slow dispersal of virus occurs in the deeper layers of water, which are almost stationary. In open water a steady decline of virus titre is noted, in contrast to the situation in lake water beneath a 2-ft-thick ice layer, where the concentration of virus remained virtually unchanged through an observation period of 15 minutes [19].

Creeks

1. *Creek B*, 7 ft wide and 3 in. deep, was dosed continuously with 7.5 log TCD_{50} of poliovirus–2 over an interval of 75 seconds. The flow rate ranged between 1.4 ft per sec at the point of addition of virus and 1.0 ft per sec at a point 60 ft straight downstream. The virus concentration at the point of addition was 2.0 log TCD_{50} per ml. Virus was first recovered from water 20 ft downstream 80 seconds after commencement of virus addition, peak titres (1.0 TCD_{50} per ml) were attained at 100 to 140 seconds, and virus was last detected at 180 seconds. At the point 60 ft downstream, a minimal amount (1 TCD_{50} per ml) of virus was recovered from water on one occasion after 260 seconds (Table IV, series *a*). Addition of virus continuously over 60 seconds at another location resulted in a virus concentration of 2.5 log TCD_{50} per ml at the point of addition. Virus was detected regularly 40 ft downstream between 60 and 165 seconds after commencement of virus addition, with a peak titre of 1.0 log TCD_{50} per ml at 75 seconds (Table IV, series *b*).

TABLE IV

CREEK B, CARRIAGE OF VIRUS AFTER ADDITION OF 7.5 LOG TCD_{50} POLIOVIRUS-2 CONTINUOUSLY THROUGH 60 TO 75 SECONDS

			Virus detected			
					Peak	
Series	Feet below	Flow (ft/sec)	Start (sec)	Finish (sec)	sec	log TCD_{50}/ml
a	Zero	1.4	0	75	5	2.0
b	Zero	1.0	0	60	5	2.5
a	20	1.2	80	180	120	1.0
b	40	1.0	60	165	75	1.0
a	60	1.0	260	260	260	+

2. *Creek D* was 6 ft. wide and 6 in. deep at the point of addition of virus, widened to 14 ft with a depth of 6 in. at the collection point 80 ft downstream, and narrowed to 10 ft with a depth of 12 in. at the 120-ft collection point located 20 ft downstream from confluence with a tributary. This creek received pulses of 6.5 log TCD_{50} of poliovirus–2 (Table V, series *c*) and 7.5 log TCD_{50} (Table V, series *d*) on separate days. The virus load passed the 5-ft collection point within 15 seconds at a peak titre of 2.0 log TCD_{50} per ml. Virus titres decreased more rapidly 10 ft and 40 ft downstream when the creek was flowing more rapidly. The steady decrease of titre with the progress of the virus load downstream suggests increasing dilution and dispersal of virus.

3. *Creek M*, 2 ft. wide and 21 in. deep at the uppermost extremity

TABLE V

CREEK D, CARRIAGE OF VIRUS AFTER ADDITION OF POLIOVIRUS-2 PULSES OF 6.5 LOG TCD_{50} (*c*) AND 7.5 LOG TCD_{50} (*d*)

Series	Feet below	Flow (ft/sec)	Virus detected: Start (sec)	Finish (sec)	Peak: sec	log TCD_{50}/ml
c	Zero	2.4	0	5	5	1.5
d	Zero	2.2	0	5	5	2.0
c	5	1.3	5	20	5	2.0
c	10	1.5	10	55	10	3.0
d	10	2.2	5	20	5	2.0
c	20	1.5	45	60	60	0.5
c	40	1.3	10	135	105	1.0
d	40	2.5	65	80	65	+
d	80	1.3	45	45	45	+
d	120*	3.1	95	155	110	0.5

*Collected 20 ft below entry of a tributary.

of the portion tested, widened to between 5 and 8 ft with a depth of 6 in. at collection points downstream. Miniature cascades were present above the upper and at the lower limits of the test portion. Poliovirus–2 was added continuously over a period of 60 seconds to water in cascades 10 ft upstream from the first point of collection in series *e*, *g*, *k*, and *l*, and at a wider point 20 ft downstream from the first site, where the rate of flow was considerably slower, in series *f* and *h*. For series *i* and *m*, virus pulses were added at the cascades, but in series *j* and *n*, *virus pulses* were added to the slowly moving portion of the stream. The total amount of virus added ranged between 7.5 and 8.5 log TCD_{50}. In collections obtained 10 ft below the point of addition of virus, persistence of virus was considerably prolonged following a continuous loading with virus for 1 minute, in contrast to the brief period of virus recovery after addition of a pulse. However, virtually no relationship was observed between the duration of persistence of virus and the flow rate at the collection point. Similar findings were obtained at points 20 ft and 30 ft downstream (Table VI). Peak titres of virus were usually observed within 30 seconds after arrival of the virus front at the sampling point. Progressively decreasing virus titres, through dilution and dispersal, were observed throughout the length of the test portion of the creek, for example in series *e*.

Sewage Treatment Columns

Column 12 contained a 32 cm length of sand. Virus was detected in the effluent as early as 1 hour after addition, when only 285 ml of liquid

TABLE VI

CREEK M, CARRIAGE OF VIRUS AFTER ADDITION OF 7.5 TO 8.5 LOG TCD_{50} POLIOVIRUS-2 CONTINUOUSLY THROUGH 60 SECONDS OR AS A PULSE

	Virus added continuously						Virus pulse added					
			Virus detected						Virus detected			
					Peak						Peak	
Feet below	Series	Flow (ft/sec)	Start (sec)	Finish (sec)	sec	log TCD_{50}/ml	Series	Flow (ft/sec)	Start (sec)	Finish (sec)	sec	log TCD_{50}/ml
10	*e*	1.4	15	105	60	1.5	*i*	0.6	10	30	15	0.5
	g	1.6	35	135	35	1.0	*m*	2.0	10	30	10	1.0
	k	1.1	45	60	45	0.5						
	f	0.4	75	165	165	1.0						
	h	0.5	30	120	60	0.5						
20	*e*	0.4	75	210	120	0.5	*m*	0.4	35	55	55	1.5
	g	0.5	85	165	85	0.5						
	f	1.0	120	180	120	0.5	*j*	0.3	25	85	75	0.5
	h	0.7	50	110	50	1.5	*n*	2.5	95	115	95	0.5
30	*e*	0.4	90	135	90	1.5	*i*	0.9	55	70	55	0.5
	l	—	30	195	45	0.5						
40	*e*	1.0	200	255	200	+						
	l	—	90	120	90	0.5						

*Series *e*, *g*, *k*, *l*, and *i*, *m*: virus added at upper cascades. Series *f*, *h*, and *j*, *n*: virus added at slow mid-portion.

had been collected. A steady decrease of virus titre in the effluent occurred until the 5th day, by which time 33,075 ml of effluent had passed through the column (Table VII), and thereafter no virus was recovered.

Column 24 was composed of silty clay 16 cm in length. Virus was detected in the effluent as long as 4 days after its addition to the column, but the first recovery from the effluent was not achieved until 7 hours after addition of the virus pulse.

Columns 37, 40, and 45 each contained 14 to 16 cm lengths of garden soil. Virus was first detected in effluents from these columns 3 hours after addition of the virus pulse. The effluents from columns 37 and 40 yielded virus for as long as 8 and 7 days respectively, but column 45 showed virus in the effluent for 3 days only.

Columns 24 and 45, which received the same virus dose, showed essentially similar transference of virus, which was last recovered at final dilutions of 1:116 and 1:107 respectively; but the slower mean daily flow in column 24 permitted the persistence of virus for one more day than in column 45. Although the quantity of liquid which flowed through column 12 exceeded the mean daily flow through other columns more than threefold (on account of the greater porosity of sand), virus persisted for 5 days, the final dilution factor being 1:94.

The persistence of virus in column effluents 3 to 7 days after the addition of virus pulses was investigated further in volumn 2, containing 17 cm of sand (E.S. = 0.26, U.C. = 1.94),* and in column 42 containing 14 cm of sand. Although virus was not detected in the effluent from column 2 beyond 4 days after addition of the pulse, virus was recovered from the sand up to 6 days after dosage. From column 42 effluent, minimal titres of virus were recovered 24 hours or more after addition of the pulse, but virus was detected in the sand at titres of 1.5 to 3 log TCD_{50} per ml at least 6 days after dosage (Table VIII). These results show that virus remains adsorbed within the sand layer for a considerable time, and it is washed away only after relatively very large quatities of liquid have been flushed through the column.

Aeration Tank

Sabin poliovirus-3 was added to an aeration tank containing 50 litres of sewage at 23° C, to give an initial concentration of 3.5 log TCD_{50} per ml. During each 24 hours, 50 litres of effluent were removed, and

*These symbols indicate the porosity characteristics of the sand: E.S. = effective size, U.C. = uniformity coefficient.

TABLE VII

VIRUS PERSISTENCE IN EFFLUENT FROM SEWAGE TREATMENT COLUMNS

Sample (hours)	12 Sand, 32 cm		24 Silty clay, 16 cm		37 Garden soil, 14 cm		40 Garden soil, 14 cm		45 Garden soil, 16 cm	
	Virus*	Fluid†	Virus	Fluid	Virus	Fluid	Virus	Fluid	Virus	Fluid
Dose	4.5+	350	5.0	60	6.0	60	5.0	60	5.0	60
1	3.0	285	—	—	—	—	—	—	—	—
3	3.5	850	0	125	2.5	590	3.5	430	2.0	135
7	—	—	2.0	310	—	—	—	—	2.5	361
24	2.0	5,015	1.5	1,830	2.0	2,145	1.5	2,149	1.0	2,206
48	2.0	12,265	0.7	4,300	1.0	4,155	1.5	4,189	0.7	4,898
72	0	18,085	0.7	5,710	1.0	6,695	2.0	6,384	0.7	6,453
96	1.0	22,675	0.7	6,963	1.0	9,115	1.0	8,819	0	8,428
120	1.0	33,075	0	9,350	0	11,040	1.0	10,974	0	11,260
144	0	38,660	0	11,245	1.0	13,019	—	13,507	0	13,750
168	—	—	—	—	0	13,874	1.0	14,410	—	—
192	—	—	—	—	1.5	15,444	0	15,765	—	—
216	—	—	—	—	0	17,639	0	18,430	—	—
Final dilution	1:94		1:116		1:256		1:238		1:107	
Mean daily flow (ml)	6,615		1,741		1,930		2,059		2,151	

*Log_{10} TCD_{50} per ml effluent.
†Cumulative total collections of effluent (ml).

TABLE VIII

PERSISTENCE OF VIRUS IN SAND WITHIN SEWAGE TREATMENT COLUMNS

Sample (hours)	Virus recovered (log TCD_{50} per ml)			
	Column 2		Column 42	
	Effluent	Sand	Effluent	Sand
0	4.5+	—	4.0	—
1	1.5	—	2.5+	—
3	2.5+	3.0	2.5+	3.5+
24	2.0	2.5	1.0	3.5+
48	1.5+	3.0	1.0	2.5
72	1.0	2.5	0	3.0
96	1.5+	2.5	0	2.0
120	0	1.5	1.0	1.5
144	0	2.0	1.0	2.5

they were replaced by 50 litres of untreated sewage. Virus was first detected in the effluent at low titre 10 minutes after the tank was dosed. A steady decrease in infectivity in the aeration tank contents was noted during the subsequent 6 days, after which no virus was detected. Virus was recovered from the effluent up to 2 days after it was added to the tank (Table IX). The effluent was run into treatment columns 37 and

TABLE IX

VIRUS PERSISTENCE IN AERATION TANK

Hours after dose	Virus content (log TCD_{50}/ml)			
	Aeration tank		Soil columns	
	Content	Effluent	37	40
0.2	3.5	1.0	1.0	1.5
22	2.5	2.0	2.0	0
45	2.0	1.0	1.0	1.0
50	2.0	1.5	1.0	1.0
69	2.0	0	1.0	1.0
97	0	0	1.0	0
116	0	0	1.0	0
142	1.0	0	0	0
164	0	0	0	0
Total volume (litres)	350	350	16.3	16.1

40. Virus was detected as long as 5 days after passage of fluid through the columns.

The persistence of virus in the aeration tank effluent at least 2 days after the tank was dosed shows that little acceleration of virus inactivation above that due to thermal degradation results from aeration treatment. Furthermore, sewage treatment columns which received the tank effluent removed virtually none of the remaining infectivity.

DISCUSSION

Spread of viruses by swimming-pools depends, first, upon the local concentration of virus in the vicinity of bathers and, secondly, on the general level of viral concentration throughout the pool [21]. Following the infection of a pool with Sabin poliovirus–2 to give a general virus concentration of 5 TCD_{50} per ml, none of 10 bathers who swam in this water developed intestinal infections with this agent [22]. However, a different situation obtains when virus is expelled at a high titre from the mouth or nose of a bather, thus creating a high local concentration of virus. This may be sufficient to infect a second bather who enters the contaminated zone of water before a sufficiently long interval has elapsed to permit either extensive dispersal of virus through the movement of water currents, or viral inactivation by disinfectant present in the pool. Continuous maintenance of minimum residuals of free chlorine at 0.5 ppm, bromine at 2.0 ppm, or iodine at 2.0 ppm will ensure inactivation of poliovirus–2 within 10 seconds following discharge from a moving point source, and after somewhat longer intervals when the source remains stationary [12].

The efficiency of water as a vehicle for viral transmission is illustrated by the effect of stasis on the distribution of virus infectivity following addition of Sabin poliovirus–2 to creeks and lakes. The flow of water in creeks induced progressive dilution of virus. The time during which infectivity was demonstrated after arrival of the virus front at points downstream was prolonged when virus was added continuously rather than as a pulse. In the light of this observation it is not surprising that discharge of untreated sewage into a river provided an efficient means of continuous addition of infectious hepatitis virus, which induced symptoms in persons who consumed water downstream [6].

In calm lake water, or water with mild superficial wave action, a virus pulse remained well localized and infectivity decreased mainly owing to dispersal factors. Considerable wave motion accelerated the dispersal of virus. However, floating objects were rapidly displaced from the site of virus addition by the action of wind and waves. This observation is important epidemiologically since virus present in floating material, such as untreated sewage, will show a greater tendency to be scattered over a wide expanse of water than virus suspended in liquid wastes which will remain localized in the static waters of bays. The accumulation of enteroviruses in sluggish terminal river branches receiving liquid wastes from sewage disposal plants during a poliovirus epidemic [13], and the epidemics of infectious hepatitis resulting from ingestion of raw clams [14] and oysters [15] raised in stagnant sea water into which city sewage was discharged, provide two epidemiological examples of the conclusions to be drawn from field experiments reported in this paper.

Enteroviruses passed readily through aeration tanks of sewage disposal units, both in the current investigations [20] and in treatment plants located elsewhere [13, 16, 17, 18], and they appeared in the effluent. Complete removal of viral infectivity was achieved only after the sewage was held in an oxidation pond, chlorinated, and filtered through sand [16], before the effluent was used to fill a recreational lake. Chlorination of effluents from sewage treatment plants therefore seems advisable before the wastes are discharged into streams or lakes, in order to remove hazards of viral infection.

SUMMARY

1. Maintenance of adequate halogen residuals continuously, combined with persistent agitation of water by bathers and a satisfactory pumping system for recirculation of water, promotes the rapid reduction of viral infection hazards in swimming-pools.

2. Movement of water in creeks results in rapid dispersal and dilution of virus loads, but continous addition of virus, together with slow movement of creek water, prolongs the duration of infectivity at sites downstream.

3. Virus dispersal occurs steadily after its addition to lake water, but surface movement only moderately augments the dispersal of suspended virus.

4. Aeration treatment of sewage exerts little or no viricidal effect, while virus passes readily through sewage disposal columns containing sand or soil, and remains adsorbed to sand for prolonged periods.

REFERENCES

1. MOSLEY, J. W. (1967), "Transmission of Viral Disease by Drinking Water," in *Transmission of Viruses by the Water Route*, edited by Gerald Berg (New York: Interscience Publishers), pp. 5–23.

2. FRASER, R. A. (1931), "A Study of Epidemic Catarrhal Jaundice," *Can. J. Pub. Health, 22*: 396–411.
3. POSKANZER, D. C. and BEADENKOPF, W. G. (1961), "Water-Borne Infectious Hepatitis Epidemic from a Chlorinated Municipal Supply," *Pub. Health Rept. 76*: 745–51.
4. FARQUHAR, J. D., STOKES, J. JR., and SCHRACK, W. D. JR. (1952), "Epidemic of Viral Hepatitis Apparently Spread by Drinking Water and by Contact," *J. Amer. Med. Assoc. 149*: 991–3.
5. MOSLEY, J. W. and SMITHER, W. W. (1957), "Infectious Hepatitis. Report of an Outbreak Probably Caused by Drinking Water," *New England J. Med. 257*: 590–5.
6. WALLACE, E. C. (1958), "Infectious Hepatitis: Report of an Outbreak, Apparently Water-Borne," *Med. J. Australia, 1*: 101–2.
7. BELL, J. A., ROWE, W. P., ENGLER, J. I., PARROTT, R. H., and HUEBNER, R. J. (1955), "Pharyngo-Conjunctival Fever: Epidemiological Studies of a Recently Recognized Disease Entity," *J. Amer. Med. Assoc. 157*: 1083–92.
8. ORMSBY, H. L. and AITCHISON, W. S. (1955), "Pharyngeal-Conjunctival Fever due to Swimming Pool Contact," *Can. Med. Assoc. J. 73*: 864–6.
9. ROBINSON, C. R., DOANE, F. W., and RHODES, A. J. (1958), "Report of an Outbreak of Febrile Illness with Pharyngeal Lesions and Exanthem: Toronto, Summer 1957. Isolation of Group A Coxsackie Virus," *Can. Med. Assoc. J. 79*: 615–21.
10. KELLY, S. and SANDERSON, W. W. (1961), "Enteric Viruses in Wading Pools," *Pub. Health Rept. 76*: 199–200.
11. BROWN, J. R. MCLEAN, D. M., and NIXON, M. C. (1963), "Swimming Pools and Bathing Places in Southern Ontario: Chemical and Microbiological Studies during 1962," *Can. J. Pub. Health, 54*: 121–8.
12. MCLEAN, D. M. and BROWN, J. R. (1966), "Virus Dispersal by Water," *Health Lab. Sci. 3*: 182–9.
13. LAMB, G. A., CHIN, T. D. Y., and SCARCE, L. E. (1964), "Isolation of Enteric Viruses from Sewage and River Water in a Metropolitan Area," *Amer. J. Hyg. 80*: 320–7.
14. DOUGHERTY, W. J. and ALTMAN, R. (1962), "Viral Hepatitis in New Jersey, 1960–61," *Amer. J. Med. 32*: 704–16.
15. MASON, J. O. and MCLEAN, W. R. (1962), "Infectious Hepatitis Traced to Consumption of Raw Oysters," *Amer. J. Hyg. 75*: 90–111.
16. ASKEW, J. B., BOTT, R. F., LEACH, R. E., and ENGLAND, B. L. (1965), "Microbiology of Reclaimed Water from Sewage for Recreational Use," *Amer. J. Pub. Health, 55*: 453–62.
17. ISHERWOOD, J. D. (1965), "The Fate of Coxsackievirus A13 in Water Reclamation," *Amer. J. Pub. Health, 55*: 1945–54.
18. CLARKE, N. A., STEVENSON, R. E., CHANG, S. L., and KABLER, P. W. (1961), "Removal of Enteric Viruses from Sewage by Activated Sludge Treatment," *Amer. J. Pub. Health, 51*: 1118–29.
19. MCLEAN, D. M., BROWN, J. R., and LAAK, R. (1966), "Virus Dispersal by Water," *J. Am. Water Works Assoc. 58*: 920–8.
20. LAAK, R. and MCLEAN, D. M. (1967), "Virus Transfer through a Sewage Disposal Unit," *Can. J. Pub. Health, 58*: 172–6.
21. MCLEAN, D. M. (1963), "Infectious Hazards in Swimming Pools," *Pediatrics, 31*: 811–18.
22. MCLEAN, D. M., BROWN, J. R., and NIXON, M. C. (1964), "Microbiological Hazards of Freshwater Bathing," *Health Lab. Sci. 1*: 151–8.

THE WATERS OF WIDE AGONY*

C. E. Dolman, F.R.S.C.

I

ON THE SANDY SHORE of the Gulf of Genoa, a mile or so above Viareggio, a sprinkling of men had gathered on a hot August morning. The beach was lapped by the blue Ligurian Sea, beyond which, in the far distance to the west, lay the dim peaks of the Maritime Alps. To the south could be seen Corsica and Elba; to the north lay an uninhabited wilderness—except for watch-towers, intended to prevent smuggling and enforce quarantine against the plague. Immediately inland were the white-marbled Apuan Alps, and over the whole coastal arc the encircling ramparts of the Appenines stood guard. It was a magnificent setting for the weird rites about to be enacted.

While a squad of soldiers kept away the curious, hired hands dug trenches in the hot sand, until a spade struck upon a skull, and a decomposed body was dragged from the shallow grave where it had been buried nearly six weeks before. The fragile corpse was manœuvred on poles into an iron frame with legs, which was placed on top of a pile of wood, and the pyre set alight. In charge of the operation was a huge man, who sprinkled the flames with wine, incense, honey, sugar, and salt, crying out: "I restore to nature, through fire, the elements of which this man was composed, earth, air and water; everything is changed but not annihilated; he is now a portion of that which he worshipped."

After several hours, when all but the heart was consumed, the furnace was dragged down to the water's edge to cool off and the ashes placed in a box. The giant master of ceremonies burnt his hands retrieving the heart, which in due course became a treasured heirloom; for it belonged to the poet Shelley, drowned when his small schooner "Ariel" capsized in a sudden squall off Leghorn on July 8, 1822. On board with him were a friend, Edward Williams, and a cabin boy. Their bodies had like-

*Presidential Address, Section III, R.S.C., June 1966.

wise been washed ashore, and only the day before the same ritual had been carried out farther up the beach on the remains of Williams.

Watching the proceedings from his coach was a devilishly handsome man with a club foot, George Gordon, Lord Byron. With him, but unable to face the gruesome scene, was a guest recently arrived from England, Leigh Hunt. Before the fire was quenched, Byron decided to match his strength against the water that had overcome Shelley and swam over a mile out to sea. Shelley could not swim a stroke, despite a romantic passion—a veritable obsession—for water in all its manifestations, and though he loved boats he was a clumsy sailor. . . . At last the party piled into the coach and drove to Viareggio, where "overcome by the two days of fascinating horror, they dined and drank heavily before returning to Pisa." As the barouche drove through the forest into the city, wrote Hunt, "We sang, we laughed, we shouted" [1].*

The cryptic title of this address is taken from "Lines Written among the Euganean Hills," composed by Shelley barely four years before the melodrama just depicted, when he was living in a villa near Venice lent him by Byron. The work, which overflows with watery metaphors, seems full of strange premonitions. The opening couplet expresses yearning for encouragement:

> Many a green isle needs must be
> In the deep wide sea of misery.

When the theme recurs nearly 70 lines later, it has become an assertion of hope in the midst of despair:

> Ay, many flowering islands lie
> In the waters of wide Agony:

I can find personal excuses for depicting that haunting scene. Leigh Hunt had his schooling at the same "Religious, Royal and Ancient Foundation of Christ's Hospital" which I attended a century and a quarter after him. When I went there, a homesick 10-year-old, the school had been moved from the City of London to the Sussex Weald, close to the Shelley family's ancestral home; and occasionally on a Sunday afternoon we walked in Shelley Wood. Edward Trelawney, who supervised the pagan ceremony upon the beach, was a fellow Cornishman. As for the other famous participant, though I never cared much for his legend or his poems, he appears to have fascinated one of my few heroes. Louis Pasteur, born in the very year of that macabre cremation, kept in the library of his home at Arbois, a beautifully bound, well-thumbed edition of Byron's Complete Works.

*Numbers in brackets refer to the list of references.

II

Pasteur never concerned himself particularly with the bacteriology of water, though he was very interested in the microbial flora of beer and wine. His name is not introduced here as talisman, but rather to evoke reflections on the hard battles fought to secure acceptance of the doctrine that some of mankind's most troublesome plagues, including those conveyed by water, are due to specific "germs," invisible to the unaided eye. In this context, Pasteur personifies the distress, persecution, and sacrifice endured by the prophets and pioneers, as well as by the victims, through whose wide agony—of body, mind, and spirit—we have arrived at our present knowledge of water-borne diseases.

In every century of human history, cholera, typhoid, and other enteric fevers—not to mention an astonishing variety of less well-known bacterial, viral, and protozoal diseases—all conveyable by water or dependent on it, have annually caused millions of human casualties. Hence it would seem a little ridiculous for this Society to organize symposia and sponsor a monograph on water resources, voicing concern over present and future supplies, distribution and reclamation projects, and various actual and potential threats to quality, without including some statement on the paramountcy of *safe* supplies. Perhaps because our generation is exposed to so many peculiar dangers unimagined in Shelley's time, we take too much for granted the public health protective measures developed since then. Nowadays, for example, we do not refuse a glass of hotel tap water and accept instead some other fluid, because the former is liable to contain cholera germs while the latter has slight antiseptic virtues. Yet only about 70 years ago—a trifling interval in the long history of man's control over his environment—the composer Tschaikowsky, within a few days of attending the première of his *Symphonie Pathétique*, drank unboiled water in a Petersburg apartment, and died of cholera.

I propose therefore to conjure up kaleidoscopically a few scenes from the past, involving persons—some familiar, others perhaps unknown—whom we should especially honour in this connection, as well as situations and episodes whose recounting may bring us reassurance and warning for the future.

III

The sanitary control of sewage and water supplies, far from being a recent innovation, was practised by such ancient civilizations as those of

John Snow, M.D., 1813–58 (London)

PLATE II

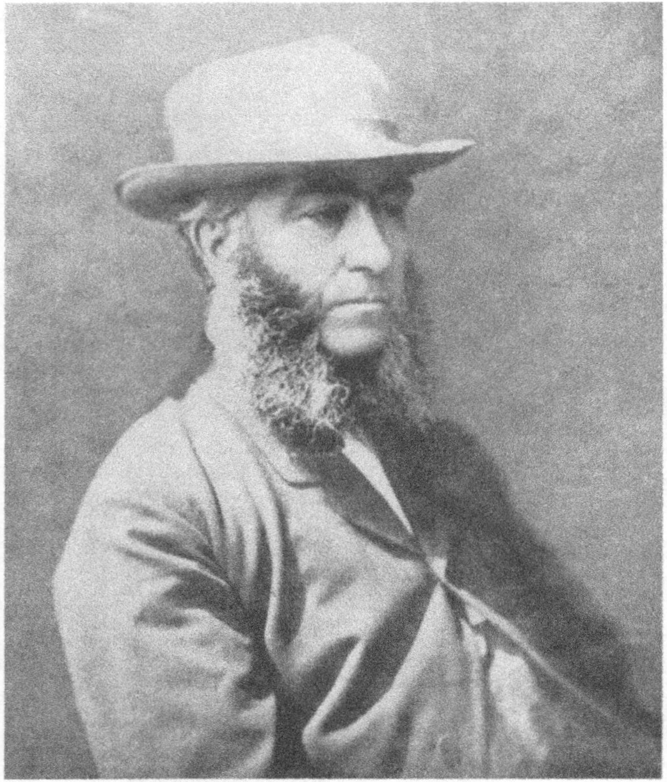

A. William Budd, M.D., F.R.S., 1811–80 (Bristol)

B. Max von Pettenkofer, M.D., 1818–1901 (Munich)

A. Theobald Smith, M.D., 1859-1934 (Washington, Boston, Princeton)

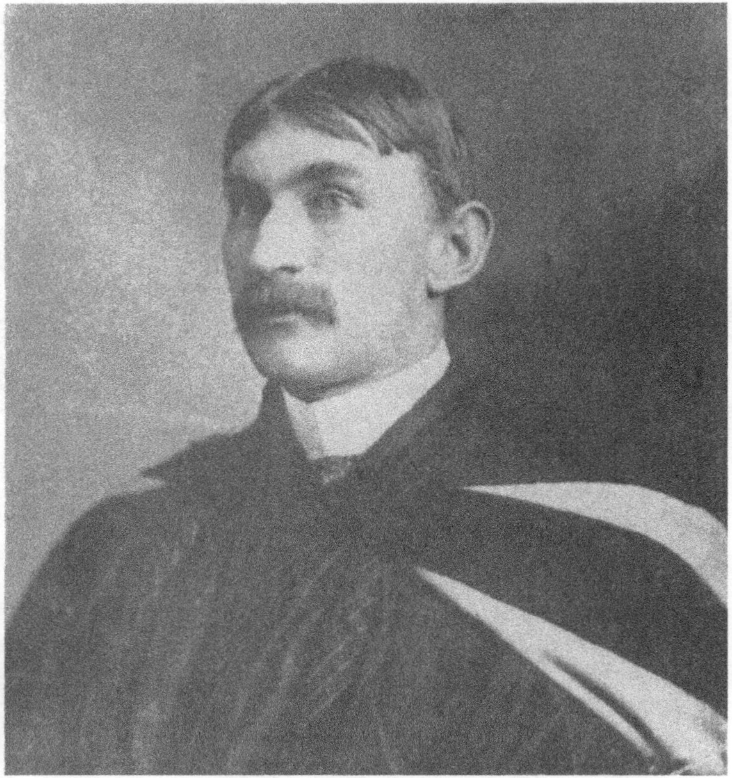

B. Wyatt G. Johnston, M.D., 1860–1902 (Montreal)

PLATE IV

Mayor Jack Loutet of North Vancouver engaged in a public debate on chlorination with the author, November 20, 1945. The Mayor threatened to retire from public life if the citizens voted to retain chlorination. At this juncture, he is, for good measure, also flaying pasteurized milk. Rats fed on such milk, he says, "get smaller, have rough coats and irritable dispositions."

Egypt, Babylon, Greece, and Rome [2]. A few years ago, within a week of having publicly complained about the sewage-polluted beaches of a certain western city, I was impressed to note in the remains of the Cretan palace at Knossos (dating from about 3000 B.C.) how carefully the terracotta sewer pipes had been aligned *below* the pipes conveying water for drinking and bathing. But in the Middle Ages, as barbarism seeped south while Christianity fanned out northward, one of the darkest features was the appalling decline in standards of personal hygiene and community sanitation. Reaction from the luxury and body-worship of Greece and Rome, expectations of an early Second Coming, and the attitude typified in St. Jerome's words "Does your skin roughen without baths? Who is once washed in Christ needs not to wash again," were some of the factors which combined to bring about a degree of communal squalor and individual filth unmatched before and since, except during modern wars or in isolated foci of contemporary slums. In those days, only the comparative paucity of urban populations, the isolation of the villages, and the traveller's slow crawl, saved mankind from virtual extinction, at least in Europe, by plague and pestilence.

However, the human spirit's resilience and resourcefulness began to break its mediaeval shackles well before the Renaissance. In those days, the king was the natural leader. Thus, in 1357, over 600 years ago, Edward III of England addressed a Royal Order to the Mayor and Sheriffs of London, telling how he had passed along the River Thames, and "beheld dung and laystalls and other filth accumulated in diverse places in the said city upon the bank of the said river . . . had perceived the fumes and other abominable stenches arising therefrom; from the corruption of which, if tolerated, great peril, as well to the persons dwelling within the said city as to the nobles and others passing along the river, will it is feared arise, unless indeed some fitting remedy be speedily provided for the same" [3].

But the Thames got no cleaner. Nearly four centuries later, Alexander Pope in the *Dunciad* (1728) refers

> To where Fleet ditch with disemboguing stream
> Rolls the large tribute of dead dogs to Thames.

Yet another century later, according to Sir Oliver Lodge's uncle Frank, an old sea captain, ". . . before a voyage, they just pumped water in from the Thames. A grid in the river sufficed to keep out all the larger impurities such as dead dogs; and for the rest, if you were very particular, you could filter it through your handkerchief, or else do as the sailors did, just set your teeth before drinking and then fling away the accumulation" [4]. Again, Sydney Smith, founder of the *Edinburgh*

Review, writes thus in 1834 to Lady Grey: "I am better in health, avoiding all fermented liquors, and drinking nothing but London water, with a million insects in every drop. He who drinks a tumbler of London water has literally in his stomach more animated beings than there are men, women and children on the face of the globe" [5]. This omnivorous English divine was less kind to the insects than the Buddhist monk of today, whose belongings include only his orange robe, an alms bowl for food, a needle, a string of beads, a razor to shave his head with, and a filter to strain his drinking-water, lest he swallow an insect and thus inflict suffering on living things. From the hygienist's viewpoint, the behaviour of the self-confident, defiant individualist may be just as antisocial as the occult death-wish of the fatalist.

Much more dirty water was to flow under London Bridge before gradual improvement came about, largely through the misery and destruction wrought in Europe and North America by cholera, which in 1832—10 years after our opening scene—broke from its ancient boundaries in India, and was spread like wildfire by the expanding routes and accelerating pace of travel. By the mid-nineteenth century, after Britain had suffered two terrifying visitations, sanitary reform was no longer a mere watchword or rallying-cry for such diverse characters as the evangelist-physician Thomas Southwood Smith (a friend of Leigh Hunt) and the lawyer-bureaucrat Edwin Chadwick, or (somewhat later) the clergyman-novelist Charles Kingsley and the martinet-nurse Florence Nightingale. All sorts of complainants were now finding expression. For instance, in 1849, *Punch* published an illustrated parody of the old nursery rhyme "This is the house that Jack built," headed "This is the water that John drinks," whose final verse read:

> This is the price we pay to wink
> At the vested int'rests, that fill to the brink,
> The network of sewers, from cesspool and sink,
> That feeds the fish that float in the ink-
> y stream of the Thames with its cento of stink
> That supplies the water that John drinks.

Again, on July 3, 1849, under the heading "A Sanitary Remonstrance," the following pathetic letter appeared in *The Times*, signed by 54 persons, half of whom had unmistakably Irish names:

> SUR,—May we beg and beseech your proteckshion and power. We are Sur, as it may be, livin in a Willderniss, so far as the rest of London knows anything of us, or as the rich and great people care about. We live in muck and filthe. We ain't go no priviy, no dust bins, no water-splies, and no drain or suer in the hole place. . . . We all of us suffur, and if the Cholera comes Lord help us.

Some gentlemans comed yesterday, and we thought they was comishoners from the Suer Company, but they was complaining of the noosance and stenche our lanes and corts was to them in New Oxforde Street. They was much surprized to see the seller in . . . our lane, where a child was dying from fever, and would not behleave that Sixty persons sleep in it every night. . . . You couldn't swing a cat in it.

Preaye Sir com and see us, for we are livin like piggs, and it aint faire we should be so ill trated. . . .

Though visited by kindly clergymen, who raised a small fund for them, many of these petitioners were no doubt still in their cellars five years later when the cholera did come again. Over 500 perished in 10 days within a radius of 250 yards in the anomalously named Golden Square neighbourhood whence came that letter.

The 1854 epidemic ended soon after Dr. John Snow (a fashionable pioneer anaesthetist who used chloroform to deliver two of Queen Victoria's offspring), persuaded the local Board of Guardians to remove the handle of a pump in Broad Street, to which he had traced the source of the outbreak [6]. Snow's demonstration that the infective agent of cholera was conveyable by a water supply containing excreta from a victim of the disease, and the acceptance of those views by the General Board of Health's chief medical officer, John Simon, facilitated the passage of an Act of Parliament requiring that by the end of 1855, all water for domestic use in London must be sand-filtered.

Before Snow died in his forties in 1858, another epidemiologist, Dr. William Budd of Bristol, made comparable claims with respect to typhoid fever, and carried the argument further (Plates I and IIA). By now, after nearly two decades of increasing emphasis on sanitary reform, to many people sin, disease, and dirt had become almost synonymous. They espoused the doctrine—anathema to St. Jerome—that cleanliness was next to godliness. The belief grew (and is still held by some) that so-called pythogenic fevers, or filth diseases, could arise as a direct result of exposure to putrescence. Noxious odours from sewage, decomposing offal, or rotting garbage became invested with infective potentialities. This concept differed only slightly from the dogma of miasms that enslaved clinical medicine for centuries; that led the Italian words for "bad air" to serve as English for that most prevalent of all water-borne diseases—stretching a point—malaria; and that allowed the famous Dr. Benjamin Rush to ascribe the 1793 epidemic of yellow fever in Philadelphia to exhalations from a cargo of putrid coffee on a wharf. Budd, however, argued in favour of distinct and specific causal agents for communicable diseases—not only cholera and typhoid fever, but also diphtheria, smallpox, and tuberculosis. His view was that in cholera and typhoid fever, the sewer (or a contaminated water supply) might be considered "a direct continuation of the diseased intestine"; and inferentially, if no disease agents were excreted into the sewage, there was no danger to health.

An opportunity to refute the pythogenic theory came in the hot summer of 1858, at the height of the Indian Mutiny, when ". . . the sewage of nearly three millions of people had been brought to seethe and ferment under a burning sun, in one vast open *cloaca* lying in their midst." Budd describes the consequences in graphic terms:

> Stench so foul, we may believe, had never before ascended to pollute this lower air. . . . For many weeks, the atmosphere of Parliamentary Committee-rooms was only rendered barely tolerable by the suspension before every window, of blinds saturated with chloride of lime, and by the lavish use of this and other disinfectants. More than once, in spite of similar precautions, the law-courts were suddenly broken up by an insupportable invasion of the noxious vapour. . . . Day after day, week after week, the "*Times*" teemed with letters, filled with complaint, prophetic of calamity, or suggesting remedies. . . . At home and abroad, the state of the chief river was felt to be a national reproach. "India is in revolt, and the Thames stinks," were the two great facts coupled together by a distinguished foreign writer, to mark the climax of national humilation . . . [7].

Yet despite highly pessimistic forecasts of pestilence, the health of the metropolis remained "remarkably good."

IV

The search for the specific causal micro-organisms of cholera and typhoid now began in earnest. Previously, at widely separated intervals, halting steps had been taken in this direction. Disease-producing agents, too small to be seen by the naked eye, had been foreshadowed long ago by Varro in *De Re Rustica* (*ca.* 35 B.C.) and Fracastoro in *De Contagione* (1546). In the seventeenth century, using primitive microscopes, Athanasius Kircher, a German Jesuit, and Anton van Leeuwenhoek, the town clerk of Delft, saw many kinds of microbes in water. Around 1720, Marten and Bradley in England, and Goiffon at Marseille, speculated ingeniously on the properties of the seeds of contagion in various diseases, especially the plague and tuberculosis. Though the Age of Reason had arrived, the technical skills needed to reveal these *seminaria* remained wanting, and the search was hampered by the still common belief that creatures of such extreme lowliness could hardly challenge man, who was made in God's image. However, before the end of the eighteenth century, the Italian polymath Spallanzani was manipulating his infusoria almost at will; and six years before Shelley was born, the great work *Animalcula infusoria et marina . . .* (1786) of the Danish naturalist Otto Friderich Müller, published posthumously, offered a classification of "animalcules" which included a genus *Vibrio*, comprising six species clearly of bacterial type.

During six decades of the nineteenth century it was a vibrio that killed hundreds of thousands in the ports and inland cities of Europe and North America, ruining trade and threatening civilization. From 1832 to 1892, cholera replaced the plague as a source of terror. By now, the old philosophical and political attitudes, challenged by the writings and conduct of rebels such as Shelley and Byron, were being infiltrated by notions of social reform and evolutionary progress. In such an era, even microbes might be considered to have ambitions worth thwarting, if man's survival and supremacy were threatened.

Since the 1830's, improved microscopes with achromatic objectives, of sufficient magnifying and resolving power to reveal some of the smaller species, had become available; but some observers, including Budd himself, mistakenly claimed that fungi conspicuously present in the rice-water discharges of cholera victims, and in the drinking-water of infected places, were the "morbific agent" [8]. Despite this false alarm, there is little doubt that the true causal organism was seen by several investigators well before the golden age of bacteriology dawned around 1875–80. For example, in France, Pouchet described immense numbers of vibrios in the stools of cholera patients as early as 1849, while the Italians claim that Pacini first described the true cholera microbe in 1854, under the name *Vibrioni colergeni*. In England, the versatile Henry Hassall noted myriads of "Vibriones" in the stools of victims in St. Bartholomew's Hospital during the 1854 epidemic, as well as in some of the impure waters they had consumed [9]. In the same year, Thomson, a lecturer in chemistry at St. Thomas' Hospital, and Rainey, a demonstrator in anatomy—both unknown for any other scientific accomplishment—found vibrios in washings from the walls of cholera wards and in the excreta of cholera cases, which were absent from control washings and stool specimens [10].

In 1865, when over 200 people were dying daily in Paris from cholera, Pasteur himself decided to set aside silkworm studies and seek the cause of the human scourge. Now the thought patterns of even the greatest minds are apt to run in grooves, and Pasteur's great fight with the spontaneous generationists had been waged mainly around the question of airborne contamination. So he did not examine the excreta of patients or the city sewage, as Snow or Budd would have urged, but set to work instead with the famous physiologist Claude Bernard in a hospital attic which communicated with a cholera ward. They opened a ventilator and drew air from the ward through a glass tube into a freezing mixture, hoping in vain to condense and isolate the noxious agent [11]. In 1883, while cholera raged in Egypt, Pasteur entered the fray again by proxy, sending his young assistant Thuillier to Alexandria, along with Roux, as members of the French Cholera Commission. Soon after their arrival, the epidemic ceased; but Thuillier inexplicably contracted the disease and died of it. Meanwhile, Koch and the German Cholera Expedition to Egypt had identified and isolated *Vibrio cholerae* [12]. Within a year, Koch's pupil Gaffky had isolated the typhoid bacillus.

Koch's fellow-countryman, Max von Pettenkofer of Munich, a remarkably public-spirited hygienist, disputed the capacity of laboratory cultures alone to induce cholera. He had postulated that a specific organism (X) needed to be "ripened" by contact with suitable amounts of moisture and decaying organic material in the soil (Y) before fully toxic germs (Z) could evolve. In his view, the simple equation $X + Y = Z$ had to be satisfied before cholera was possible.

To test this theory Pettenkofer drank 1 cc of a culture of *V. cholerae*, recently isolated from a patient dying in the 1892 Hamburg epidemic, in which, within a few months, some 18,000 people had been stricken with the disease, mostly from drinking the unfiltered water of the sewage-polluted River Elbe. Although he developed mild diarrhoea and excreted cholera vibrios for several days, Pettenkofer claimed to have proved his point, ignoring the fact that his junior colleague Emmerich (who swallowed a larger dose of the culture) had a severe choleraic syndrome. Pettenkofer was then 74 and indulged in some rather pompous heroics over this episode. "Even if I had deceived myself and the experiment endangered my life," he wrote, "I would have looked death quietly in the eye, for mine would have been no foolish or cowardly suicide: I would have died in the service of science like a soldier on the field of honour. Health and life are, as I have so often said, very great earthly goods, but not the highest for men. If man would rise above the animals, he must sacrifice both life and health for the higher ideals." Born in 1818, four years before Shelley was drowned, the world's first professor of hygiene survived into the twentieth century. But one midnight, early in 1901, the lonely old man took a pistol and shot himself dead [13] (Plate II B).

When the 1892 outbreak of cholera, which originated in Russia, reached France, the self-exiled microbiologist Metchnikoff, then working at the Pasteur Institute in Paris, deemed it opportune to try his hand at settling the question of the cholera vibrio's pathogenicity. He failed to produce the disease in a variety of animals, so after some fuss and soul-searching he swallowed a culture, without effect. The experiment was repeated on a volunteer assistant, likewise with negative result. Thus emboldened, he accorded the privilege to another volunteer, who promptly developed most alarming choleraic symptoms. The young man recovered, but Metchnikoff himself—a rather neurotic type—nearly died of fright [14].

These crucial experiments in Munich and Paris, and similar ones carried out in other laboratories, gave the coup de grâce to the anti-contagionists, whose doctrines had been mainly sustained by the fact that in every cholera epidemic some people managed to escape, despite their apparent close contact with the disease; and by the general failure of experimental animals to develop significant ill-effects, regardless of the route by which cholera discharges were administered. Such animal experiments, which had been conducted periodically ever since 1832 (the year of cholera's first epidemic invasion of Europe), reached a climax in 1866, when Burdon-Sanderson reported to the Privy Council that he had failed to transmit the disease to 26 guinea pigs, 90 mice, 6 hedgehogs, 4 pigeons, and 5 dogs [15]. This large-scale negativity should have pleased and yet shocked the still extant sanitary reformers, whose mid-Victorian religiosity usually involved anti-contagionist and anti-vivisectionist complexes.

Incidentally, self-experimentation with cholera was not inaugurated by Pettenkofer and Metchnikoff. In 1854, the year of the Broad Street pump outbreak, a 37-year-old doctor of American and French ancestry went to Mauritius, intending to start a practice. Finding a cholera epidemic afoot, he took charge of the island's hospital, treating his cases with opium, as advocated by the great physiologist Magendie. With a view to testing both contagiousness and remedy on himself, he swallowed the vomit of cholera patients. "When he felt that he had caught cholera, he took a huge dose of laudanum, and was found semi-conscious in his room, curled up in a corner, strong enough only to signal for coffee" [16]. Brown-Séquard recovered and lived another 40 years, becoming a celebrated neurologist.

An even more dramatic though unintentional experiment occurred during the 1861 epidemic in Calcutta, where 19 persons drank the rice water stools from a case of cholera. That so many could do this by mistake is a sad commentary on the general palatability of the local water supply. Five of the thirsty ones developed cholera . . . [17].

Cholera has been chosen as the exemplar of water-borne disease because it is unsurpassed in the sudden ferocity of its attack upon individuals and communities; in the panic its visitations have inspired in affected or threatened citizenry; in its relative indifference to questions of climate, colour, or class; and in its capacity to spur sanitary reform and public health legislation. As William Welch, the great American pathologist, wrote in the wake of the Hamburg disaster:

Cholera has destroyed millions of human lives, but it has been the means of saving millions more. It has been one of the levers of progress in modern sanitation. The same measures which are needed to protect a city against occasional epidemics of cholera are needed at all times to protect it against other infectious diseases, such as typhoid fever, which is spread in a similar manner, and which, although they do not come with the terrible impetuosity of cholera, steadily do their deadly work, and in the course of time destroy among us far more lives than cholera [18].

V

For the purposes of this essay, an Old World setting has offered hitherto a richer cast of dramatis personae, but now it is time to change the emphasis. During several decades of the nineteenth century, the ravages of cholera were as violent and as recurrent in North America as in Europe. No major city in the United States or in Lower and Upper Canada—from Boston and New York to Sacramento, from Quebec to Toronto—escaped the scourge. The Hudson, Ohio, Mississippi, and St. Lawrence rivers played comparable roles to the Thames, the Seine, and the Elbe in transporting the infected hosts and the infective agent. Very readable historical accounts of cholera in the United States are available [19, 20]; but although references to epidemics of the disease in Canada are plentiful and colourful, they are scattered and sorely in need of compilation [21, 22].

For example, the following letter, sent from the Comptroller's office, Albany, under the date of 15 June 1832, to Felix Alden, Esq., Collector of Canal Tolls, Fort Edward*, came into my possession many years ago:

Dear Sir; The Reports of the dreadful scourge called the Asiatic Cholera in a variety of places in Canada has made considerable excitement here, and has called upon our board of health to take such measures as are in their power to stop the importation of this contagion into the state and especially

---

*The toll collector was a direct descendant of John Alden, cooper, recruited at Southhampton just before the "Pilgrims" set sail, who was the emissary in Longfellow's *The Courtship of Miles Standish*, and in due course became the last male survivor of the "Mayflower Compact" of 1620.

its dissemination in the populous towns where it is most dangerous. In corroboration of their efforts I think it proper to request you to inspect the state and condition, as to health and cleanliness, of the passengers upon the canal boats which pass your office and especially such as appear to be foreign emigrants or from the Canadas.* I do not know whether your village is incorporated but if it is you had better confer with the Trustees and get them to designate a physician to make this examination. If it is not incorporated you had better confer with some of your principal inhabitants and with your physicians and determine what you will do on this subject. I am aware you can do nothing authoritatively but much by persuasion and advice with the masters, and by a show of authority as far as you can carry that without personal liability. This letter will be handed to you by J. D. Wasson, the agent of the board of health of this city—I am very Truly Yrs SILAS WRIGHT, JR.

The remarkably sensible instructions contained in the letter did not avert an outbreak of the disease in Albany itself, which, though then a small city, spent $19,000 of public funds in fighting it.

Passengers from "the Canadas" were of course not necessarily to blame for that outbreak. But Quebec was sorely stricken, recording 3,451 fatal cases, which decimated its total urban population of not more than 30,000, despite the fact that a quarantine station had been instituted in 1832 at Grosse Ile, 30 miles below the city, with a squad of soldiers and artillery stationed there to enforce *pratique*. Only two years later, the city suffered a further 2,509 deaths, and in 1849 another 1,185 were buried in the cholera cemetery [22]. In those days Quebec was the sole port of entry into this country from Europe, so that as quarantine was more effectively enforced, the risk of direct transoceanic importation of cholera could be minimized. The last Canadian outbreak of 1866 was probably introduced from the United States.

At mid-century, echoes of the sanitary reform movement, which in England culminated in the Public Health Act of 1848, had crossed the Atlantic. Their impetus was side-tracked in the United States by the Civil War, but once this tragic disruption was over, problems of sanitation were attacked with vigour. To that end, the Commonwealth of Massachusetts, always a leader in this field, established a State Board of Health in 1869, and the American Public Health Association was founded in 1872. Within a decade or two, the emergence of the science of bacteriology, reinforcing the drive and vision of such zealots as

*Canadian passengers from Quebec and Montreal travelled down the Richelieu River to Lake Champlain, crossed the lake, and took the Champlain Canal to Fort Edward via Whitehall, New York. If they proceeded by boat along the Hudson Valley, they eventually joined the Erie Canal, which would take them to Albany.

Lemuel Shattuck, Henry Bowditch, Stephen Smith, and George Sternberg, was making possible the modern development of what Whipple has called "the greatest of the sanitary arts—the art of water purification" [23].

Upper and Lower Canada had customarily organized Central Boards of Health for the duration of epidemic emergencies, but after the latest visitation of the Almighty had been thus brought under scrutiny, the sanitary folly, ignorance, and carelessness of man tended once more to prevail. In the very year of Confederation, "in the ancient capital of Quebec, the Canadian Medical Association was formed and a resolution adopted providing for the appointment of a strong committee on public health, to promote the establishment of a federal board of health." A key phrase in the committee's report, presented a year later, already seems to foreshadow the emphasis on a "soft approach," which has generally characterized and sometimes enfeebled our federal government's handling of public health issues: "A necessity therefore exists for the introduction by the government of a comprehensive system of sanitary laws, not so complete, perhaps, as those of the Mosaic code nor so severe in the punishment of any violations of them" [24]. We need not discuss here the reasons why over half a century passed before the Parliament of Canada enacted a bill, in 1919, which made provision for a Department of Pensions and National Health. Fortunately, long before then, all the provinces and many of the bigger cities had set up departments of health, beginning with Ontario's Provincial Board of Health in 1882, and Quebec's Conseil de Santé in 1886.

In their unravelling of the bacteriology of cholera, Koch and his associates in Germany had a clear lead. But Americans did their best to bridge the gap. In July 1884, within a few months of the discovery of the "comma bacillus" (*Vibrio cholerae*), two young doctors, William H. Welch and T. Mitchell Prudden, enrolled in the first public course in bacteriology given by Koch. Welch had organized the first laboratory for teaching and research in medical bacteriology in the United States in 1878, at the Bellevue Hospital Medical College; and in the following year, Prudden had done likewise at the College of Physicians and Surgeons (later Columbia University) in New York. They were keen to take home with them not only the latest techniques, but also some live cultures of *V. cholerae*. Knowing Koch's exaggerated fear of releasing such cultures, they had each procured a culture from Professor Flügge at another institute. But one evening, as Koch sat talking with them about cholera, he remarked that "It would be better a man had never been born if he introduced a disease germ into a region where it previously had not existed." After a sleepless night, Welch rose from his bed at dawn, unlocked his desk, took out the tube of cholera culture, and poured bichloride of mercury solution upon it to kill the germs. Then he slunk through the streets to a bridge over the Spree, only to find another guilty-looking figure approaching, bent on a similar mission. It was Prudden. As both men threw their cultures into the river, they were disconcerted to observe their tubes bobbing up and down as they floated slowly away, instead of sinking immediately out of sight [25].

Notwithstanding Koch's knowledge and prestige, he was powerless to avert the last great cholera pandemic of 1892. Within about six months, nearly 400,000 persons died of the disease, not counting those in India. In Hamburg there were roughly 17,000 cases within three months, of whom 8,600 died. From this focus, distributed mainly by the waterways, the disease took hold in 269 places in Germany, yet failed to establish itself anywhere in the United States or Canada.

The disaster at Hamburg, which still haunts a few memories, hastened the introduction of bacteriological controls of water supplies. In this field, the earliest initiatives were European, but by the end of the century, North America was displaying leadership. In 1871, Burdon-Sanderson in England had systematically demonstrated the presence of bacteria in water, and in 1880, the first exact methods of enumerating them were developed by Miguel, in Paris. By 1885, when Percy Frankland applied Koch's new culture techniques to Thames water [26], a dedicated young American of German ancestry, Theobald Smith, was already adapting the same techniques to the needs of the United States Bureau of Animal Industry, and within a few months had published findings on the bacterial flora of the Potomac River. In 1893, Smith introduced his gas fermentation tube, whose applications included the quantitative estimation of faecal bacteria in water supplies, and reported its use in studies of the Mohawk and Hudson rivers. In the development of internationally accepted standard methods for the bacteriological analysis of water, Theobald Smith played a key role for many years (Plate IIIA).

The need for uniform methods of water analysis was emphasized in 1894 by a Canadian bacteriologist, Wyatt Johnston,* at a meeting of the American Public Health Association in Montreal (Plate IIIB). His pleas resulted in a convention of bacteriologists being held in New York

*Dr. Johnston had a brilliantly versatile but short-lived career. In 1890 he carried out a careful bacteriological study of Montreal's water supply, and in 1895 published a well-regarded report on methods of classifying water bacteria. Just before his untimely death, in 1902, he was appointed McGill University's first Professor of Hygiene.

in June 1895, at which there was general agreement on the need to secure precise, standardized methods for identifying bacterial species. A committee was appointed, with Welch as chairman, which presented reports in 1896 and 1897. The eventual outcome was the publication, in 1905, of the first edition of *Standard Methods of Water Analysis* [27], a work now in its twelfth (1965) edition.

The need for tax-supported laboratories to carry out such work became evident. The Massachusetts State Board of Health led the way, by establishing its experiment station at Lawrence and instituting systematic examinations of all municipal water supplies in the state, in 1887. Only three years later, the government of Ontario sponsored the first state or provincial public health laboratory in North America. My own province (blessed as it is with a superabundance of virgin snow and pure rain-water) was one of the last to do so, in 1931. Yet by the first decade of the twentieth century, many of the great rivers, lakes, and estuaries in the New World had become as sewage-polluted as those of the Old, and there was a high and increasing incidence of water-borne epidemics of enteric infections. To estimate and combat these hazards, sewage commissions, research stations, and control laboratories were set up, whose activities have tended always to expand. In England, for example, the Water Pollution Research Laboratory, established in 1927 under the Department of Scientific and Industrial Research, has furnished the River Authorities with invaluable information and advice. This institution has recently completed a Survey of the Thames Estuary [28]—probably the most ambitious project of its kind yet undertaken anywhere—climaxing at least a half-century of intensive bacteriological studies of that noble river, during which time no serious outbreak of water-borne disease has been traced to it. "Many a green isle needs must be. . . ."

Bacteriological testing alone, however thoroughly done, will not protect cities from suddenly or intermittently polluted water supplies. By the time the danger has been spotted in the laboratory, many citizens may have swallowed multiple infective doses of some pathogen. Though sand is a much better filtering device than a handkerchief or clenched teeth, as a safety measure nothing compares with sterilization by a halogen. The bactericidal properties of chlorine were first applied to the Maidstone water supply in 1897, at the suggestion of Sims Woodhead, who investigated a local outbreak of nearly 2,000 cases of typhoid fever. The mains were effectively sterilized by use of chloride of lime, and the epidemic ceased. Again, early in 1905, during a severe outbreak of typhoid fever at Lincoln, Alexander Houston recommended the addition of sodium hypochlorite to the city water supply, after *Bacillus typhosum* had been isolated therefrom. The epidemic was soon controlled. On this continent, Jersey City became the first municipality to have a continuously chlorinated water supply, in 1908. Subsequently, no other process of water purification showed such astounding growth all over the world, or proved so promptly and cheaply prophylactic, against almost all forms of water-borne infection.

Of course, health officers concerned with water nowadays realize they have much more than cholera vibrios and typhoid bacilli to reckon with. Many hundreds of species of paratyphoid-like bacilli (the so-called Salmonella group), most of them capable of affecting animals as well as man; a considerable number of dysentery bacilli (the Shigella group); the bacillus of tularaemia, and numerous leptospira, again shared by man and animals; and uncounted varieties of enteroviruses—all are potentially water-borne. These are so much in our own midst that we scarcely need to strengthen our argument by referring to that Pandora's box of protozoal and helminthic diseases, from amoebiasis and malaria to ancylostomiasis, paragonimiasis, and schistosomiasis, in which water is important or essential to propagation of the parasites or their vectors.

In confronting the challenge of these resilient, persistent, and invisible antagonists, mankind everywhere displays extremely variable degrees of wisdom, energy, and social conscience. If a community pays heed to its best-informed minds, water-borne epidemics (like many other kinds of disasters) can be avoided; otherwise not. The weak links, the loop-holes, the Achilles heels may be too numerous and flagrant for any one person to be blamed, as applies to the endemic cholera of Bengal, or the recurrent epidemics of southeast Asia, e.g. the 1958 outbreak of nearly 10,000 cases of cholera in Thailand. Alternatively, a single anonymous carrier may bring trouble to an overconfident, underchlorinated community, as in the 1963 outbreak of over 300 cases of typhoid fever in Zermatt, or the 2,000 cases of water-borne salmonellosis in 1965 at Riverside, California.

VI

Quite apart from such direct kinds of implication in epidemics, citizens sometimes take violent umbrage at efforts to protect them from their own sanitary short-comings. Nearly 100 years ago, a doctor in a Bavarian health resort was persecuted and ostracized until, sick in mind and body, he was forced to leave the scene of his labours, because he had reported a case of cholera to the authorities. Ibsen's play, *An Enemy of the People,* which appeared in 1882 (the year before Koch isolated the cholera vibrio), is said to be based on that occurrence. In this drama, as you may recall, the impetuous Dr. Stockmann incurred the wrath of the burgomaster and local populace, because he wanted to publicize a laboratory report confirming his suspicions that "typhoid and gastric attacks" among visitors to the town baths were due to a polluted water supply, containing "millions of infusoria." Stockmann was naïve enough to disavow in advance any reward for his conduct, "such as an address of thanks, a subscription for a testimonial, a civic banquet, or a procession with banners." Instead, when he tries to explain his stand to a meeting of citizens, they hoot insults at him, tear his clothes, stone his windows, and boycott his family; while the mayor (who happens to be his brother) relieves him of his job, reminding him that as an official he had no right to any individual conviction.

Again, in 1911, a young medical officer of health in Upper Austria was persecuted mercilessly because he had notified the proper authorities of a case of proven typhoid fever in the town. Army manoeuvres had been proceeding in the vicinity, and when no further troops were allowed to billet there, shopkeepers refused to sell the doctor food, he was overwhelmed with abusive letters, threatened with violence, became involved in a law suit, and was dismissed from his post. He died of heart failure, leaving behind a dependent mother, as well as his widow and small son [29].

Since you may want to demur at this point that such things surely cannot happen in Canada today, I propose to close this long series of lessons from history by dispassionately citing a personal experience. When World War II began, aside from being involved in university teaching and research commitments, I was in charge of the Provincial Laboratories of British Columbia, in which capacity I had noted that the city of Vancouver's water supply now and again failed to meet internationally accepted bacteriological standards. Though at first the war was so distant, one felt increasing disquiet that the city's supply, from a splendid but not inviolable watershed in the North Shore mountains, remained unchlorinated; that the local Water Board, and also the Mayor and City Council, were fanatically proud of their water's pristine purity and determined not to sully it with "chemical poisons"; and that the city and provincial health officers to whom the laboratory reports were sent had no apparent intention of stirring up trouble by suggesting, still less insisting, that the bacterial counts be brought within acceptable limits through chlorination. Perhaps they knew their Ibsen.

After the Pearl Harbour episode, one's concern deepened to alarm.

A saboteur could easily have polluted our water supply by walking into the watershed with heavy enough suspensions of cholera vibrios or typhoid bacilli in his pocket to pollute the city's water supply and place the lives of thousands in jeopardy; or an enemy plane could have sprayed the whole watershed with various pathogens. For a time, I used to carry around a small sealed vial of killed cholera vibrios, to produce when opportunity offered for the edification of key politicians and officials. I would explain to them that if the contents of this vial could be evenly distributed among a day's water supply to the whole city, each glassful of water would contain about 100 cholera vibrios. But though this caused momentary shock, some were obviously incredulous and all remained recalcitrant.

When it was evident that the customary "channels" were likely to remain obstructed, I felt it devolved on me to get that water supply chlorinated without further delay. This, in brief, was the background of the Greater Vancouver water chlorination scandal, fiasco, or vendetta, which started some decades after most other cities had willingly adopted the process, and went on for quite a while after the war had ceased. For the federal government, using its emergency war-time powers, installed chlorination equipment and supervised its operation; but as soon as Ottawa ceased "interfering" in Vancouver's civic affairs, the Water Board, backed by the Mayor and City Council, carried out their frequently uttered threat and turned off the chlorine. The battle was therefore rejoined.

It would be out of place here even to outline the chronology of events. The intensity of the feud has been alluded to in an earlier account [30]. Suffice it to say that representatives of the Water Board did their utmost to get me discredited, dismissed, and sued, while the city health officer made allusions to "armchair professors" and his provincial colleague kept very quiet. Numerous threatening, abusive, or merely ludicrous letters were received, some of them bearing such pithy addresses as "Dolman, Chlorinator," "Bugologist, UBC," or "Water Wizard, Vancouver." For months, complaints abounded in the newspapers from people claiming the poisoned water had caused their wives to become spotty, their cows barren, and the birds to leave the area. A few people wrote or telephoned encouraging messages, and one daily paper—long since gone out of business—took a refreshingly intelligent stand. But when the whole dismal business was over, one had learned the hard way that there is no public issue in which the misconceptions and wilfulness of the ignorant and foolish, the venom of the bigoted, the cowardice and opportunism of fence-sitting politicians and officials, and the mischief-making potentialities of the Press may find freer rein than in what Stockman called "so clear and straightforward a matter" as the securing of a safe water supply.

Twenty years or more afterwards, it is fairly easy to feel tolerant, and to enjoy sharing the funny side of some of the headlines and cartoons of those days (Plate IV and Figs. 1–3). Even at the time, some cold comfort could be squeezed from those well-known words of Ibsen's hero: "The strongest man upon earth is he who stands most alone"—a sentiment cribbed from Schiller, whose Wilhelm Tell says: "Der Starke ist am mächtigsten *allein*." But such bravado rings hollow in the face of the propinquities and complexities of tomorrow's world. Besides, the philosophy behind it will not solve one of the most awesome problems facing mankind today, that of reconciling the prodigal usage of water for drinking, bathing, recreational, and industrial purposes by a proliferating population, with diminishing surface water supplies subject to increasing pollution, while the water table inexorably falls. Quite apart from the knotty scientific and technical considerations involved, discussions and trials of possible remedies will demand all the wisdom, restraint, and oecumenicalism of which *Homo sapiens* is capable. In organizing several symposia bearing on a question of such ramifying, overall importance, I believe our Society is setting a good example. In our self-indulgent civilization, it is hard to bring home the message that if posterity wishes to enjoy "many flowering islands" it faces a continuing and intensifying struggle to maintain them "in the waters of wide Agony." But this is the unmistakable warning of history, and by emphasizing it our fellowship is doing a public service.

Finally, whenever our duties as scientists or citizens chance to be concerned with the use and abuse of water, I suggest we may be spared many disappointments and surprises if we bear in mind that human nature changes more slowly than Father Thames; that we all had gills at one stage of our embryological development; and that about 65 per cent of our body weight comprises indispensable water. Thomas Mann—obviously, like Shelley, a lover, if not a worshipper, of that all-pervading element—eloquently defines our intimate indebtedness to it: "The attraction which water exercises upon the normal man is natural and mystically sympathetic. Man is a child of water. . . . True abstractedness, true self-forgetfulness, the real merging of my own circumscribed existence in the universal, is granted to me only when my eyes lose themselves in some great liquid mirror . . . " [31].

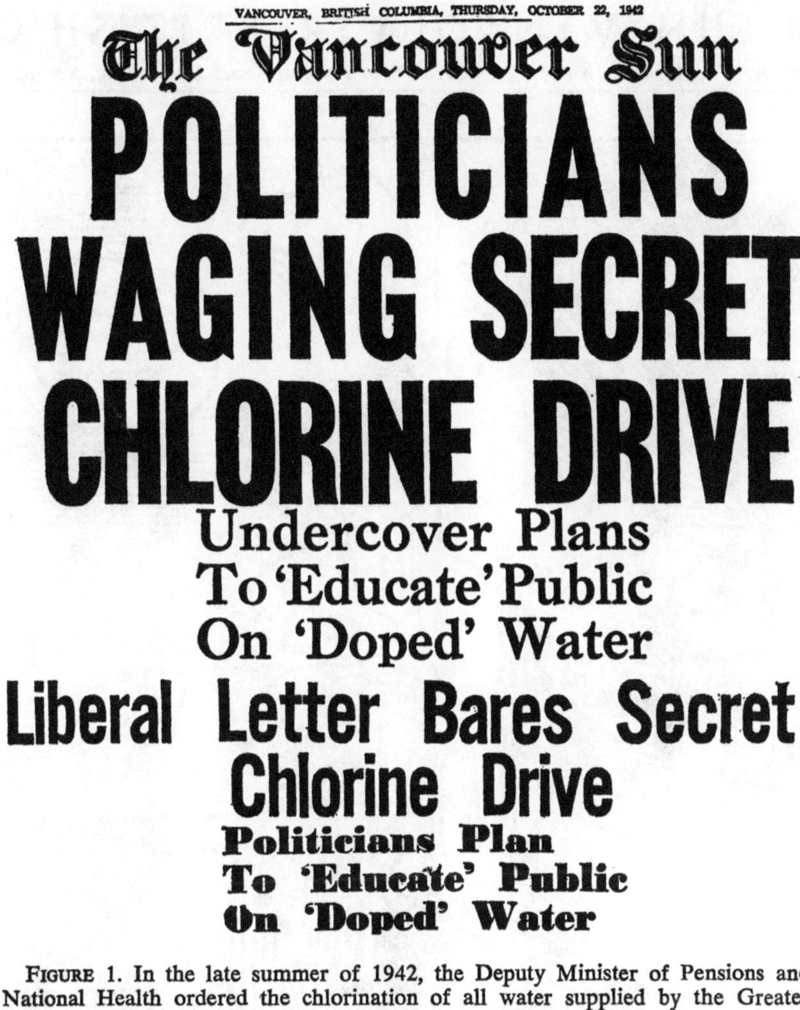

VANCOUVER, BRITISH COLUMBIA, THURSDAY, OCTOBER 22, 1942

The Vancouver Sun

POLITICIANS WAGING SECRET CHLORINE DRIVE

Undercover Plans To 'Educate' Public On 'Doped' Water

Liberal Letter Bares Secret Chlorine Drive

Politicians Plan To 'Educate' Public On 'Doped' Water

FIGURE 1. In the late summer of 1942, the Deputy Minister of Pensions and National Health ordered the chlorination of all water supplied by the Greater Vancouver Water District. The Water Board and the City Council disputed the order, and several weeks elapsed before it was finally implemented under the War Measures Act. Meanwhile it was hoped that "persuasion" might make coercion unnecessary. The Minister of Pensions and National Health, the Honourable Ian Mackenzie, happened to be M.P. for a Vancouver riding.

OCTOBER 31, 1945

R SUN, VANCOUVER, BRITISH C

ıcouver People, Is a Newspaper Devoted to Progress and Democracy, Toleran

Putting a False Face On It

FIGURE 2. After the war, the War Measures Act was rescinded. The federal government offered to hand over to the Greater Vancouver Water District, for the sum of one dollar, all the chlorination equipment it had installed. Efforts to ensure that the water supply should not revert to its prewar unchlorinated state were resisted and scorned by various devices.

FIGURE 3. E. A. Cleveland, Chief Commissioner of the Board of the Greater Vancouver Water District, had hired three carefully selected "experts" to make a secret report disavowing the need for chlorination. They never visited the Provincial Department of Health Laboratories which had provided the crucial evidence indicating pollution. Their report was released as a "bomb-shell' to scatter and discredit pro-chlorination arguments.

REFERENCES

1. Marchand, L. A. (1957), *Byron: A Biography* (New York: Knopf), Vol. 3, pp. 1021–4.
2. Garrison, F. H. (1929), "The History of Drainage, Irrigation, Sewage-Disposal and Water-Supply," *Bull. New Acad. Med. 5*: 887–938.
3. Winslow, C.-E. A. (1923), *The Evolution and Significance of the Modern Public Health Campaign* (New Haven: Yale University Press), pp. 6–9.
4. Lodge, Oliver (1931), *Past Years. An Autobiography* (London: Hodder & Stoughton), p. 17.
5. Smith, Sydney (1834), In a letter to Lady Grey, Nov. 19, 1834. Cited in H. & P. Massingham's *The London Anthology* (London: Phoenix House, 1950).
6. Snow, John (1855), *On the Mode of Communication of Cholera* (London: Churchill).
7. Budd, William (1873), *Typhoid Fever; Its Nature, Mode of Spreading, and Prevention* (London: Longmans, Green & Co.).
8. ——— (1849), *Malignant Cholera: Its Mode of Propagation and Its Prevention* (London: Churchill).
9. Hassall, J. (1893), *Narrative of a Busy Life* (London: Longmans, Green & Co.), p. 74.
10. Wildy, P. (1957), "Dr. Thomson and Mr. Rainey," *St. Thomas's Hosp. Gaz. 55*: 91–94.
11. Vallery-Radot, R. (1937), *The Life of Pasteur* (New York: Sun Dial Press), pp. 380–32.
12. Bochalli, R. (1954), *Robert Koch der Schöpfer der modernen Bakteriologie* (Stuttgart: Wissenschaftliche Verlagsgesellschaft M.B.H.), pp, 71–74.
13. Hume, E. E. (1927), *Max von Pettenkofer* (New York: Hoeber, Inc.).
14. Metchnikoff, Olga (1921), *Life of Elie Metchnikoff, 1845–1916* (New York: Houghton Mifflin Co.), p. 155.
15. Sanderson, J. B. (1866), *Reports of the Medical Officer of the Privy Council*, 9th Report, Appendix No. 9, pp. 434–56.
16. Gooddy, W. (1964), "Some Aspects of the Life of Dr. C. E. Brown-Séquard," *Proc. Roy. Soc. Med. 57*: 189–92.
17. MacNamara, C. (1873), "Cholera in Calcutta during the Year 1872," *Ind. Med. Gaz. 8*: 33–35.
18. Welch, W. H. (1893–94), "Asiatic Cholera in Its Relations to Sanitary Reforms," *Popular Health Magazine, 1*. Reproduced in *Papers and Addresses by William Henry Welch* (Baltimore: Johns Hopkins Press, 1920), Vol. 1, pp. 599–606.
19. Chambers, J. S. (1938), *The Conquest of Cholera, America's Greatest Scourge* (New York: Macmillan Co.).
20. Rosenberg, C. (1962), *The Cholera Years* (Chicago: University of Chicago Press).
21. Heagerty, J. J. (1928), *Four Centuries of Medical History in Canada* (Toronto: Macmillan Co.), Vol. 1, pp. 179–211.
22. LeBlond, S. (1954), "Cholera in Quebec in 1849," *Can. Med. Assoc. J. 71*: 288–92.
23. Whipple, G. (1921), "Fifty Years of Water Purification," in M. P. Ravenel's *A Half Century of Public Health* (New York: American Public Health Association), pp. 161–80.

24. BRYCE, P. H. (1921), "The Story of Public Health in Canada," in Ravenel, *ibid*, pp. 56–65.
25. FLEXNER, S. and FLEXNER, J. T. (1941), *William Henry Welch and the Heroic Age of American Medicine* (New York: Viking Press), pp. 148–9.
26. WINSLOW, C.-E. A. (1950), "Some Leaders and Landmarks in the History of Microbiology," *Bact. Rev. 14*: 99–114.
27. *Standard Methods of Water Analysis*, 6th ed. (New York: American Public Health Association, 1925), Preface. p. ix.
28. EDEN, G. E. (1966), "The Water Pollution Research Laboratory," *Air & Water Pollut. Internat. J. 10*: 57–67.
29. EDITORIAL (1911), "Persecution of a Medical Health Officer," *Brit. Med. J.* i: 642–3.
30. DOLMAN, C. E. (1948), "The Sanitarian's Place in Public Health," *Can. J. Pub. Health, 39*: 41–51.
31. MANN, THOMAS (1930), *A Man and His Dog* (New York: Knopf), pp. 137–9.

www.ingramcontent.com/pod-product-compliance
Lightning Source LLC
Chambersburg PA
CBHW020249030426
42336CB00010B/683